WHERE

Third Edition

THE
JOBS
ARE

The hottest careers for the 21st century

WHERE

Third Edition

THE

JOBS

ARE

—— Joyce Hadley Copeland

CAREER PRESS

Franklin Lakes, NJ

WHERE THE JOBS ARE, 3RD EDITION
Cover design by Barry Littmann
Printed in the U.S.A. by Book-mart Press

To order this title, please call toll-free 1-800-CAREER-1 (NJ and Canada: 201-848-0310) to order using VISA or MasterCard, or for further information on books from Career Press.

The Career Press, Inc., 3 Tice Road, PO Box 687, Franklin Lakes, NJ 07417
www.careerpress.com

Library of Congress Cataloging-in-Publication Data

Copeland, Joyce Hadley.
    Where the jobs are : the hottest careers for the 21st century / by
Joyce Hadley Copeland.—3d ed.
        p.   cm.
    Includes index.
    ISBN 1-56414-422-4 (pbk.)
    1. Job hunting—United States. 2. Job vacancies—United States. 3. Career development—United States. 4. Vocational guidance—United States. I. Title.

HF5382.75.U5 C66 2000
331.7'02—dc21   99-059035

Acknowledgements

A very special thank you to all the people who so generously shared a slice of their career-lives through the professional profiles within these pages. A new generation of career-choosers may take their next steps more confidently after looking through your eyes!

I am especially grateful to Alexa Armanino, Matt and Kathy Dailey, Kimberly Friddle, Cole Garrett, Dick Hadley, Chris and Nannette Mahar, Josh and Rena Malkofsky-Berger, Barbara Oertli, Betsy Sheldon, and Meredith West for making those introductions.

As always, I bless my family for their constant support—especially my wonderful husband, Gary Copeland.

Contents

Contents

Get Ready for the Revolution

When I grow up, I want to file all day.
I want to claw my way to middle management.
Be replaced on a whim.
I want to have a brown nose.
I want to be a yes-man...yes-woman.
Yes, Sir. Coming, Sir. Anything for a raise, Sir.
When I grow up,
I want to be underappreciated.
Be paid less for doing the same job.
I want to be forced into early retirement.
—from a TV commercial for the **Monster.com** career Web site

Say *what*??

The economy is booming, unemployment is at an all-time low, and technology is throwing you the keys to brand-new careers that didn't exist 10 years ago. You're definitely in the driver's seat when it comes to the world of work. Companies of all sizes are intent on wooing you into their ranks with fatter paychecks, stock options, and a host of creative perks. **Monster.com**'s commercial spoofs the way things used to be...before. Before you had hundreds of job listings at your fingertips. Before you could job-hop to advance your career and compensation without getting busted for it in your next interview. Before you dreamed of working from home, bringing your dog to work, using your signing bonus for a down payment on a new car.

To say the dynamics of the job market have changed is an understatement. You ain't seen nothin' yet. Work as we know it today will continue to be reinvented in the next 10 years. According to management guru Tom Peters: "They aren't in charge of our careers—and by extension our lives—

anymore. We are. It's up to us to fashion ourselves." He calls it the "Liber-ating-New-World-Order-of-Brand-New-Brand-You."

Launching your career as "Me, Inc."

Today, more employees—especially Generation X-ers under 30—view themselves as "free agents" who must actively manage their own careers just as they might manage a brand-name product like Coca-Cola or Nike.

With change difficult to predict—but sure to continue—it's impor-tant to think of yourself as a "package" of marketable skills rather than a former or even prospective title. Why? Skills are transferable. If need be, you should be able to repackage yourself to take advantage of a range of new opportunities. For example, the technical knowledge and people skills prized in a nurse can build a bridge to a new career in medical equipment sales or as a consultant on health-related legal issues, such as insurance fraud.

A new attitude

This new attitude has created a savvier job seeker. Class of 1999 graduates entering the market are focusing more on the challenge of the work they'll be doing and what kinds of people they'll be working with than on salary, according to a survey of seniors and M.B.A. candidates from more than 50 schools across the country. Conducted by **WetFeet.com**, a career research site, the survey found that students spend 20 hours a week on average researching, searching, or interviewing for full-time employment.

Of course, once you land that job, you'll be putting in long hours—initiating projects, keeping your skills on the cutting edge—without the promise of security that your "underappreciated" predecessors had as they "clawed their way" to middle management.

Yes, restructuring and reductions are expected to continue. But many of the firms planning to restructure also expect to be hiring. Throughout your career, your security will come from your experience. If you're caught in a layoff or are ready for more responsibility, just pack up your skills and sell your track record to the next company or client.

The U.S. Bureau of Labor Statistics (BLS) estimates that most of us will change jobs as many as seven times over the course of one career—by choice or by chance. Rather than follow a prescribed path, you're likely to find yourself taking part in a number of ad hoc teams created for specific purposes—to develop a software application, design a Web site, market a new financial service, or find a cure for a disease.

As companies continue to downsize and outsource more work, prepare yourself for a future that may include temping, consulting, running your own business, returning to college, transitioning to a new career—or all of the above.

What counts in the new millennium?

Knowledge. Updating knowledge and skills is essential for everyone—from a college freshman to a senior manager. Of course, you'll have to keep pace with changes in technology. But the race for efficiency and innovation will challenge you to improve the quality of your thinking as well. Smart managers will take advantage of company-based training programs and continue building broad-based experience by earning more college credit, and even voluntary certification that is available.

With the growth of intranets, a new class of "knowledge worker" is carving out a niche on the cutting edge within forward-looking organizations. Technical gurus with a good sense of how information should flow to computer users working in specific business environments are creating "expert" systems. From stock market predictors to job competency modeling systems to Internet search engines, expert systems use artificial intelligence to identify and track specific information, providing the right amount of detail precisely at the moment of need.

Technical savvy. As the world becomes more and more networked, technical computer illiteracy will become as debilitating as reading illiteracy. More business will be conducted online—and not just by techies. Associates can attract the attention of law firm partners by networking through online legal forums, and advertisers will market-test and advertise new products in cyberspace. In addition, more software applications will be developed to provide intelligent support to managers who are making key decisions.

Problem-solving skills. Leave the time- and work-intensive tasks to technology. You are free to focus on a new crop of situations that defy rational methods of problem-solving. Using technology as a tool, you will be challenged to blend creativity and analysis in pursuit of innovative products, services, and programs, and more efficient processes.

Business sense. From law to public relations to travel, there is a new respect for the bottom-line realities. Clients and top executives are holding managers and professionals accountable for producing results and keeping costs down. In many jobs, a business degree or key business courses can be the ticket to credibility and advancement.

Communication ("people") skills. These days, technical people are talking to customers. Managers are motivating multidisciplinary teams. Writing and language skills, including public speaking, are crucial to leadership.

A global perspective. International borders continue to blur in the business world. A new multinational company needs people who can speak more than one language and understand cultural differences to staff international offices, negotiate joint ventures, and develop marketing materials. In fact, experience working abroad is becoming a prerequisite for moving into the executive ranks at many companies.

Where the jobs are

This book will help you survey dozens of jobs that promise career opportunities throughout the coming decade. In the 15 chapters that follow, you'll find the detailed information you need to gain perspective and begin to think strategically, not only about finding your next job, but about placing yourself in the best position to take full advantage of career opportunities you can't even begin to dream about.

Most of the hot jobs listed reflect the issues and concerns we will continue to face now that the new millennium has begun. Some career choices are as brand-spanking new as the technology that spawned them. Others answer the needs of an aging population, changing consumers, or environmentally conscious companies. Almost all new jobs in the next decade will be created by service industries. One in three will be in health care, business, or social services. It pays to tune into the trends, no matter what stage you're at in your career.

Let's begin by taking a look at how the job search will change as we go further into the new millennium.

How to get the most from this book

Each of the following sections will preview career opportunities in 15 growing industries and professions. They will give you a feel for what it might be like to work in industries poised for growth in the new millennium. You'll learn about the best and newest career opportunities and how to prepare for them. Rather than rush blindly into the next "gold rush," you should take this opportunity to assess:

* Whether you will enjoy working in the industry.
* Whether a particular job meets your salary goals.
* Where potential employers can be found.
* How to find more information.

Let's take a close look at the format of each section.

Forecast

This provides a general sense of how well the industry is growing overall, and highlights specific occupations described later in the section. Most statistics are drawn from the U.S. Bureau of Labor Statistics (BLS), which uses business and economic trends and changing demographics to chart expected growth in employment for occupations in every industry over a 10-year period. The most current set of projections (issued in November 1999) covers 1998-2008 period.

Although the fastest growing occupations generally offer the best opportunities, the size of the occupation can significantly affect the number of new jobs expected to open up. For example, there will be many more jobs projected for corrections officers (103,322) than for paralegals (76,426), even though the projected growth rate for paralegal jobs is 67.7 percent compared to a growth rate of 32.2 percent for corrections officer positions.

If you really want to crunch these numbers, spend some time online at **www.stats.bls.gov**.

The National Industry-Occupation Employment Matrix will allow you to perform searches by occupation or by industry. Searching by occupation allows you to see which industries will have the most growth in number of jobs in 500 occupations. Searching by industry allows you to see which occupations in 240 different industries will grow fastest or have the largest increase in jobs.

Refer to the *Occupational Outlook Handbook* to delve into more detail on your occupation of choice. You can find it at **www.stats.bls.gov/ocohome** or in the business reference section of your local library. This valuable career reference covers 250 occupations. Each listing includes sections on working conditions and related occupations. Most traditional occupations are covered; however, if you're hot on the trail of an emerging occupation, such as a Webmaster, you're better off talking to people who hold those jobs.

Growth

Generally, certain industries seem headed for quicker growth than others. How fast does one industry grow compared to other industries? According to the BLS, the average growth rate for all industries between 1996 and 2006 is between 10 and 20 percent. You're likely to find the strongest prospects in industries growing faster than the average (21 percent to 35 percent) or much faster than the average (36 percent or more).

Overview

If you're unfamiliar with a particular industry, this brief introduction will outline what kind of work is done in the industry (focusing on the occupations listed in the beginning of the section) and where you're likely to work if you join the ranks.

For example, the majority of health care professionals work in hospitals, but increasingly there are very good opportunities opening up in a growing number of outpatient facilities and medical group practices. Webmasters and computer security specialists were once outside consultants, but are increasingly moving inside companies. Civil engineers tend to work for state and federal governments, but may also be on the payroll at engineering services and architectural firms.

Industry snapshot

It's often useful to take a quick look back at the previous decade. What was "business as usual" during the 1990s? How did that change? How an industry coped with a scandal, or its own growing pains, often proves to be illuminating.

Almost without exception, most of the industries profiled in this book are fundamentally changing—or entirely transforming—the way they conduct business in reaction to a range of special circumstances. For most, change is far from over.

Trends to track

Global competition. Revolutionary advances in technology. Changing demographic patterns and consumer preferences. Major trends like these are changing the scope and substance of opportunities within many industries.

In some industries, such as banking and telecommunications, companies are consolidating to remain competitive. Some industries, such as sales, are transforming the way they do business—taking orders via the Web. Others (such as the travel industry) are finding strength in specialization.

Make it a habit to track these changes in the trade periodicals, as well as national publications such as *The Wall Street Journal*, available on the Web and in print. Watch the progress of local companies in the business section of your newspaper. And begin to think about ways your skills can be used to solve problems before you meet your first interviewer.

Old standards...and still winners

Nurses. Paralegals. Engineers. Teachers. This section will highlight the shortages in key areas within these broad occupations.

In some cases, basic responsibilities are changing with the times. In others, specialization (often possible with some extra education) can lead to new opportunities. For example, advanced practice nurses are handling many of the tasks of a physician. (See Health Care & Health Care Services on page 137.) Increasingly, self-employment offers bright prospects. Most chapters suggest which careers are "best bets for entrepreneurs."

A new generation of opportunities

Since this book was last published, the Internet has transformed most of the industries covered and created an explosion of new opportunities.

But it is also a generation of niche specialists. Web developers (see Telecommunications & the Internet on page 259), forensic accountants (see Accounting, page 43), destination marketers (see Travel & Hospitality, page 275), and geriatric care managers (see Health Care & Health Care Services, page 137) are occupations that have sprung up in the last decade.

Keep in mind that many niche opportunities covered in this book may not create a vast number of jobs—at least in the short term. But they are serving distinct needs in today's changing marketplace. Let your own interests—and research—guide you.

Do you have what it takes?

Do you have the technical aptitude it will take to be a systems analyst or a corporate network manager? The temperament to be a special education teacher or customer service representative? This section will help you focus on the personal qualities and values that are essential to success in a variety of occupations.

If your options are still wide open, be careful not to dismiss a "technical" industry, such as banking and financial services if you enjoy helping people or a "help" industry, such as health care, if your interests run more toward business. Like families, industries have room for many kinds of individuals.

Education and training

Will you need an advanced degree to get a foot in the door? A license to practice? Continuing education to move ahead? This section will tell you what types of education and training are acceptable—and which are preferred by employers.

If you haven't chosen a college or university, do some research. According to *Forbes* magazine, more M.B.A. schools offer specialized degrees—the Massachusetts Institute of Technology (MIT) in real estate and technology, Northwestern University in marketing, the University of Pennsylvania's Wharton School in international management, and Duke University in small business studies.

Many community colleges have teamed up with local businesses to provide job training in key areas such as computer-aided design and hazardous waste management. If you're thinking about one of these programs or are headed to a vocational or technical school, get the thumbs up from prospective employers as well as from industry and professional associations.

Professional licensing and certification

If voluntary certification is available, it may be to your benefit to pursue it, especially in highly competitive occupations or if you want to become a consultant.

Continuing education, such as formal seminars and informal reading, is a requirement—the price of participation—in most industries.

Career path

This section will introduce you to career paths for traditional occupations. But keep in mind, this trail has yet to be blazed for many of the emerging occupations covered by this book. Even traditional paths to advancement are taking some interesting twists and turns of late. Some companies are offering parallel career tracks to challenge and compensate scientists and other professionals who are not interested in or adept at management. Some offer additional training to managers who are stuck in a "flat" organization.

Lateral moves may provide your best opportunities. Temporary work and self-employment are also becoming viable options for an increasing number of experienced technicians, managers, and executives in many industries.

Tips on breaking in

Take advantage of any specific insights offered by recruiters to get a leg up on the competition or to save some time during your job search.

Tips range from what to ask recruiters to how to get experience to how to beef up your design or writing portfolio if you don't have a lot of experience.

How much can you earn?

Education, geography, and the size of a company all can influence the compensation you receive. While this section provides average salaries, and in many cases a range of earnings as you move through a career, you should view this information as a guideline. In most cases, you will be evaluating a total compensation package. It will be up to you to weigh the value of health benefits, bonus potential, stock options, or even lifestyle perks such as an on-site health club.

In the years ahead, compensation and salary adjustments will increasingly be based not on seniority, title, age, or annual "entitlements" as they have in the past, but on your skills and how innovative you are.

Where will you work?

Will geography affect your career choice? Possibly. Some professions, such as nursing and teaching, offer opportunities for challenge and advancement anywhere. Others, such as law and entertainment, draw people interested in top earnings to prestigious firms and studios in New York City and Los Angeles. That used to be true of advertising agencies, too, but increasingly, small boutique agencies and Web specialists are making news in cities like Portland, Ore. So things change.

In general, employment is growing in Western Mountain states such as Utah and Colorado and in the Sunbelt, especially the South and Southwest.

Jobs also seem to be gravitating to the suburbs and smaller cities, where more people live and where it is more economical for companies to operate. Fairfax County, Va., outside of Washington, D.C., and Marietta, Ga., outside of Atlanta, are two suburban growth spots. Austin, Tex.; Des Moines, Iowa; Orlando and Kissimmee, Fla.; and Raleigh/Durham, N.C., are a few small-town meccas.

How about working from home? Telecommuting is catching on with more and more companies. If this appeals to you, explore this option early in your interviews.

Resources

This extensive list of resources will help you extend your search—and research. If you don't find a listing for a database in an industry section, check the general business resources at the end of this introduction.

Web sites. Today your entire job search can be conducted online. With a computer and modem, you can dial up a database containing tens of thousands of detailed, current job listings in your industry or occupation or conduct research on prospective employers. You can also multiply your own visibility by placing your resume online where it can be viewed by an increasing number of employers, agencies, and recruiters with jobs to fill.

Where to find them. Most companies and industry associations have a button for current job opportunities on their home page. There are also a wide range of general and industry-specific sites on which you can post your resume, scan job opportunities, and get career and job hunting information. You'll find a listing of general Web sites at the end of this Introduction. Just type the location address, or URL, into your Web browser. Or perform a search using key words such as "jobs" and "careers," as well as specific occupation, industry, and company names.

Bulletin board systems (BBSs). These precursors to the Web sites are accessible via your modem. They typically have a very narrow occupation or regional focus, but job seekers can often find an abundance of information on topics of interest, as well as free software and public chat rooms. Most BBSs are free. Some charge fees for additional access and services.

Where to find them. You'll find some BBSs listed at the end of this Introduction. Try them out, with this caveat: BBSs are known for being somewhat "nomadic," moving and sometimes disappearing altogether.

Industry directories. These compendiums contain a wealth of information on the participants in a particular industry or occupation. You can add names and addresses to your mailing list and use other information to update your research. However, this detailed information can come at a very high price. Association directories tend to be expensive even for members.

Where to find them. Many directories are available at your city or college library. Be sure to check the general business resources at the end of this chapter.

Industry magazines. Major industry and trade journals provide an excellent way to get a feel for a career or job and to identify progressive and growing companies you'd like to target. Many magazines offer insight on what to say in an interview and whom to write or call for a job lead. Most also carry job listings.

Where to find them. If you can't find an issue on the newsstand or in the library, call the magazine and ask to see a sample issue before you subscribe. Also, check the general business resources at the end of this introduction.

Job hotlines. These telephone numbers will connect you to a prerecorded bulletin about jobs available in government, corporations, or associations. Depending on the sponsoring agency, the service may be free or charge a fee. Tip: stay away from hotlines that charge high fees for hundreds of job leads. In many cases the ads are taken directly from newspapers.

Where to find them. Most hotlines are run by associations. Look for information on the association's Web site or call the association for more information.

Job profiles

For every chapter in this book, you'll meet a real person who is working in one of the jobs highlighted. This may be your first glimpse of what the real world is like in your chosen profession—what happens on a typical day. You'll also get some expert advice on how to land a similar job.

Resources

General Web sites for job seekers

1ˢᵗ Steps to the Hunt
www.interbiznet.com/hunt/companies
Access to 4,000 companies' job pages.

4Work
www.4work.com
Volunteer opportunities, internships, and jobs across the United States.

America's Employers
www.americasemployers.com
A wealth of career resources and job listings.

America's Job Bank
www.ajb.dni.us
Access to 1,800 state employment services.

Ask the Headhunter
www.asktheheadhunter.com
An information resource for job hunters.

Career Magazine
www.careermag.com
Articles about a variety of career-related topics and searchable Usenet newsgroup postings.

Career Resource Center
www.careers.org
A wide range of information with more than 7,500 job-related links.

CareerMosaic
www.careermosaic.com
Tens of thousands of detailed, searchable listings.

CareerPath
www.careerpath.com
Access to 200,000 classified job ads from more than 32 major metropolitan newspapers.

careers.wsj.com
www.careers.wsj.com
One of the online offerings from Dow Jones & Co. providing top notch reporting from *The Wall Street Journal*.

CareerWEB
www.cweb.com
JobMATCH guide to the perfect job. Virtual career fairs. Resources for job seekers, entrepreneurs, and recruiters.

College Grad Job Hunter
www.collegegrad.com
Tips on which companies are hiring, how to ace an interview, putting together an attention-getting resume, and so forth.

E*SPAN's Job Options
www.joboptions.com
More than 10,000 detailed searchable listings.

Hoover's Business Resources
www.hoovers.com
In-depth profiles of thousands of hiring companies and a wide range of business information.

JobBank USA
www.jobbankusa.com
Compilation of listings from all major Web-based job databases along with excellent career resources.

JobCenter
www.jobcenter.com
Matches applicants with employers for a fee.

JobHunt
www.job-hunt.org
Guide to the premier Internet employment resources.

JobTrak
www.jobtrak.com
Available to students and alumni of more than 600 member colleges and universities.

The Monster Board
www.monsterboard.com
Tens of thousands of detailed, searchable listings.

Net Temps
www.net-temps.com
Temporary and permanent job listings from employment agencies.

Online Career Center
www.occ.com
Career fairs, career guidance, and links to recruiting sites.

The Riley Guide
www.rileyguide.com
A comprehensive guide to employment opportunities and job resources on the Internet.

Vault Reports
www.vaultreports.com/career
Provides an "insider's" view of companies, complete with information on current events from mergers to layoffs to IPOs.

U.S. News Online Career Center
www.usnews.com
Career guide offering research and data on the job market.

WetFeet.com
www.wetfeet.com
Industry research and career advice and resources.

Yahoo Careers
www.careers.yahoo.com
A wealth of information about occupations, companies, salaries, and more than 500,000 job listings.

BBSs

CapAccess Career Center
Modem: (703)671-9382
Job listings for the federal government.

Career Connections
Modem: (414)258-0164
Employment listings and networking opportunities.

Digital X-Connect BBS
Modem: (972)517-8443
Nationwide job opportunities.

Employer's Network
Modem: (206)476-0665
Contains a resume database and federal, Internet, and local (Tacoma, WA) job listings.

Fjob BBS
Modem: (912)757-3100
Federal Job Information Center with nationwide federal job listings.

SBA Online
Modem: (800)697-4636
Small Business Administration

General business directories

AMA's Executive Employment Guide
American Management Association
135 W. 50th Street
New York, NY 10020

AMBA's M.B.A. Employment Guide
Association of M.B.A. Executives
227 Commerce Street
East Haven, CT 06512

America's Corporate Families and International Affiliates
Dun's Marketing Services
3 Sylvan Way
Parsippany, NJ 07054
(201)526-0651

Association Yellow Book
Monitor Publishing Co.
104 Fifth Avenue
2nd Floor
New York, NY 10011
(212)627-4140

Business Organizations, Agencies, and Publications Directory
Gale Research Inc.
645 Griswold
835 Penobscot Building
Detroit, MI 48226
(800)877-4253

Business Publications Rates & Data
Standard Rate & Data Service, Inc.
3004 Glenview Road
Wilmette, IL 60091
(708)256-6067

Career & Job Fair Finder
College Placement Council, Inc.
62 Highland Avenue
Bethlehem, PA 18017
(215)868-1421

Directories in Print
Gale Research Inc.
645 Griswold
835 Penobscot Building
Detroit, MI 48226
(800)877-4253

Directory of Corporate Affiliations
Reed Reference Publishing
P.O. Box 31
New Providence, NJ 07974
(800)323-6772

Directory of Leading Private Companies
Reed Reference Publishing
P.O. Box 31
New Providence, NJ 07974
(800)323-6772

Dun & Bradstreet Million Dollar Directory
Dun's Marketing Services
3 Sylvan Way
Parsippany, NJ 07054
(201)526-0651

Dun & Bradstreet Reference Book of Corporate Management
Dun's Marketing Services
3 Sylvan Way
Parsippany, NJ 07054
(201)526-0651

Dun's Career Guide
Dun's Marketing Services
3 Sylvan Way
Parsippany, NJ 07054
(201)526-0651

Dun's Directory of Service Companies
Dun's Marketing Services
3 Sylvan Way
Parsippany, NJ 07054
(201)526-0651

Dun's Regional Business Directory
Dun's Marketing Services
3 Sylvan Way
Parsippany, NJ 07054
(201)526-0651

Encyclopedia of Associations
Gale Research Inc.
645 Griswold
835 Penobscot Building
Detroit, MI 48226
(800)877-4253

International Directory of Corporate Affiliations
Reed Reference Publishing
P.O. Box 31
New Providence, NJ 07974
(800)323-6772

Moody's Industry Review
Moody's Investors Service, Inc.
99 Church Street
New York, NY 10007
(212)533-0300

National Trade and Professional Associations
Columbia Books
1212 New York Avenue, NW
Ste. 330
Washington, D.C. 20005
(202)898-0662

Peterson's Job Opportunities for Business and Liberal Arts Graduates
P. O. Box 2123
Princeton, NJ 08543
(609)243-9111

Source Directory
Predicasts
1101 Cedar Avenue
Cleveland, OH 44106
(216)795-3000

Standard & Poors' Register of Corporations, Directors, and Executives
Standard & Poors Corporation
25 Broadway
New York, NY 10004
(212)208-8702

Thomas' Register
Thomas Publishing Company
1 Pennsylvania Plaza
New York, NY 10110
(212)695-0500

General business magazines

Barron's
Dow Jones & Company
200 Liberty Street
New York, NY 10281
(212)416-2759

Business Week
McGraw-Hill Inc.
1221 Avenue of the Americas
New York, NY 10020
(212)997-3608

Forbes
Forbes, Inc.
60 Fifth Avenue
New York, NY 10011
(212)620-2200

Fortune
The Time Inc. Magazine Co.
Time & Life Building
New York, NY 10020
(212)522-1212

Inc.
38 Commercial Wharf
Boston, MA 02110
(617)258-8000

Industry Week
1100 Superior Avenue
Cleveland, OH 44114
(216)696-7000

Nation's Business
U.S. Chamber of Commerce
1615 H Street, NW
Washington, DC 20062
(202)463-5650

National Business Employment Weekly
420 Lexington Avenue
New York, NY 10170
(212)808-6791

The Wall Street Journal
200 Liberty Street
New York, NY 10281

Chapter 1

Getting Started

An 8-step job-hunting strategy for the new millennium

If your ship doesn't come in, swim out to it!
—Jonathan Winters

Recruiters respect job hunters who show resourcefulness and determination during the hiring process. Most consider it evidence of how you'll perform on the job.

The following eight-step strategy will save you from random (and fruitless) action from the outset. You'll make steady progress toward your goal—and quite possibly, enjoy the journey more.

1. Assess your skills and abilities

It's easy to be drawn to a glamorous industry or prestigious occupation. Or to bank on the industry with the hottest growth potential.

But think of it this way: The career you choose will shape the life you lead. Even if you can set off in almost any direction, be practical. Let your interests, skills, natural talents, and personality guide you to work that will challenge you and a job you'll enjoy showing up for every day.

Let's begin making a few lists

What skills and talents do you already have? What subjects were a breeze for you in school? What do you have a passion for or always find yourself gravitating toward? What do other people say you're a genius at? These are your talents.

Now, distill the specific responsibilities you handled in the jobs you've held (even volunteer work), as well as extracurricular activities you've participated in, into a set of general skills. Your list might include influencing people, advising professionals, observing and recording information, even something as basic as listening (very few people are good listeners).

Your talents and skills may suit you for many more fields than you realize. Say you're a high school history teacher who has coached and raised funds for the basketball team, but want to change careers and sell sports equipment. Do you have what it takes? Your list includes working with people (students), communicating game strategies, a knowledge of sports equipment, and persuading people to donate money. You shouldn't have much of a problem making a move.

What motivates you? Helping people? Making money? Solving problems? Be honest about what sparks your interest and makes you go the extra mile. Do you expect hours from 9 to 5? A corner office?

What kind of person are you? Do you thrive on stress? Are you naturally assertive? Detail-oriented? Compassionate?

These lists will help you focus your search and at the same time expand your thinking. There is room for many different skill-sets and temperaments in almost every industry. You just may find yourself in a job you might never have considered...including CEO.

Do you have what it takes to be an entrepreneur? By 2005, the number of self-employed workers will increase by a third, creating half a million jobs. Many professionals, managers, and executives who are laid off or whose careers seem to be on hold are choosing to become independent consultants or "interim" managers, rather than searching for another corporate job. Answer yes or no to the following questions:

1. Do you easily get along with all kinds of people—even difficult people?
2. Do you enjoy working independently?
3. Do you have a talent, skill, interest, or good idea that others admire?
4. Do you consider yourself smarter than most of the bosses you've worked for?
5. Do you feel that most of the events in your life are determined by you?
6. Are you self-motivated and willing to work long hours?
7. Do you make learning a top priority?
8. Are you persistent, even in the face of rejection or failure?

9. Are you able to handle a lot of tasks and projects at once?
10. Are you comfortable with a certain element of uncertainty and risk?

If you answered yes to at least seven questions, you may have what it takes to go it alone...but you still need to do more research.

For more help:

Sign up for entrepreneurship training. Many colleges and universities have added entrepreneurship programs to their curriculum. San Francisco University has started a Center for the Study of Enterprise.

Visit franchising expos. If you're intrigued by the current boom in franchise ownership, you can find out more by visiting a franchising expo in your city or contacting the International Franchising Association at (800)543-1038 (**www.franchise.org**) or the American Franchise Exhibition at (800)334-0232 (**www.afexpo.com**). Entrepreneur Magazine also lists the Franchise 500 (**www.entrepreurmag.com/resource/franchise.hts**).

Visit the SBA online. The U.S. Small Business Administration (SBA) Web site (**www.sba.gov**) offers a wealth of free information as well as online courses to guide you in starting and financing a business.

Resources

* *The Best Work of Your Life*, Patricia V. Alea, et al., Pergiee, 1998.
* *Careers, Aptitude and Selection Tests,* Jim Barrett, Kogan Page Ltd, 1998.
* *Do What You Are: Discover the Perfect Career for You Through the Secrets of Personality Type,* Paul D. Tieger, Barbara Barron-Tieger, Little Brown & Co., 1995.
* *Do What You Love, the Money Will Follow: Discovering Your Right Livelihood*, Marsha Sinetar, Dell Books, 1989.
* *Find Your Calling, Love Your Life: Paths to Your Truest Self in Life and Work*, Martha Finney, Deborah Dasch, Simon & Schuster, 1998.
* *How to Choose a Career Now that You're All Grown Up: Evaluating Your Interests, Abilities & Goals to Find the Career That's Right for You,* Anna Mae Walsh Burke, Lifetime Books, 1997.
* *The Pathfinder: How to Choose and Change Your Career for a Lifetime of Satisfaction and Success*, Nicholas Lore, Fireside, 1998.

* *What Color is Your Parachute? A Practical Manual for Job-Hunters & Career Changers,* Richard Nelson Bolles, Ten Speed Press, 1998.
* *Zen and the Art of Making a Living: A Practical Guide to Creative Career Design,* Laurence G. Boldt, Penguin USA, 1999.

2. Explore your options

That's why you bought this book! The 15 sections will introduce you to the industries and professions with the healthiest prospects for growth in this century. A quick read will give you a sense of the challenges each industry faces, and how changes in demographics, technology, and the economy are likely to have an impact on your career prospects. Make note of the industries and occupations that interest you and seem to mesh with your goals.

For more help:

Conduct information interviews. If you're just not sure whether a particular industry or job is for you, start interviewing—for information only.

Friends, professors, and colleagues may be able to direct you to someone they know who works in the position you're considering. If not, call a local company and ask for the name of the person who holds your target position. Be sure to emphasize to the receptionist that you are simply seeking information—not a job—or you may be funneled directly to human resources.

Before the interview, draft a list of questions similar to those answered by the people profiled in this book. In addition, you might ask:

* How did you get started in this business?
* What are the current career opportunities for college grads?
* What are the basic requirements for an entry-level position with this company?
* Could you suggest trade publications or Web sites I should be reading/visiting regularly?
* Where do you see the opportunities in this industry in the next five years?
* Could you recommend someone else for me to contact for more information?

Most people are more than happy to talk about the work they do. At the conclusion of the interview, ask if there is anyone else you should speak with. An important side benefit to information interviewing: The more you do this, the more you become known to important people in the industry. When a job opens up, you may be remembered. (You'll find more on the crucial practice of networking further in this chapter.)

Resources

* *30 Great Cities to Start Out In*, Sandra Gurvis, Arco Pub., 1997.
* *America's Top Internships: 1999*, Mark Oldman, Princeton Review, 1998.
* *The Back Door Guide to Short Term Job Adventures: Internships, Extraordinary Experiences, Seasonal Jobs, Volunteering, Work Abroad*, Michael Landes, Ten Speed Press, 1997.
* *The Jobbank 1999* (city-by-city) series, Adams Media Corporation, 1998.

3. Write a resume

Your resume is simply an advertisement. It won't generate job offers. But hopefully it will generate an interview.

There is a library of excellent books attending to every detail and question you might have as you create your resume. A handful of the best are listed here. In a nutshell, there are two standard resume formats:

The chronological format. The chronological resume presents your experience in chronological order, starting with your current or most recent job. This is a good choice if you have had impressive job titles, steady upward mobility, and no gaps in your work history.

List the responsibilities and scope of each job, as well as the skills you used, but focus on specific accomplishments. Action words will help you describe projects you organized, created, established, initiated, developed, supervised, or designed. Wherever possible, list tangible, quantifiable results—the amount of money and time saved, percentage of productivity improvement, or sales growth.

The functional format. But what if your career path doesn't fit the corporate mold (an increasingly common situation these days)? Or what if you want to change careers, are entering the job market for the first time, or are staging a "re-entry" after raising children full-time? The functional resume format allows you to spotlight your accomplishments, especially if they were more impressive than your job titles. You can also use a functional resume to hide gaps in employment and give weight to experience and skills you gained while participating in extracurricular activities or performing volunteer work. Employment dates and job titles can be omitted or briefly listed in chronological order at the bottom of the resume.

As a general rule, your resume should be no longer than two pages (preferably just one) and end with a section describing your education (the name[s] of your college degree[s] and dates of graduation), as well as any professional credentials or awards you've earned. You may also list job-related training. But leave out personal information, such as personal hobbies. And never, **never** include salary information.

The electronic resume. If you're conducting part or all of your job search online, your resume should be studded with "key words"—skills, industry terms, company names, years of experience, degrees, and other credentials. Most companies and recruiters use specialized software to scan and sort resumes using these identifiers. Of course, key words vary by industry and profession. For example, key words for a device analysis engineer might include "device physics," "failure analysis," "material science," and "B.S." (degree).

Most of the same rules apply to electronic resumes, with a few important exceptions:

* Computers don't read cover letters. Your electronic resume has to do the selling job of both.

* Computers tend to bypass action verbs in favor of nouns—job titles, departments, skills. Reuse terms used in advertisements and don't spare the industry jargon. Computers like buzzwords.

* An electronic resume can be longer—two pages, or even three. This leaves room for a maximum of carefully chosen key words. Don't send volumes, however, because your resume will ultimately be reviewed by a real live human being who may have fairly traditional ideas about resumes.

* Steer away from boldface, underlined, and italic type. A computer scanner may not be able to recognize an unusual typeface or may get confused if it has to switch from boldface to underline to italic often.

The bottom line is to convince a recruiter that your background is a "fit" with a specific job opening. It is often worth the effort to create a new resume for every opening you apply for.

For more help:

Hire a consultant. Look in the yellow pages under "Resume Services" for the names of consultants who will create a resume from scratch for about $200—or simply critique your current resume for much less. Some community colleges and career resource centers offer consulting and conduct seminars on effective resume writing.

Try multimedia. Many advertising agencies and companies are looking for people with multimedia skills. If yours are impressive or if you have a portfolio of work to show a creative director, you might call on multimedia technology to create an interactive resume.

Just don't get too carried away. Substance is still more important than style. Dazzling special effects will never make up for sloppy editing and poor quality graphics. It's also a good idea to make sure that your recipient has the hardware and software necessary to view your portfolio.

This can be a time-consuming and costly route, and it is not recommended for computer novices. Most colleges and universities have tools on hand to create multimedia effects.

Resources

* *Electronic Resumes & Online Networking: How to Use the Internet to Do a Better Job Search, Including a Complete, Up-to-Date Resource Guide*, Rebecca Smith, Career Press, 1998.
* *Portfolio Power: The New Way to Showcase Your Job Skills and Experiences*, Martin Kimeldorf, et al, Petersons Guides, 1997.
* *Power Resumes*, Ron Tepper, John Wiley & Sons, 1998.
* *Resume Writers*, David F. Noble, Jist Works, 1998.
* *The Smart Woman's Guide to Resumes and Job Hunting*, Betsy Sheldon and Julie Adair King, Career Press, 1995.
* *Your First Resume*, Ronald W. Fry, Career Press, 1995.

4. Do your homework

You may be tempted to gloss over this step. But that will leave you at a disadvantage when making contact with a prospective employer, whether through a cover letter, at a job fair, or via the Web.

Facts and figures. The best way to stand apart from the crowd is to know enough about a company's products and services, competition, and current challenges to convince the person you're interviewing with that your skills would make a difference.

Reviewing the trade publications listed in the "Resources" section of each chapter will give you a good foundation of knowledge. There is also an enormous amount of information on specific companies, as well as their industries at large on the Web. Who are the most powerful players in your industry of choice? What do they say about themselves on their Web sites, and in the latest annual report and press releases you download? What kinds of jobs are available? How detailed are the job descriptions?

Of course, the companies listed at the end of each chapter are only a few of the universe of potential employers. Check the industry directories and publications for more names. Also check some of the following general business directories (available in the business section of your local library) for information about companies advertising job opportunities on the Web:

* *Standard & Poors Register of Corporations, Directors and Executives.* Lists more than 45,000 corporations.

* *Dun & Bradstreet's Million Dollar Directory.* Lists 160,000 public U.S. corporations and 30,000 private companies with a net worth of $500,000 or more.

* *Moody's Industry Review.* Annual reference that's updated weekly. Includes 4,000 leading businesses in more than 100 industries.

* *The Career Guide: Dun's Employment Opportunities Directory.* Features companies with more than 1,000 employees in fields in a variety of technical and professional areas. Listings include information about occupations, training programs, and hiring requirements.

* *The Guide to American Directories.* Lists 330 directories covering 400 topics.

* *Who Owns Whom.* Contains information on companies that may be difficult to find.

* *Thomas' Register of American Manufacturers.* Lists 140,000 product manufacturers.

* *World's Business Directory of U.S. Private and Public Companies.* Lists 133,000 companies.

The cultural component. Facts and figures are not enough information. As a job seeker, you have to gain a sense for what life will be like after you land a job. In other words, what's the culture like? What do the company's competitors and industry analysts say about it? Are employees passionate about working there?

A good resource for finding out this kind of "inside" information is WetFeet.com Insider Guides. Each 30- to 70-page book in this series gives you the lowdown on:

* Average starting salaries for undergrads and M.B.A.s.
* What the recruiting process is like.
* Tips from company insiders on how to sail through interviews.
* Key publications and articles that will help you complete your research.
* What employees love most—and like least—about working for the company.

Check out **WetFeet.com** for a host of other research tools, as well as up-to-the-minute news, career self-assessment, and expert advice to help you quickly get up to speed for your interviews, negotiate the best compensation package, and excel after you're on the job.

Magazines like *Fortune* and *Working Women* also annually rank companies according to specific cultural criteria such as availability of telecommuting or childcare.

5. Cast your net

Once you've targeted the type of job, the industry, and the companies that interest you, it's time to get your resume out for review. There are a multitude of ways to do this. Although it's possible to spread yourself too thin during the "seeding process," it's also not a good idea to go to the other extreme and focus on only one medium.

The Web. In the last edition of this book, "online resources" came up next to dead last in this section listing. Newspaper classified ads led the way! Well, as you've already noticed, technology (and especially the Internet) has fundamentally changed the way we conduct our lives—and certainly our job searches. There are dozens of company, association, and career-specific sites where you can assess you skills, post your resume, and browse hundreds of thousands of job listings and respond to those that sound like a fit. Some sites will e-mail you job listings that match your specifications.

Most companies and associations have a button for current job openings on their home page. If you see a listing that you like, you can respond using the contact information provided. For addresses of some of the best general career Web sites, check out the resource section at the end of the next chapter.

A word to the wise: There is so much available, you might feel like a kid in a candy store. But rather than post your resume everywhere, spend some time comparing sites. Narrow down your options to two or three strong ones, including at least one specifically focused on your industry. Your goal is to reduce the amount of time you spend finding the right job rather than inviting a deluge of calls that send you down blind alleys.

Professional associations. No matter what industry, occupation, professional level, race, or gender you represent, there is at least one—and probably half a dozen—of these nonprofit organizations representing you. Once you're a member, you can take advantage of a range of services from training and certification to salary surveys. In addition to a Web site, most associations publish magazines with job listings and many have established hotlines, placement, or referral services to help members list and find jobs. You can bet that top employers in your industry use these services extensively. Industry-specific associations are listed in the "Resources" section at the end of each chapter.

The classifieds. Look at your Sunday newspaper and you'll see classifieds are still going strong. So it doesn't hurt to keep an eye out for jobs you haven't found during your Web surfing.

Here a few tips to maximize your effectiveness:

Check out every section of the Sunday classifieds. Ads are run alphabetically rather than clustered by position or industry. An ad for a "personnel" position might appear under "human resources," "compensation," "benefits," or "management." Many newspapers also publish classified advertising directed toward experienced professionals seeking middle-management opportunities in the business section.

"Shop" trade journals and business publications. *The Wall Street Journal* is a good resource, as is its *National Business Employment Weekly*, a compilation of ads that have appeared in various regional editions during the previous week.

Concentrate on "open" ads. In other words, ads that appear with the name and address of the company. Companies running blind ads (with only a post office box number) may just be trying to get a feel for what talent is available and what kinds of salaries people are asking for. Even if there is a job opening, you won't have much of a chance to display the research that will set you apart from other applicants. And never reveal salary information in your resume or cover letter. If you're well qualified for a job, you'll still get a call—and be in a better position to bargain.

Job fairs. What better way to personally meet and talk with recruiters from dozens of companies of all sizes that are actively seeking people with your education and skills? To ensure that you stand out from the crowd of hopeful candidates, treat this experience just as seriously as you would a job interview. Do your homework on the companies you know will be attending. Dress professionally, and confidently introduce yourself to each recruiter. As you present your resume, sum up your background and the type of job you're looking for in a few sentences. If the recruiter doesn't offer you a business card or offer to schedule an interview, don't be afraid to ask for both. Always close the conversation by asking about the next step. After the fair is over, follow up in your contacts by sending a thank you note and another copy of your resume.

Resources

* *100 Best Nonprofits to Work For,* Leslie Hamilton, Robert Tragert, IDG Books Worldwide, 1998.

* *Directory of Executive Recruiters 1999,* Liz Kennedy Information, Kennedy Publications, 1998.

* *The Directory of Jobs and Careers Abroad,* Jonathan Parker, Vacation-Work, 1997.

* *Get What You Deserve!: How to Guerilla Market Yourself,* Seth Godin, Jay Conrad Levinson, Avon Books, 1998.

* *The Global 200 Executive Recruiter: An Essential Guide to the Best Recruiters in the United States, Europe, Asia and Latin America,* Nancy Garrison Jenn, Jossey-Bass Publishers, 1998.

* *The Guide to Internet Job Searching,* Margaret Riley-Dikel, et al, Vgm Career Horizons, 1998.

* *Job-hunting on the Internet,* Richard Nelson Bolles, Ten Speed Press, 1999.

* *Job Searching Online for Dummies,* Pam Dixon, Dummies Technology Press, IDG Books Worldwide, 1998.

* *Job Seekers Guide to Wall Street Recruiters,* Christopher W. Hunt, Scott A. Scanlon, John Wiley & Sons, 1998.

* *M.B.A. Employers: The VaultReports.com Guide to the Top 50 M.B.A. Employers, an Industry Guide for Job Seekers,* Marcy Lerner, et al, VaultReports.com, 1998.

* *Strategic Job Jumping: Fifty Very Smart Tactics for Building Your Career,* Julia Hartman, Prima Pub, 1997.
* *Using the Internet and the World Wide Web in Your Job Search,* Fred E. Jandt and Mary B. Nemnich, JIST, 1997.

6. Network, network, network

What do your former employer, your college professor, and your dentist have in common? They're part of your network, which means they may be able to introduce you to people they know who work in the industry you're targeting. One of these people may offer you your next job, or introduce you to someone else who can.

That's the "magic" process of networking, and as you can see from the profiles of real people in this book, it is an essential ingredient in any job hunter/career builder's strategy. But there are some rules and etiquette involved.

Begin by asking 15 of your own professional, school, and personal contacts to give you the names of three people they know who work in a particular company, industry, occupation, or part of the country that you're interested in.

Agree on how you should introduce yourself. Ideally, your friend or colleague will offer to pave the way by calling or writing a letter of introduction. At a minimum, make sure you have your contact's permission to use his or her name whenever you call a networking referral.

Send each of your new contacts a package containing a cover letter describing your career goals and the list of companies you are interested in working for.

Follow up with a telephone call. It's helpful to write a short script so you will be concise and direct about the purpose of your call. Most people enjoy talking about their profession and are flattered when they are asked for advice, especially when they are referred by someone they know and respect.

In the course of an informal telephone or face to face chat, ask your contact if he or she knows anyone who works for any of the companies you're targeting. If not, ask if there is anyone else in his or her circle of business who might be interested in receiving your resume. Check back with people periodically to see if anything may have changed.

For more help:

Keep your ears open. You could hear about opportunities as easily at a family gathering as a conference. Don't be afraid to step up to a group or even a stranger and explain your interests and situation.

Get an alumni referral. Have your college alumni office refer you to other alums already employed in your career of choice.

Resources

* *Networking for Everyone: Connecting with People for Career and Job Success*, L. Michelle Tullier, JIST Works, 1998.
* *Power Networking: Using the Contacts You Don't Even Know You Have to Succeed in the Job You Want*, Marc Kramer, Vgm Career Horizons, 1997.
* *The Secrets of Savvy Networking,* Susan RoAne, Warner Books, 1993.
* *The Smart Woman's Guide to Networking*, Joyce Hadley and Betsy Sheldon, Career Press, 1995.

7. Interview

Believe it or not, wall-to-wall books on interviewing have not created better interviews according to many recruiters and interviewers.

With employers toughening up on interviewing practices to avoid expensive hiring mistakes, it's a good idea to make sure you won't be guilty of the following complaints:

Most candidates ask superficial questions. If you arrive at the interview without a passing knowledge of the industry or company, the interviewer has no choice but to assume that you aren't serious about working for the company. The way to impress a recruiter or hiring manager is to do your homework and apply it in the interview.

How much should you be expected to know? According to recruiters, you should be familiar with information that is generally available to the public. Even for privately held companies, you have a broad range of reference resources—from business and industry directories to the company's own advertisements and marketing materials. Prepare yourself to ask thoughtful questions during the interview.

Many candidates have bad manners. It's hard to believe, but interviewers report that candidates lack basic social and professional etiquette.

If you are abrupt with the receptionist, expect the human resources to have an extra copy of your resume, and lack basic manners, you are likely to earn a reputation—but certainly not a job.

If you need to brush up on social skills, scout around for a book or seminar. Students in "Wine, Dine and Act Fine," offered by Lycoming College, Williamsport, Penn., learn how to dress for professional situations and actually practice their table manners during mock luncheon interviews.

Most candidates are easily flustered. More and more, interviewers are using a technique called the stress interview to test your professional and confidence under pressure.

Typically, this interview begins with a few friendly questions, Just as you begin to think you've gotten off on the right foot, the interviewer will throw you a curve.

> *Q.* *"Your resume does a fine job of pointing out your professional strengths and skills, but I'd like to find out more about you as a person. What would you say is your greatest weakness?*

It's natural for first-time interviewers to leap to the defensive, but that would be a mistake. Rather, respond calmly and thoughtfully—focusing on the positive.

> *A.* *"When I started in sales, I tended to overbook my appointments. Then I realized I wasn't devoting enough time to each call. I've learned not to schedule more calls than I can handle effectively."* Then, try to turn the discussion back to the job itself.

On a related subject, as many as 30 percent of employers in some industries routinely use lengthy psychological tests to probe for personal attributes and values such as honesty, competitiveness, self-confidence, and initiative. Sharpen your pencil.

Nothing can substitute for practice. Use current books on interviewing to help you think through the answers to tough questions. Role-play with friends or associates, or videotape a mock interview and ask for feedback.

Resources

* *101 Answers to the Toughest Interview Questions,* 4th Edition, Ronald W. Fry, Career Press, 2000.
* *Your First Interview*, Ronald W. Fry, Career Press, 1995.

8. Negotiate the best compensation package

"What salary were you hoping for?" After months of hard work, it comes down to this. Do you shoot for the moon because you know you'll be negotiated down? Or do you accept less than you know you are worth—less than you know the same position pays in other companies—rather than risk walking away from this job?

Keep in mind that a compensation package is more than just a paycheck, It can include everything from a signing bonus with stock options (that can make you rich one day) to discretionary telecommuting privileges. You may decide to take a lower salary if you can work toward a healthy quarterly bonus, make good use of the fancy on-site health club, and can look forward to a six-week paid sabbatical in a few years.

It pays—literally—to negotiate. If you are unskilled in the art of negotiation, there are many excellent books to help you formulate strategies and counter objections. Perhaps you can quantify the value you can bring to the company in real dollars (increased sales, immediate cost savings). Or arrange an early performance review and another salary negotiation. It may be early in the game, but remember not to give this area short shrift. You'll be living with your decision for at least a year.

Resources

* *24 Hours to Your Next Job, Raise or Promotion*, Robin Ryan, John Wiley & Sons, 1997.

* *College Grad Job Hunter: Insider Techniques and Tactics for Finding a Top-Paying Entry-Level Job,* Brian D. Krueger, Adams Media Corp, 1998.

* *Dynamite Salary Negotiations: Know What You're Worth and Get It!,* Ronald L. Krannich, Caryl Rae Krannich, Impact! Publications, 1997.

* *Get More Money on Your Next Job: 25 Proven Strategies for Getting More Money, Better Benefits & Greater Job Security*, Lee Miller, McGraw-Hill, 1997.

* *Negotiating Your Salary: How to Make $1,000 a Minute*, Jack Chapman, Ten Speed Press, 1996.

* *The Smart Woman's Guide to Interviewing and Salary Negotiation*, Julie Adair King, Career Press, 1993.

A final word

Persist! Nothing will take the place of persistence. Your job search may seem formidable today, but once you reduce it to manageable tasks, you'll begin to see progress. Send out a certain number of resumes every day, resolve to spend one evening a week, or every Saturday afternoon doing research on the Web. With every step, you'll move closer to your goal—and, in the process, you'll develop skills you'll use over the life of your career.

Best of luck to you!

Chapter 2

Accounting
From "bean counter" to "business consultant"

Auditor
Certified Public Accountant (CPA)
Cost accountant
Environmental accountant
Forensic accountant
International accountant
Management accountant
Tax accountant
Best Bet for Entrepreneurs: *Independent CPA*

Forecast

Expect more than 122,000 new jobs for accountants and auditors by 2008, according to the U.S. Bureau of Labor Statistics (BLS).

Growth

Employment is expected to grow as fast as the average for all occupations, increasing 11.3 percent through the year 2008.

Overview

So you're interested in making a career of crunching numbers? You've made a practical choice. But that shouldn't come as a surprise to someone like you. You're probably accustomed to weighing the odds and consulting the law of averages.

But anybody who dares to call you a "bean counter" in this age of information is clearly out of step with the times. Today, technology handles most of the tedious number crunching, leaving accountants free to serve as business consultants and strategic advisors to new and established companies as well as individuals.

In a Robert Half International poll of 150 executives at the nation's largest companies, 71 percent said that accounting professionals have become increasingly critical to their overall operations. Accountants have an insight into bottom-line business issues that many executives need to make better decisions. For example, they may advise against a seemingly lucrative contract because it is likely to create an accounting nightmare.

As competition heats up at the global level, corporate giants and blossoming startups will need accountants and auditors to help them grow bottom -line profits, often by acquiring or partnering with other businesses. A study by Gunn Partners predicts that by the year 2002, management accountants at the controller level will be spending 30 percent more time on business partnership issues.

No matter what the future holds, all companies will need to manage more complex and creative (yes, creative!) accounting methods, regularly report on earnings to investors and stockholders—and keep the taxman at bay. In the final analysis, accounting remains one of the most secure career paths you can choose for the long term.

Accounting firm or company?

Starting out, you'll follow one of two paths. One leads through the ranks of one of the "Big Five" public accounting firms, such as PricewaterhouseCoopers. Once you've passed the rigorous exams that qualify you to be a *Certified Public Accountant (CPA)*, you'll handle a range of activities for clients of the firm. Or you may choose to specialize in tax accounting or perform financial audits.

As a *tax accountant*, you'll have a full-time job following the often circuitous route of the U.S. Tax Code. Your close scrutiny will be the basis for answering questions and developing tax and investment strategies many individual clients and companies will use to make key business decisions.

Sound cut and dried...and dull? Any tax accountant worth his or her stuff will tell you that the real challenge of the job lies in understanding the black and white well enough to work in the gray area. That is, while some deductions are blatantly illegal, written rules can often be interpreted in ways lawmakers didn't intend. Your judgement will help you advise your company and clients on how conservatively or aggressively to interpret the ever-changing rules.

As an *auditor*, you will carefully analyze the detailed financial records, or "books," of publicly held companies to ensure that the money coming in and going out is properly accounted for. You may also specialize in electronic data interchange (EDI), systems that allow companies and selected vendors to exchange orders, invoices, and other accounting "paperwork" entirely online.

Working inside a public or privately-held company as an *internal auditor, management accountant,* or *cost accountant*, you will examine and evaluate your company's financial and information systems, management procedures, and internal controls to ensure that records and controls are adequate to protect against fraud and waste. Working with people from many departments, you'll track and manage financial information, perhaps focusing on financing, collections, payables, receivables, budgeting, or cost analysis. You'll also prepare financial reports for non-management groups, including stockholders, creditors, regulatory agencies, and tax authorities.

Many companies are generating half or more of their revenues abroad. This opens up opportunities for accountants with training and experience in an international marketplace. Corporations concerned about the security of the worldwide business systems are looking for a special cadre of accounting "sleuths"—part auditor, part detective—to safeguard profits. Hundreds of billions are lost each year to white collar crime and fraudulent health care claims.

You may also manage the activities of an outside accounting firm, as well as other financial consultants such as *mergers and acquisitions specialists* (see Banking & Financial Services). With your finger on the pulse of your company's financial health, you're likely to gain the attention—and frequently the ear—of top management as you rise through the ranks. Later on you may decide to hang out your own shingle as an *independent CPA*.

Industry snapshot

Since the 1980s, the accounting industry's "Big Eight" multinational public accounting firms have been consolidated into the Big Five: Andersen Worldwide, Deloitte Consulting, Ernst & Young, KPMG Peat Marwick, and PricewaterhouseCoopers.

The double whammy of a recession with the savings and loan crisis began with layoffs and laid the groundwork for increased competition between firms. For the first time in many years, job security was no longer a given—even for partners. Firms that rallied added new services—most notably business advisory and consulting—to the traditional audit and tax functions. Firms that faltered were absorbed.

Public accounting firms will continue to lure corporate clients with a range of business services related to accounting, such as management consulting. Many firms have chosen to limit the services they offer in order to provide expertise in key areas, such as health care or banking. As in many other industries, look for alliances and associations between CPA and non-accounting firms. For example, client demand for financial services has sparked new alliances between accounting firms and Wall Street brokerage houses, transforming some accountants into investment advisors, who sell a host of products from equity funds and annuities to insurance.

Internally, growth through diversification continues to create power struggles between consultants and accountants. As consulting revenues grow by leaps and bounds, accounting partners maintain their grip on management—and monetary rewards.

In the process, the total number of independent, local accounting firms that offer only tax and accounting services is shrinking.

Trends to track

The new investment advisors. Despite regulatory concerns over conflicts of interest, accounting firms are responding to customer demand for financial services by forming alliances with some of the nation's largest brokerage houses. In return for pitching investments to their clients, accountants get a portion of the sales commissions or fees. Wall Street's Salomon Smith Barney already has alliances with 200 accounting firms in 32 states.

Clients clearly like having a one-stop shop for tax, accounting, and investment advice. The top 100 tax and accounting firms rang up $25.5 billion in sales in 1999, a whopping 21 percent increase over fiscal 1997. The Big Five accounting firms aren't sharing the spoils because of past auditing missteps. The key to continued success is training on new products.

The technology ticket. A growing number of accountants and auditors are developing extensive computer skills. Some specialize in correcting problems with software or developing software to meet unique data needs. Because so many computer systems affect financial data, many companies are tapping management accountants for advice on financing of new hardware, implementing software updates, and training financial personnel to use new systems.

Figuring on changing business. A continued explosion of new startups and small businesses whose growth is fueled by electronic commerce on the Internet, as well as the ongoing consolidation of existing companies through mergers and acquisitions will keep accountants plenty busy.

Old standards...and still going strong

Auditors. Auditing remains an excellent place for new accounting graduates to "get their feet wet" in the field by combining training with on-the-job experience. Extensive travel tends to lead to higher-than-average turnover in this area of public accounting. Internal auditors have a much better chance staying put, working within one company.

Cost accountants. There is currently a demand for accountants skilled in startup situations as well as with manufacturing experience to keep tabs on inventory movements, adjustments, or corrections and analyze workorder variations.

Tax accountants. As long as death and taxes are certainties, this career avenue promises the closest thing to job security you're likely to find anywhere. Tax accounting is so highly specialized that it tends to demand an all-or-nothing commitment. Watch for new challenges as businesses continue to expand into international markets.

Management accountants. After recruiters from top CPA firms swoop down on the nation's college campuses, corporations are often left wanting for entry-level accountants. If you're interested in developing a broad business perspective in a particular industry, step forward and be recruited. A bonus for some: As a management accountant, you'll spend less time away from home than you would as a member of a public accounting firm.

A new generation of opportunities

Environmental accountants. How will mandated ecomeasures affect profits? An environmental accountant is trained to crunch the numbers on all the alternatives. Chrysler saves $18,000 in regulatory fees annually after swapping one car part for its mercury-free alternative. Environmental accountants at Baxter International recommended less bulky product packaging and recycling as pollution control measures, saving the company $100 million.

International accountants. Working abroad for several years can be your ticket to becoming a partner at a public accounting CPA firm or netting the top spot in a corporation. Most internationally trained accountants work for Big Five firms serving multinational U.S. companies and foreign companies operating in the United States.

Forensic accountants. This "elite" force of auditors—many with experience in law enforcement—use financial records to ferret out white-collar crimes, such as tax fraud. Because they are trained to question witnesses and suspects as well as to testify in court, they are in great demand by government agencies and the corporate world.

Do you have what it takes?

Excellent math skills are a prerequisite—that goes without saying. But in a field in which cultivating long-term relationships with many types of people is critical for success, good people skills tip the scales when it comes to hiring and promoting accountants in all areas. Accounting is much more of a team effort these days. Your ability to work well with others on departmental and interdepartmental teams will set you apart.

You'll be expected to analyze, compare, and interpret facts and figures quickly and to make sound judgements based on this knowledge. You should also be able to clearly communicate the results of your work, orally and in writing, to non-accounting managers and clients. You should also be counted on for accuracy and the ability to handle responsibility with limited supervision.

Tax accountants, for example, may spend considerable time advising clients on investment strategies. Auditors often walk into tricky situations in which employees resist handing over financial records. Management accountants must establish relationships with people at many levels of the company, and feel comfortable making presentations and briefing top management.

In addition, you should have a high level of integrity and feel comfortable working on your own much of the time.

A "needle in the haystack" brand of curiosity helps auditors and forensic accountants trace large sums of money through a series of complex financial transactions. Tax accountants must also love research.

Education and training

An undergraduate degree in accounting will launch your career as an accountant or auditor. Based on recommendations from the American Institute of Certified Public Accountants, a small number of states currently require CPA candidates to complete 150 semester hours of college coursework—an additional 30 hours beyond the usual four-year bachelor's degree. If you're a prospective accounting major, you should carefully research accounting curricula and the requirements for any states you hope to become licensed in before enrolling.

If you've got your sights set on joining one of the Big Five, your grade point average should remain safely inside the 3.5 to 4.0 range. That may mean retaking a class or two before you graduate. Requirements tend to relax a bit for accounting firms at the regional and local levels.

Corporations place less emphasis on grades than on leadership skills and your interest in the industry. What about an M.B.A.? Some companies, particularly larger companies, still prefer to hire recent M.B.A. recipients for management track positions. In a recent survey of CFOs, 70 percent said it is valuable for accounting and finance professionals to earn an M.B.A.

With or without an M.B.A., it may be more useful to gain knowledge in a specialized area, such as international business and current legislation.

Auditors charged with analyzing nonpaper financial transactions, made via electronic data interchange (EDI) systems are increasingly making the transition to accounting from information services (IS) departments.

Tax accountants enter with a master's degree in business, tax, or law.

Environmental accountants need a multidisciplined background, including accounting, finance, and engineering or environmental science courses.

Forensic accountants should combine an undergraduate degree in accounting with training or experience in law enforcement with an emphasis on white collar crime. Many have previous experience working for the Internal Revenue Service (IRS), Federal Bureau of Investigation (FBI), or the U.S. Customs Service.

If you plan to step into the international arena, take advanced conversational courses in Japanese, French, Spanish, and/or Portuguese.

Continuing education is becoming vital for accountants in all areas. Many public accounting firms offer excellent training programs. Tax accountants must burn more midnight oil than most just staying up to date on the continually changing tax code.

Regularly taking software courses through a university extension program may also benefit your career.

Professional licensing and certification

More than 40 percent of the one million accountants and auditors working today have earned one of four types of professional certification.

Certified Public Accountant (CPA). The majority of accountants, especially those planning a career at a public accounting firm, take the rigorous CPA exam within the first five years of employment. In fact, only about a quarter of those who take it each year pass each part they attempt. Most CPA firms enroll newly hired accountants in a preparation course.

The CPA exam tests your knowledge in four areas: law, audit, theory, and practice. You are allowed to pass the exam in increments, one area at a time. However, many states require all sections to be passed within a certain period of time. And, of course, your prospects for promotion will be limited until you've passed all four parts.

Even after you pass the exam, in most states you must spend two years working before you can sign your name to a tax form or audit statement as a CPA. Nearly all states require CPAs and other public accountants to complete a certain number of hours of continuing professional education before their licenses can be renewed. Professional associations sponsor numerous courses, seminars, group study programs, and other forms of continuing education.

Certified Management Accountant (CMA). Accountants who make their careers in corporations may opt for this professional certification in addition to or instead of the CPA. With a bachelor's degree and at least two years of management accounting experience, you can take the four-part exam to become a CMA from the Institute of Management Accountants (IMA). Pairing an M.B.A. degree with a CMA credential is a great way to position yourself for the top management rungs in large companies.

Certified Fraud Examiner (CFE). Forensic accountants can enhance their professional credibility by earning the CFE. Contact the Association of Certified Fraud Examiners for more information. (See "Resources" section.)

Even if certification is not required in your area, it can give you a distinct advantage when competing for the best jobs.

Certified Internal Auditor (CIA). The Institute of Internal Auditors awards the Certified Internal Auditor to graduates of accredited colleges and universities who have completed two years of work in internal auditing and have passed a four-part exam.

Certified Information Systems Auditor (CISA). The Information Systems Audit and Control Association awards the Certified Information Systems Auditor to graduates who pass an exam and have five years of experience auditing electronic data interchange (EDI) systems. (Auditing or data processing experience and a college education may be substituted for up to three years.)

Tips on breaking in

Keep your grades up. The good news for new graduates is that there are relatively few contenders for entry-level positions. The number of accounting degrees awarded today has changed little since the early 1980s. But the reality is that competition for jobs with the best firms is hotter than ever. And new hires face more rigorous training and work standards according to the American Institute of Certified Public Accountants (AICPA). More now than ever, a strong academic background is the foundation you need just to stay in the game. In a recent nationwide survey by Accountemps, 54 percent of CFOs said their organizations' hiring procedures have become more in-depth over the past five years.

Stay local. Unless you have your heart set on becoming a rising star in the New York office of Arthur Andersen, consider joining a respected public accounting firm close to home. Regional firms are rarely represented by the army of Big Five recruiters on campus, so your best bet is to research local firms listed in the yellow pages or contact your local chapter of the National Association of CPAs and apply directly.

Or go corporate. Many college graduates don't even think about starting their careers in industry, so a lot of jobs go unfilled each year. If you think you might be interested in working for a company, apply directly to the controller or chief financial officer of companies in industries you have an interest or work experience in. It's also much easier to enter a corporate accounting job mid-career. Remember, corporations value people with leadership skills who have broad backgrounds with some specialized experience.

Start early. Summer or part-time internship programs are offered by most public accounting firms, as well as by many companies. Take advantage of this opportunity to try an accounting career if you're not sure it's right for you. The contacts you make during your short tenure will be extremely valuable resources when it comes time to look for a "real" job. You may even receive an offer from the firm or company you interned for.

Career path

In a large public accounting firm, you'll follow a fairly structured route from day one. As a staff accountant, you'll assist with work for several of the firm's clients. Or you may go into the audit pool, a large group of accountants who are chosen to work on audits under the supervision of a more senior accountant. Increasingly, even staffers are beginning to specialize in particular industry audits—it's great training. Just be prepared for long hours, a huge workload, and lots of travel.

With two or three years of experience, you'll move on to senior accountant and then supervisor, managing the activities of other accountants. (Or once you have your CPA, you may choose to leave the firm for a job as a management accountant.)

When you step up to manager a few years later, you'll begin to have extensive contact with clients as you direct major portions of client business. To make the leap from senior manager to partner, 12 years or so into your career, you'll need to demonstrate skill in developing new business for the firm. There are more than 5,000 partners at a multibillion dollar company like Andersen Worldwide. For the large percentage of people who don't stay around and become partners, a stint at one of the Big Five makes you a hot commodity when you leave.

By contrast, the career path of a management accountant can lead in a variety of directions, depending on the company and your own career aspirations. You may begin your career as a junior internal auditor or trainee. As a trainee, you may rotate through a series of jobs to get exposure to accounts payable, accounts receivable, and finance. You may advance to accounting manager, cost accountant, budget director, or manager of internal auditing. However, the larger the company, the more likely you'll specialize in a certain kind of task: cost accounting, tax, or government reporting, for example.

It can take 15 years to reach a top spot—controller, treasurer, vice president of finance, or chief financial officer, for example—in a major corporation, or as few as 10 years in a smaller company. Many senior corporate executives, such as CEOs and general managers, have backgrounds in accounting, auditing, or finance.

To move ahead, you must be prepared to spend more time on people and strategic management issues than on managing the finance function.

How much can you earn?

The following national averages come from the 1999 Accountants Salary Guide from Creative Financial Staffing, a direct hire and temporary placement agency, specializing in accounting and financial personnel.

The range for entry-level public accountants is from $34,000 to $43,300. Entering the field with a graduate degree usually adds $6,000 to $7,000 to that base. Within four to six years, you can be earning $48,800. Managers make an average of $74,000. Partners earn well over $100,000 to $200,000 or more at Big Five firms. You can earn another 10 to 15 percent working overtime. (Corporations generally don't compensate employees for overtime.)

Beginning salaries for management accountants working in private industry average about $30,500. With four to six years of experience, you can expect to earn $44,000. Managers earn more, with salaries ranging up to $80,000. CFOs and CEOs with accounting backgrounds earn $100,000 plus.

Internal auditor trainees average $34,000. Experienced internal auditors can earn $42,600 to $65,500. Salaries for tax accountants range from $35,500 to $72,600 in management positions. Cost accountants generally start at $32,400, topping out at around $56,100.

The starting range for environmental accountants is $29,500 to $32,750. After five years, you can be making $38,500 to $48,000. With experience and seniority, you can make $47,000 to $67,000.

Of course, these are national averages. The highest salaries go to accountants working at large public accounting firms. A rule of thumb: The larger the firm and the larger the city, the higher the salary. The deepest pockets are found in New York and Los Angeles. Geography aside, there are two key factors that directly impact your earning power, according to Abbott, Langer & Associates, Inc., Compensation and Benefits Report (**www.abbott-langer.com**): earning a CPA and moving into management. On average, CPAs earn 34 percent more than non-CPAs. Accountants who supervise 25 or more people take home as much as 169 percent more than non-supervisors.

Where will you work?

Although the Big Five still dominate the industry, good regional and local public accounting firms exist in almost every city. The hours are often much less grueling at regional firms and the path to partnership may be a little quicker. During a stint at a Big Five firm, your only responsibility may be to audit the cash account for one corporation. As a bigger fish in a small pond, you'll have more interesting work.

Management accountants work for mid-sized and large companies in almost every industry throughout the country. Opportunities are best in health care, financial services, insurance, and real estate. If you should rise to the level of controller or CFO, you'll be involved in running and developing the business. Most accountants in the private sector stay in one place in one job working with the same colleagues for fairly extended periods.

Accounting skills are portable, making it easier to keep your professional options open.

Job Profile
Tim Oertli, cost accountant

What general job responsibilities does your position encompass?
I'm responsible for the following:

* Reconciling perpetual inventory records with our general ledger (G/L).
* Invoicing for our turnkey program. (This is the program we use to outsource the manufacture of key components for the products we sell.)
* Auditing the cycle counting of inventory and analyzing work orders.
* Managing demo warranty and contingent sales inventories.
* Month-end close journal entries.
* Year-end inventory.

How many years have you been in this business?
I have 15 years in general accounting and one year in cost accounting.

How many years of education do you have?
I have a B.A. in accounting and business administration.

How many hours do you typically work per week?
I work 50 hours per week.

What hours do you work on a typical day?
8:30 a.m. to 7 or 7:30 p.m.

How big is the company you work for?
400 employees.

Have you earned professional certification?
No.

What is your annual salary?
$55,000-$65,000.

How did you get your job?
I was working in the General Ledger department when I learned about an opening in the Cost Accounting department and I applied for the position.

Please describe one of your "typical" days?
8:30-9:30: Check my e-mail and voice mail for (updated) information concerning inventory movements, adjustments, or corrections. Gather paperwork for turnkey program.
9:30-12: Different activities, according to where we are in the month. They may include working with the turnkey program paperwork, requesting invoices of turnkey vendors, and updating the turnkey spreadsheet.
12-1: Lunch and socializing with colleagues.
1-7: Again, different activities. I may:

* Analyze work order variations and meet with my boss to convey any problems or discrepancies in the process.
* Publish results and graphs relating to missing documentation in turnkey system.
* Run reports and graph how accurately we were in meeting established completion dates for work orders.
* Work on special projects—such as compiling data for the program recalling defective equipment sold by our company.
* Answer questions from G/L personnel relating to my old position (my move has involved training my successor).

What are your career aspirations?
I'd like to get back into G/L—this time at a supervisory or management level.

What kind of people do really well at this business?
People who are detail-oriented. You should be able to deal with large amounts of data and have good spreadsheet skills. You should also know how to use accounting software, such as ASK, FAS2000 fixed asset software, etc. Organizational skills, an ability to work independently, and resourcefulness are also important.

What do you really like about your job?

I'm getting trained in some new areas both on the job and in classes. It's interesting being "at the heart" of a manufacturing company and knowing that the things you do (such as finding ways to save money) really affect the bottom line of the company.

What do you dislike?

Some of the work is monotonous and involves a lot of data entry. My eyesight has suffered from staring at my computer screen for long periods. Dealing with so many different departments can also be frustrating. Change is slow in coming, and sometimes it's hard to get answers out of people. Because I'm not a manager, people in other departments sometimes ignore my requests (which makes my work hard to complete).

What is the biggest misconception about this job?

The nerdy "bean counter" image. Actually, nerds wouldn't do well. You need to be people-oriented, persuasive, and resourceful to get your job done.

How can someone get a job like yours?

I had an accounting degree and some cost accounting experience. It's easier to get into G/L accounting. With cost accounting, you do need experience. I am lucky to be able to get this from making the lateral move that I did. A lot of younger accounting job applicants have M.B.A.s or CPAs, but experience in an actual cost accounting work environment is at least as important. Even with an M.B.A., getting a job in cost accounting would be difficult.

Resources

General accounting

American Accounting Association
5717 Bessie Drive
Sarasota, FL 34233
(941)921-7747
Publications: *The American Accounting Review*

American Society of Women Accountants
1255 Lynnfield Road, Suite 257
Memphis, TN 38119
(901)680-0470

Public accounting

American Institute of Certified Public Accountants
More than 330,000 members.
Harborside Financial Center
201 Plaza III
Jersey City, NJ 07311-3881
(201)938-3000
www.aicpa.org
Publications: *CPA Letter, Journal of Accountancy*

National Society of Public Accountants and the Accreditation Council for Accountancy and Taxation
1010 North Fairfax Street
Alexandria, VA 22314
(703)549-6400
www.nspa.org
Publishes: *National Public Accountant*

Tax accounting

American Society of Tax Professionals
P.O. Box 1024
Sioux Falls, SD 57101
(605)335-1185
Publishes: *Firm on Firm Directory*

Management accounting

Institute of Management Accountants
10 Paragon Drive
Montvale, NJ 07645-1760
(201)573-9000
www.imanet.org
Publishes: *Management Accounting*

Auditing

The Institute of Internal Auditors
249 Maitland Avenue
Altamonte Springs, FL 32701-4201
(407)830-7600
www.theiia.org
Publishes: *Internal Auditor*

Information systems auditing

The Information Systems Audit and Control Association
Accredited programs in accounting and business.
3710 Algonquin Road
Suite 1010
Rolling Meadows, IL 60008
(708)253-1545
www.isaca.org

American Assembly of Collegiate Schools of Business
605 Old Ballas Road
Suite 220
St. Louis, MO 63141
http://www.aacsb.edu

Accounting publications

Accounting Today
425 park Avenue
New York, NY 10022
(212)756-5155

The Practical Accountant
Faulkner & Gray
1 Penn Plaza
New York, NY 10001
(212)971-5000

Chapter 3

Banking & Financial Services
A boom in personalized investment services

Certified Financial Planner (CFP)
Financial analyst
Financial services marketer
Financial services sales specialist
Loan officer
Mergers & acquisitions specialist
Treasury officer
Private banking specialist
Software programmer
Venture capitalist
Best Bet for Entrepreneurs: *Certified Financial Planner (CFP)*

Forecast

As the population and economy grow, applications for commercial, consumer, and mortgage loans will increase, spurring demand for loan officers and counselors. Some of the most promising prospects in banking are for financial services sales and marketing professionals as banks offer increasingly complex financial services.

Growth

While employment in banks—where most loan officers and counselors are found—is projected to decline, a growing number of individual investors are turning to financial planners to assist them in sorting through a wide variety of financial alternatives. In addition, demand should increase as banks and credit institutions expand the range of financial services they offer and issue more loans for personal and commercial use.

Overview

Remember the day you stood in line, clutching the birthday money that would become the very first deposit in your new savings account? Back then, you probably didn't realize that the bank you were depending on to keep your money safe was really in the business of selling money—yours and every other depositors'—to large corporations. Traditionally, the interest collected on sizable loans was the lifeblood of a banking institution.

Things have changed quite a bit. If you have a computer (and who doesn't these days?) you may never have to see a teller or talk to a broker. With a few mouse clicks, you can pay your bills, apply for a credit card or a mortgage, and follow up on a hot stock tip by purchasing 100 shares of a high tech start-up—all in the same afternoon. With 24-hour-a-day access to stock quotes, corporate reports, even brokerage firm research, savvy consumers are getting a better return online than from a broker.

The borders continue to blur between banks, insurance companies, and brokerage houses. At this writing, new legislation is being considered that would allow banks, securities firms, and insurance companies to merge, giving customers a one-stop shop for banking transactions, loans, insurance, stocks, and securities. Some recruiters think that the future banking/finance industry will consist of a dozen or so very large, broad spectrum financial services firms.

Even more competition comes from another sector: venture capital funds. In the first quarter of 1999, U.S. venture capitalists poured $3.6 billion into 464 fledgling companies—the majority earmarked for Internet-based businesses.

The bottom line? You will find plenty of opportunity as the $486 billion banking industry continues to restructure. Creativity and innovation—not words you'd traditionally associate with the staid banker or money-mad broker of the 1980s—will be the key ingredient for competing in a new service economy powered by the Internet.

Taking money, making money

Not everything has changed. Bank *loan officers* continue to carefully evaluate the credit of prospective consumer and corporate borrowers. *Treasury officers,* and *financial analysts* continue to scout out and capitalize on op-portunities in emerging and changing markets around the world.

Meanwhile, *financial services marketers* and *sales specialists* are creat-ing, packaging, and promoting specialized services to lure new customers and make sure that customers return often. For example, newly wealthy entrepreneurs can engage the services of a *private banking specialist.* And *certified financial planners* are helping customers of all ages and demo-graphic profiles build investment portfolios to meet short and long-term goals.

With all this growth into new markets here and abroad, corporations in transition may work with a *mergers and acquisitions specialist.* Venture capital-ists are having a heyday helping startups grow into formidable competitors.

Industry snapshot

How did we get to this point? Well, it all started in the 1980s when a plump cushion of federal deposit and loan guarantees lulled savings and loans (S&Ls) into making too many loans to too many "risky" customers. When the loans went bad, the S&Ls failed—more than 1,000 during the 80s alone. And after the dust cleared, scores of commercial bank employees (from bank tellers to top executives) were out of a job.

Meanwhile, the thunder of a bull market on Wall Street became a siren song for thousands of college graduates. The story was that with an M.B.A. and two or three years of experience, you could pull down six figures a year. (While your boss was working on a cool million, or more.)

New investment vehicles—including mortgage-backed securities dubbed Fannie Maes and Freddie Macs—were created or marketed more aggres-sively. Hefty fees from a flurry of mergers and acquisitions padded the pockets of investment bankers. Just when there seemed to be no end to the party, the lights went on.

In October 1987, a drop in earnings brought the stock market abruptly to its knees—and thousands of investment professionals face-to-face with reality. Some securities firms were able to ride a wave of continued mergers, but when the tide ebbed in 1989, liquidity dried up. In the next three years alone, about 70,000 professionals nationwide (one-fifth of the pre-1987 Wall Street workforce) received their pink slips.

Mergers and consolidations were the only way to cut costs and stream-line banks for a new kind of competition with more cautiously aggressive financial services firms. Although cutbacks and layoffs, especially of bank tellers, are likely to continue, banks will usually and quickly gain lost ground.

Trends to track

Do-it-yourself investing. At this writing, one in three stock trades is done online by average Americans using discount brokers such as Charles Schwab and upstarts such as E*Trade. On average, these firms charge $15.75—about one-tenth the cost of full-service firms like Merrill Lynch. However, even Merrill Lynch finally relented, letting its five million customers bypass its force of 15,000 stockbrokers to trade stocks online. To say that the number of online brokerage customers is exploding would almost be an understatement. Gomez Advisors, an electronic commerce consulting firm, estimates the number of online accounts will more than double—totaling 18 million by 2001. Now the nation's biggest retail brokerage faces the challenge of flourishing in the electronic age without completely dismantling the infrastructure that allowed it to succeed.

Step up to the online window. While online banking has caught on more slowly, it has excellent prospects. Internet-based companies such as WingspanBank.com and E-Loan have broken new ground by conducting 100 percent of their business online rather than in downtown offices with high overhead and long lines. FDIC-member WingspanBank.com offers customers a one-stop resource for everything from personal checking with interest to home equity solutions. E-Loan advertises an average saving of $1,000 on mortgages from more than 70 lenders nationwide. Both offer unprecedented hours—open for business around the clock. You can even apply and get approved for a credit card on the Internet. The number of online credit applications is expected to mushroom from 5.3 million in 1999 to 28.3 million in 2002, according to Cyber Dialogue, a New York-based Internet research firm.

Old standards...and still winners

Loan officers. Part analyst, part salesperson, loan officers follow set bank guidelines to determine the credit-worthiness of prospective borrowers. It may not be enough for a prospect to clear every hurdle, however. The loan officer must stand up to senior management and sell the mortgage as a business deal, often only after extensive presentations. Professional credibility comes with a sound track record of proposals. Thanks to lower interest rates, mortgage banking, and personal credit, loans have been booming in the short term and are expected to be good business for many banks well into the new millennium. Specialize in commercial, consumer, or mortgage loans.

Treasury officers. Buying and selling money on the international market can generate substantial income for banks. Operating in a Wall Street-like environment, treasury officers play on fluctuations in exchange rates to make quick profits.

Financial analysts. Which stocks are good buys? Brokers and investors turn to financial analysts for guidance. Analysts spend a good deal of their time poring over the day-to-day financial performance of companies in a particular industry, such as technology. After researching a company's financing strategies, product development, and pricing models, as well as economic forecasts for U.S. and international markets, financial analysts develop a picture of each industry player. Their "buy," "sell," and "hold" recommendations wield enormous clout.

A new generation of opportunities

Mergers and acquisitions specialists (M&As). Since 1995, over 200 large and small banks have merged. There were more than 500 mergers in the banking industry alone in 1998, leading experts to predict that 50 banks will control 80 percent of the industry at the cusp of the millennium. And there seems to be no end to it, this trend in growth-by-consolidation. Companies with the "urge to merge," or acquire-smaller competitors need the guidance only an M&A can provide. By closely analyzing a company's financial performance, M&As develop an understanding of how its strengths and weaknesses might mesh with those of another company. With this knowledge, M&As can identify companies ripe for a merger or acquisition and put together a proposal in the best interests of both parties.

Financial services marketers. With banks and financial services firms vying for the same customer, increasing market share demands innovative marketing strategies. After researching the marketplace, financial service marketers may blend banking services, such as electronic banking, with a range of investment products and services to create a comprehensive package. Then, using direct mail campaigns or a mix of media, they communicate the benefits of this package to a community or nation of prospective customers.

Financial services sales specialists. As banks offer increasingly complex financial services, financial sales specialists will focus on selling customers a broad spectrum of banking and financial products—ranging from deposit accounts to bank credit cards—depending on their short and long-term needs. Look for service-oriented salespeople (called "financial planners" in some firms) who are able to sell a total financial services package as banks offer increasingly complex financial services. Conversely, the demand for stockbrokers or registered sales representatives who only sell securities—stocks, bonds, mutual fund shares, and insurance annuities—tends to fluctuate with the economy. Even during an economic boom, competition for securities sales training positions—particularly in larger firms—can be fierce.

Certified financial planners (CFPs). Working for a financial services firm or independently, financial planners prepare comprehensive long-term plans to manage cash, trusts, or private portfolios. Since the best approach for a single working professional is rarely right for a retiree, financial planners begin by interviewing their clients to determine their assets, liabilities, cash flow, insurance coverage, tax status, and financial objectives. Then they analyze this information and—using their knowledge of tax and investment strategies, securities, insurance, pension plans, and real estate—work up a detailed financial plan tailored to each client's needs.

Private banking specialists. An average bank client generates about $1,000 in annual revenue to the bank. Most major banks have established services to focus on the special needs of wealthier clients. Entrepreneurs and principal stockholders in these special programs can generate $5,000 annually.

Software programmers. Technology has not only opened the door to new services—such as electronic funds transfer—but indeed is redefining how banking is done. So it should come as no surprise that people who understand technology are in great demand. The *New York Times* recently reported that banks and other financial firms need to fill close to 400,000 job openings in information technology alone. Citibank boasts that its software programmers outnumber those at Microsoft. Specific responsibilities can range from managing network systems to coding applications for a wide variety of transaction-oriented processes to modeling bank functions such as loan approvals and risk management. These positions usually go to technical pros with experience working on specific platforms and software programs. (For more detailed information, see Computer & Information Systems.)

Venture capitalists (VCs). Some of America's most successful companies, such as Apple Computer and Federal Express, funded their ride to the top with the help of venture capital. Venture capital funds make money for investors (and the firm) by giving money and expertise to companies that appear to have a promising future. The money comes from investors such as corporations, financial institutions, private foundations, and wealthy individuals. The expertise comes from the VCs themselves, who remain involved in important business decisions and often take a seat on the company's board of directors. When the company is sold or goes public in an initial stock offering (ISO), the investors and the VC firm take the profits.

By all accounts, the venture capital market is booming. Although the competition for jobs is intense, opportunities for M.B.A.s and even undergraduates will increase as the industry continues to mature.

Do you have what it takes?

As you may already have gathered, there is room for many different types of people in banking and financial services firms. In addition to the requisite quantitative and analytical skills, good communication is important at every level of banking and financial services. This business is, after all, very much focused on building long-term relationships.

Certified financial planners and financial services sales specialists need to couple broad-based financial expertise with the ability to gain the trust of many different kinds of clients, many of them first-time investors. In this area, many employers consider personal qualities and skills more important than academic training. In addition to sales experience, the self-confidence to handle frequent rejections is an ingredient of success.

Loan officers should also relate well with prospective clients, but need top-notch presentation skills to sell their proposals to upper-level management.

Step into bank operations and you'll find organized, detail-loving people who would probably be uncomfortable operating on the "sixth sense" that seems born in successful stockbrokers. Private banking specialists spend a lot of time lavishing attention on individual customers. Financial analysts, treasury managers, and mergers and acquisitions specialists are more concerned with speculating about business and financial trends, and world markets.

Venture capitalists need exceptional networking skills as well as entrepreneurial experience.

Education and training

With a bachelor's degree in accounting, finance, or business administration (and an emphasis on accounting or finance) most entry-level bankers go directly into a year-long in-house training program that covers everything from accounting and corporate finance to business law.

Banks and other credit institutions prefer to hire college graduates for financial services sales and marketing jobs. A business administration degree with a specialization in finance or a liberal arts degree including courses in accounting, economics, and marketing serves as excellent preparation for this job.

Most financial services firms provide on-the-job training to help sales representatives meet the requirements for registration. This training period takes months and may include classroom instruction in securities analysis, effective speaking, and the finer points of selling. On-the-job training may last up to two years. Many firms like to rotate their trainees among various departments, to give them a broad perspective of the securities business. In small firms, sales representatives often receive training both from outside institutions and on the job.

An M.B.A. is essential for breaking into some banking positions. If you want to become a treasury manager, financial analyst, M&A specialist, or venture capitalist you'll find yourself on the outside looking in without an advanced degree in business and economics. In fact, established VC funds generally hire people with either Harvard or Stanford M.B.A.s because both schools offer specialized venture capital tracks.

Continuing education in the form of advanced courses and industry conferences is an important part of career advancement for most banking and financial services professionals. Industry associations commonly sponsor national and local training programs that cover accounting management, financial analysis, and international banking. And because technology has revolutionized financial analysis and management, a good working knowledge of computers and management information systems is very recommended.

Professional licensing and certification

Financial services sales specialists and certified financial planners who sell stocks and securities are required to register with the Securities and Exchange Commission (SEC). Financial planners earn their CFP credential by passing an exam administered by the Certified Financial Planners Board of Standards.

Financial services sales specialists working in banks must meet state licensing requirements. Most often this requires passing an examination. In cases, they must also furnish a personal bond. Financial services sales specialists also must register as representatives of their firms according to the regulations of the securities exchanges where they do business or the National Association of Securities Dealers, Inc. (NASD). Before beginners can qualify as registered representatives, they must pass the General Securities Registered Representative Examination, administered by the NASD, and be an employee of a registered firm for at least four months. Most States require a second examination—the Uniform Securities Agents State Law Examination. These tests measure the prospective representative's knowledge of the securities business, customer protection requirements, and record keeping procedures.

Tips on breaking in

Choose the right boss. Like any sales job, financial sales is marked by peaks and valleys. When you're starting out, it helps to have a supervisor with a successful track record who will freely offer advice and is willing to help you navigate the inevitable lows. It pays to do some research on sales managers while you research firms.

Bring experience, and clients, with you. Financial sales applicants with some experience can sweeten an employment deal with a new firm by bringing specialized knowledge of a hot industry such as health care, as well as a built-in clientele. Venture capital funds prize people with expertise in the industries they serve. If you're a software engineer or scientist, you're already well-positioned to evaluate high tech or biotechnology startups.

Resolve to know at least a little about a lot. Developing a broad knowledge of many areas, such as banking, credit, insurance, real estate, and securities will also help you build your career.

You may also be asked for your opinion on the dramatic changes taking place in the industry.

If you're a woman, go where the natives are friendly. For women managers, they tend to be friendlier at banks and in brokerage firms. If you're a woman interested in building a career as a financial planner, focus on the market of working women (30 million strong) with money to invest and an interest in future security.

Start small—or at a startup. If you lack an Ivy League education—or blue chip net worth—sign on with a startup. Even if it fails, you'll have gained a lot of hands-on operating experience, as well as exposure to the company's investors—who may become your next boss. The flip side of this is to establish a track record at a smaller, regional VC firm, where you'll plug into the industry knowledge you need to impress established firms.

Career path

These days, a safe and stable "tenure track" banking career has been replaced by something less certain, but a lot more challenging.

Many executives start as loan officers and advance to larger branches of the firm or to a managerial position, usually becoming a supervisor over other loan officers and clerical staff. Loan officers in banks and lending institutions are less likely to lose their jobs during an economic downturn because loans are a major source of income.

Vice presidents still abound in banking. You can often become an assistant vice president after three years and a full vice president within eight years. The real clout, however, comes with the title of senior vice president, 15 to 20 years into your career. At this level, you may run a department such as operations, or manage a number of important client relationships. Executive vice presidents make up the top-level management committee that determine the bank's strategic direction.

Some firms prefer candidates for financial services sales specialist to have commission sales experience in areas such as real estate or insurance. The principal form of advancement for securities sales representatives is an increase in the number and size of the accounts they handle. Although beginners usually service the accounts of individual investors, eventually they may handle very large institutional accounts, such as those of banks and pension funds. Some experienced sales representatives become branch office managers and supervise other sales representatives while continuing to provide services for their own customers. A few representatives advance to top management positions or become partners in their firms.

A financial services marketer may begin as a sales assistant, move on to investment consultant, and ultimately become a sales manager.

Financial analysts and mergers and acquisitions specialists tend to shun management in favor of doing what they love to do best. For M&As, career milestones are measured by bigger and more lucrative, high profile deals.

Certified financial planners may gain experience and certification working for a bank or brokerage house before making the break to work independently.

In a major venture capital firm, you may spend three years as an analyst, screening business plans and performing due diligence or research on promising industries and entrepreneurs before moving on to vice president or associate. At this stage, you'll screen business plans, make cold calls on prospective investments, and make occasional site visits to companies in the funds portfolio. You'll need to accumulate a wealth of business expertise as well as industry contacts to make general partner.

What can you earn?

Salary levels vary with the size and location of the bank or financial services firm, with the rule of thumb being that the bigger the bank or firm and the bigger the city, the higher the salary. For example, smaller banks pay at least 15 percent less than large institutions.

Loan officers start at $30,000 to $35,000. With promotions and raises, they can earn as much as $85,000. Some loan officers make a salary plus commission.

The average annual salary for an entry-level sales assistant or trainee is $26,000. In five years, with raises and promotions, middle-level financial managers may earn from $30,000 to $60,000. Financial analysts earn from $40,500 to $55,600. Treasury managers average $66,900. With commissions and performance bonuses, investment consultants can make from $75,000 to $85,000. Salaries of $200,000 or more are common for senior vice presidents.

Private banking specialists earn income from fees for banking services paid by their clients.

Financial services sales specialists can earn from $24,300 to over $100,000 depending on where they work and their commission structure. Securities sales specialists working for brokerages and mutual funds often tack on hefty bonuses—$250,000 or more—when their firm does well.

Only 17 percent of financial planners work as fee-only consultants. After an initial consultation, an independent certified financial planner may charge $50 to $200 an hour or a percentage of the client's invested funds. Most also earn a commission on sales of financial products, earning from $60,000 to $120,000 a year. The very best can earn over $250,000 typically working on a fee or commission basis.

Financial analysts and M&As start with a base salary ranging from $50,000 to $60,000. Analysts top out at $150,000 to $200,000 plus bonuses. Bonuses and periodic raises for financial analysts are closely tied to the accuracy of their quarterly earnings projections. The best analysts are ranked annually by Institutional Investor magazine. M&As often earn an annual bonus of 25 to 50 percent and six figures, but have been know to make millions on transactions.

Even at the analyst and associate levels, a venture capitalist's compensation is directly tied to performance of the fund and indirectly to the market as a whole. Analysts earn $30,000 to $70,000, plus a bonus. Associates earn from $50,000 to $100,000. Partners earn $100,000 at the junior level to more than $250,000 at the top tier—plus a percentage of profits that can run to the millions at the highest level. Compensation at corporate venture funds is lower.

Where will you work?

Three out of five loan officers are employed by commercial banks, savings institutions, and credit unions. Others work at nonbank financial institutions, such as mortgage brokerage firms and personal credit firms. New York is also the center for most of the best opportunities for financial analysts and M&A specialists (although some work in Los Angeles, Chicago, and Atlanta.)

While the powerhouses of multinational banking are found in and around New York City, banks exist in virtually every city and town in America, so you don't have to live in a major city to pursue that career.

Financial services marketers, financial sales specialists, and certified financial planners can work in banks, brokerage firms, and credit institutions anywhere in the country. At many small and medium-size banks, branch managers and commercial loan officers are responsible for marketing the bank's financial services. Opportunities for inexperienced sales representatives should be best in smaller firms.

Some of the larger mutual find companies (Merrill Lynch, Franklin, Fidelity) and brokerage houses have active campus recruiting programs.

Venture capital funds are increasingly focusing on technology and Internet companies. Many of the top funds have headquarters in Silicon Valley. Some high tech companies, notably Microsoft and Intel, have started their own internal venture capital operations, as have many financial services firms.

Job Profile
Rhoda Israelov, financial consultant, CFP, CLU

What are your general responsibilities?
I manage investments and financial planning for more than 450 client households. I meet with each client on an ongoing basis to determine his or her

needs. Then I recommend investments and insurance products that will help clients reach their goals.

How many years have you been in this business?
20 years.

How many years of education do you have?
I have bachelor's degrees in secondary English and Hebrew education and a master's degree in financial services, with a major in charitable and estate planning. I have continued to take many education courses through the Financial Planning Association, the National Association of Life Underwriters, and the Society for Financial Service Professionals. We have to keep documentation of attendance to turn in for the credentialing and licensing agencies.

How many hours do you typically work per week?
I put in approximately 70 hours a week on work or work-related activities.

What are your activities on a typical day?

* Three or four face-to-face meetings with prospective clients or going over portfolios with existing clients.
* One or two board meetings for professional financial planning or insurance organizations, charitable organizations, or business networking group meetings.
* Phone contact with clients, or with their attorneys or CPAs.

How big is the company you work for?
I work for the largest financial institution in the world (Citigroup). I am one of more than 12,000 financial consultants.

Do you have (or need) professional certification?
It is not necessary to have professional certification to be a financial consultant. Technically, financial consultants are Registered Representatives under the National Association of Securities Dealers and have licensing requirements. I have two professional designations that I voluntarily studied and qualified for: Chartered Life Underwriter (CLU) and Certified Financial Planner (CFP).

In what general range does your annual salary fall?
I have no salary whatever. I am considered to be an employee of Salomon Smith Barney, and am 100 percent commission paid. Most of this is for product sales, but some are "trails" (small percentage-of-value fees given to

reward continued service to an account). Around one-sixth of my compensation is quarterly percentage fees on professional managed accounts).

I receive a paycheck with taxes and insurance withheld. My gross pay (before business expenses and taxes) is now in the range of more than $250,000 a year.

How did you get your current job?

I was recruited by EF Hutton Financial Services in 1981. At the time, I was an insurance agent with Connecticut Mutual Life Insurance Company. EF Hutton is the forerunner (through various mergers) of my current firm.

Please describe one of your "typical" days.

7 a.m. Attend a meeting of Circle Business Network, where I meet with owners of different kinds of companies, learn more about different industries, and promote my own business.

8:30 a.m. Meet with estate planning attorney to plan joint seminars on trust investing.

10 a.m. Meet with a client at my office.

11 a.m. Read mail, return phone calls, talk to three or four clients by phone. Obtain insurance proposals for various clients from different insurance companies and order materials for clients from different investment companies.

Noon-1 p.m. Go to lunch with a client.

1:30 p.m. Conference call with a client who lives in another state to go over the portfolio. (I mailed my report ahead of time).

2 p.m. Meet with client.

3:30 p.m. Leave my office for an outside appointment at a client's home.

5:30 p.m. Client meeting in a restaurant.

7:30 p.m. After a light supper, type letters to clients on my laptop and read through materials I've received by mail.

What are your career aspirations?

I am first vice president of investments. The next appointment will be senior VP—a combination of longevity and "production" numbers. I want to do more traveling around the country to see different clients, give a greater number of seminars and speeches, and possibly write a book.

What kind of people would do especially well in your job role?

Outgoing people who are empathetic and nonjudgmental would likely succeed as financial planners. In addition, a love of numbers and of abstract concepts would be of help. There is a lot of detailed information to learn and manage, lots of paperwork, lots of regulation. The ability to "teach" abstract concepts and to paint a verbal picture of the future is important, as are listening skills. Any commissioned salesperson must be able to deal with rejection and to have the tenacity to stay with it. Long, hard hours of work and study are prerequisites for ultimate flexibility and success.

What do you especially like about your job?

I especially enjoy the public speaking aspects of my position. I also value my clients' trust in me and their willingness to allow me to share in their dreams, plans, and concerns. The closeness with people is of great joy to me.

What do you like least?

I least enjoy paperwork and legal restrictions.

What are some common misconceptions about your job/profession/industry?

Some common misconceptions (fostered in large part by the press, I might add) include the following:

* Stockbrokers or insurance agents simply sell a commodity, rather than serve as advisors—on par with an attorney or accountant.
* Fees are high. Concentrating more on—"How much does it cost?" than on "How much can I benefit?"
* Last year's best mutual fund—as reported in the magazines—is still this year's best investment.
* Timing is everything—that there is a quick road to riches.

What is the best way to going about landing a job like yours?

Ask for a meeting with people in your community who are working in the financial profession. Even looking in the yellow pages and calling a brokerage firm and asking for a ten minute "networking" interview would be of enormous help. Express your interest in working as an apprentice or intern. Take courses in finance. Read financial columns in the paper.

Resources

Top multinational banks

Chemical Bank and Trust Company
333 E. Main
Midland, MI 48640-0231
(517)631-9200
www.chemicalbankmi.com

Citicorp
Citgroup corporate college recruiting
575 Lexington Ave.
New York, NY 10043
www.citigroup.com/newgrads

BankAmerica
Bank of America Center
555 California Street
San Francisco, CA 94104
(415)953-6273
www.bofa.com

J.P. Morgan
60 Wall Street
New York, NY 10260-0060
(212)483-2323
www.jpmorgan.com

EquiServe
First Chicago Division
Shareholder Relations
P.O. Box 2500
Jersey City, NJ 07303-2500
www.fctc.com

Chase Manhattan
1 Chase Manhattan Plaza
27th Floor
New York, NY 10081
(212)552-2222
www.chase.com

Top securities/financial services firms

Merrill Lynch
World Financial Center
New York, NY 10080
(212)449-1000
www.ml.com

A.G. Edwards & Sons
1 N. Jefferson Street
787 Seventh Ave.
St. Louis, MO 63103
(314)289-3000

Goldman Sachs Group
(800)292-2552
www.gs.com
e-mail: gs-funds@gs.com

Charles Schwab Corp.
101 Montgomery St.
San Francisco, CA 94104
(415)627-7000

Banking industry associations

American Bankers Association
1120 Connecticut Ave. NW
Washington, DC 20036
(202)663-4000
www.aba.com

Financial Institutions Insurance Association
21 Tamal Vista Blvd., Suite 162
Corte Madera, CA 94925
(415)924-8122
Fax: (415)924-1447
www.fiia.org

Independent Bankers Association of America
1 Thomas Circle NW, Suite 950
Washington, DC 20005
(202)659-8111
www.ibaa.org

Bank Administration Institute
One North Franklin, Suite 1000
Chicago, IL 60606-3421
(800)224-9889 or (312)683-2464
Fax: (800)375-5543 or (312)683-2373
www.bai.org

Bank Marketing Association
1120 Connecticut Avenue NW
Washington, DC 20036
(800)433-9013 or (202)663-5268
Fax: (202)828-4540
www.bmanet.org

Mortgage Bankers Association of America
1125 15th Street NW
Washington, DC 20005
(202)861-6500
www.mbaa.org

Financial services industry associations

Association for Investment Management and Research
P.O. Box 3668
Charlottesville, VA 22901
Fax: (804)980-9755

Commercial Finance Association
225 West 34th Street, Suite 1815
New York, NY 10122
(212)594-3490
Fax: (212)564-6053
postmaster@cfassn.com
www.cfa.com

Financial Executives Institute
100 Madison Avenue
P.O. Box 1938
Morristown, NJ 07962
(201)898-4600

Securities Industry Association
120 Broadway
New York, NY 10271
(212)608-1500

Banking and financial industry directories

American Banker Directory of U.S. Banking Executives
American Banker Inc.
(800)221-1809 or (212)803-8333

CFP Board
1700 Broadway, Suite 2100
Denver, CO 80290-2101
(303)830-7500
Fax: (303)860-7388
www.cfp-board.org
E-mail: mail@CFP-Board.org

National Association of Personal Financial Advisors
355 West Dundee Road, Suite 200
Buffalo Grove, IL 60089
www.napfa.org

Securities Industry Yearbook
Securities Industry Association
120 Broadway
New York, NY 10271
(212)608-1500

Directory of American Financial Institutions

McFadden Business Publications
6195 Crooked Creek Road
Norcross, GA 30092
(404)448-1011

Chapter 4

Computer & Information Systems
Surfing the wave of innovation

Computer game developer
Computer engineer
Geographic information systems (GIS) practitioner
Information archivist
PC technical support specialist
Project manager
System programmer/analyst
Technical trainer
Technical writer
Best Bets for Entrepreneurs:
Independent consultant, technical trainer, technical writer

Forecast

The five fastest-growing occupations are computer-related! Experts predict that more than 100,000 qualified candidates will be needed to fill the one million-plus jobs expected to be created by 2006. However, a continued shortage of qualified technical professionals may result in a workforce gap of 200,000 by the year 2010.

Growth

Employment of computing professionals is expected to grow much faster than the average for all occupations between 1998 and 2008 according to the latest BLS employment projections. The number of jobs for computer engineers will grow 108 percent by 2008, closely followed by computer support specialists (102 percent) and system analysts (94 percent).

Few of us can imagine life without our computers. How would we perform our jobs—or manage our lives, for that matter—without our word processing software, scheduler, and online checkbook?

Overview

More than 125 million personal computers, workstations, and laptops have put more power at users' fingertips around the world, for far less money than in the past. Once a major investment, entry-level PCs are being sold for $400. Computer technology—from supermarket bar codes and computer-aided design to online stock trading—has fueled an unprecedented two-decade-long economic boom, according to Federal Reserve Chairman Alan Greenspan. Yet a serious shortage of qualified technical professionals costs Silicon Valley, California, firms as much as $4 billion per year in recruiting expenses and lost productivity. And the problem may get worse, because two-thirds of local, middle, and high school students seem uninterested in pursuing high-tech careers.

This translates into plenty of opportunity for anyone who wants to step in and fill the gap. But if you want to be part of the action, get ready for a wild ride. Layoffs and cutbacks are a way of life in this highly competitive industry. Whether you join the ranks of a superpower like Microsoft or hit the ground running for a 10-person startup, your biggest challenge will be keeping your skills current. New generations of technology are here before there's time to sharpen your expertise on the current state of the art.

If you want advancement, you'll have to be relentless about walking the cutting edge. What's in store for tomorrow is anybody's guess. Look for computers capable of voice recognition and artificial intelligence hardware or software.

Computer engineers design and produce the complex circuitry for every size and shape of computer available—from the mammoth supercomputers and mainframes still used by the government, large corporations, and university resource centers, to the personal computer sitting on your desk. As more compact products such as laptops and hand-held computers are developed, the focus will remain on finding ways to manufacture them more quickly and make them more affordable to the masses.

If hardware is the body of the computer, then software is its brain. *System programmer/analysts* write code to create applications that perform a range of specialized tasks, from word processing to complex suites of business applications. In a highly competitive marketplace, corporate data is a company's most valuable asset. Packaged and custom software helps people at all levels and in all areas of a company transform data into meaningful information that can be used in making decisions and developing strategic direction.

Just as there is no end in sight of upgrades to the functionality of "workhorse" applications such as Microsoft Word, there is no limit to the scope of applications that can be developed to meet the very specialized needs of businesses operating in every industry.

For example, *geographic information systems (GIS) practitioners* combine databases with computerized geographic maps or models to compare information about sites struck by environmental or natural disasters. *Consultants* employ a range of skills to help companies define and solve specific business problems. They may recommend purchasing hardware or software, or customize existing software to streamline data management and reporting.

Software development or implementation may employ a cast of thousands, but one project manager is typically responsible, keeping everyone on schedule. Project managers work closely with development teams and related business areas to ensure that new systems will achieve their objectives.

As PCs proliferate, support issues can make or break a company's competitive advantage. PC technical support specialists safeguard the productivity of every PC user. A new breed of database librarians, *information archivists,* help organizations decide what records to keep and for how long.

Even as operating standards take shape and applications are designed to be more "user friendly," *technical writers* will be called upon to write detailed documentation to explain technical operation and software features to database managers and systems users. *Technical trainers* (see Education and Training) will take things a step further to provide hands-on instruction designed to hasten productivity and reduce service calls.

On a lighter note, computer games have become big business. Consumers purchased 141 million home computer games in 1998—accounting for $4.5 billion in sales. To put that figure in perspective, the total U.S. box office take for feature-length movies was $6.95 billion for the same year. This is more than enough to bring game developers out of the "closet" (actually, this business was started by people working out code in their bedrooms) and into the limelight.

Industry snapshot

Talk about a revolution! Walking into a computer room in the early 1960s, you would never have dreamed that the room-sized "monster" you faced would have any impact on your personal life. Expensive to purchase and operate—and plodding by today's standards—computers were feasible only for the largest corporations and universities. Enter Apple Computer.

With the introduction of the first desktop computer specifically designed for home use in 1977, the revolution was underway. But like a rollercoaster ride, an initial sales boom was followed by a steep dip that resulted in industry-wide layoffs. The recession compounded losses. In fact, in the years from 1988 to early 1992, the computer industry cut nearly 192,000 jobs—more than the defense, aerospace, and automobile industries.

Like almost every other industry, the computer industry will continue consolidating and restructuring for intense competition, both in America and abroad. Intense price-cutting has forced most hardware companies to relocate manufacturing "off shore." But software is still on a roll. Even during the peak of layoffs, employment in the software industry grew—by as much as 7 percent in prepackaged software alone.

The combination of technological advances and global competition will keep computer professionals plenty busy, developing customized software solutions for companies in a range of industries and making sure every user is prepared to take full advantage of the power at his or her fingertips.

Trends to track

The Internet connection. The Internet's impact on software development has been substantial (see Internet and Telecommunications). Many consumer applications now include some sort of Internet tie-in, such as a multi-player Internet version of a popular CD-ROM game, so most technical professionals need at least a passing familiarity with popular Web-based languages, such as Java.

Aim for the middle. The word among recruiters is that there are plenty of mid-level jobs begging to be filled. If you're a fast learner and motivated, you can jump from entry- to mid-level within a couple of years. There aren't too many fields where you can make that kind of move. Beware of getting stuck in a mid-level job, however. Doing the same thing for too long can mean career death if you're not learning about new technologies that can advance your career—and your market value. By the way, one entry-level job that provides a fast track to the mid-level jobs is *PC technical support specialist,* described later in this chapter.

The female perspective. When Carleton "Carly" Fiorina moved in as President and CEO of Hewlett-Packard Co., the world's second largest computer maker, women took a step toward balancing gender inequity. Still, Fiorina is only the third woman running a Fortune 500 company, and the high-tech industry is slow to lose its male-dominated image.

While women have successfully infiltrated marketing and technical support areas, engineers are almost always men. The National Research Council reports that 9.8 percent of working engineers in the U.S. in 1997 were female. Why does this matter so much? Because women will ultimately be left out of decisions about our technical future, according to the Institute of Women and Technology (IWT). The PalmPilot, for example, was shaped to fit a man's breast pocket and most calendar software programs are designed to track one person's—not a family's—life.

In its effort to interest more women in becoming engineers and computer scientists, IWT plans to open virtual development centers where female college students work with faculty members and engineers from sponsoring companies to develop prototypes of products.

A new way to operate? Virtually every home computer sold today comes with Microsoft Windows operating pre-installed. (Some industry insiders refer to the Windows license fees hardware manufacturers must fork over as "Microsoft tax.") But balance may be shifting. Several manufacturers are introducing PCs without Windows—or any other Microsoft software—pre-installed. Proponents of "Window-less" PCs are hoping that the lower prices resulting from software licensing and hardware savings will help them reach 50 to 60 percent of American households currently without computers—and also help them open new markets abroad.

Old standards...and still winners

Computer engineers. Engineers design and test integrated circuits or other electronic components that make computers work. As a member of a small group or project team, a computer engineer often focuses on a particular component in the overall design or manufacturing process. In addition to developing detailed cost estimates for production, many engineers are being tapped to develop strategies and budgets for research and development by companies that face a tough battle for shares of an international market.

System programmer/analysts. These high-tech gurus design, develop, and help implement software that supports various business functions. Working from an overall design, programmers use a computer language such as C++ or Visual Basic to write or automate the writing of lines of code. Often, small teams of programmers within a development team work together on different aspects of a complex application, such as a user interface. Powerful applications, such as Microsoft Word, can keep up to 100 programmers busy. Programmers working for software companies may be involved in writing upgrades or enhancements to applications they've already developed. Others work independently to tailor an existing application to the specialized needs of an individual, company, or industry

Technical writers. Computers and software may be getting more user-friendly, but they are also becoming more powerful and more complex. Certainly, on-screen "help" won't begin to replace the prose of a skilled technical writer anytime soon. In fact, demand for straightforward, easy-to-use product documentation is expected to grow with the increase in operating systems and applications. Some technical writers concentrate on writing detailed documentation for data processing managers and other highly skilled technical staff members. Others have a flair for translating technical terms and concepts into everyday language for the lay user.

Technical trainers. Even the best documentation or user manual should be supported by training. Independent trainers, as well as members of corporate training departments, design courses and structure curricula to help users build comprehension quickly. Hands-on training can take place in a classroom via interactive television, or through guided video or computer-based training courses that, once completed, can be consulted for future reference. (See Education & Training.)

Consultants. These professional problem-solvers work closely with programmers, as well as the information systems (IS) managers and computer users in a company to answer a range of business requirements. They begin by nailing down specific requirements. They may recommend the purchase of specific hardware, operating systems, or software applications. Before the job is done, they may implement new systems, integrate new components (such as networks) to existing systems, tailor applications to individual departments, and teach employees how to maximize overall computing performance.

A growing number of programmers move from contract to contract customizing software and solve short-term problems for a range of companies. Typically, they bring a familiarity with programming, technical operations management, and business to customer-companies in specialized industries. Many are also asked to conduct training and customize software to solve a wide variety of business problems.

PC technical support specialists. With profitability riding on hundreds of thousands of PCs in the field, companies are designating PC technical support specialists as the first line of support for technical and nontechnical users. Often part of a team manning a company's internal help desk, these PC pros coach individuals through situational problems, install and upgrade desktop software, monitor equipment purchases, and manage software license agreements.

Project managers. The buck stops with the project manager when it comes to making sure new technology meets business needs within a company. Project managers carefully manage the progress of a systems development team according to specific business objectives. The challenge is to marry the advanced functionality of new technology to detailed and very specific tasks and processes—while ensuring that standard business processes and procedures are maintained across different locations and functions.

Computer game developers. In a matter of a few years, computer games have emerged from the realm of the bedroom-developer into the bright lights of an extremely competitive market segment that spans role-playing software, car and flight simulation, sports, strategy games, and children's games. Working in large companies or small developer shops, computer game developers devise game concepts and create the characters and story lines that compel players to keep returning. The growing complexity of game platforms, such as the Sony Playstation II with DVD-ROM and super-fast processors, means "gamers" are demanding lush, realistic games that involve a huge investment in equipment and personnel hours. Development costs can easily be in the tens of millions, which means the days of independent developers may be numbered.

Information archivists. In past, archivists have worked in libraries, museums, and colleges. These days, they're increasingly at home in profit, nonprofit, and government organizations.

For example, tobacco companies have sensitive legal documents that must be preserved. High-profile technology companies such as Microsoft, Digital Equipment, and Sun Microsystems have trade secrets that must be protected from industrial espionage. Archivists also deal with other organizational issues, such as which records are accessible to what departments, divisions or customers. Information archivists should have a fascination for documenting and preserving data contained in information systems. This requires knowledge of how database systems are designed to work. Successful archivists have a flair for understanding very detailed information and records in terms of the bigger picture related to business and industry requirements.

Geographic information systems (GIS) practitioners. By combining a database with a computerized geographic map or model, a GIS practitioner can compare information about sites struck by environmental or natural disasters. GIS workers planned evacuation routes after Hurricane Floyd swept the coasts of the Florida, Georgia, and the Carolinas in 1999. In the event of an oil spill, specialists can create a computer map of the area and trace the likely course of pollutants. Environmental data on clean sites can also be stored to track and assess future pollution.

Do you have what it takes?

Those aspects of the industry that make it exciting are the same that account for the lack of stability within the field. Company priorities (and prosperity) change quickly. Being this year's "big hit" doesn't guarantee a company's long-term stability. Some claim that software companies both big and small often lack clear decision-making hierarchies and road maps for getting things done. Regardless of that, most jobs in the computer industry call for a proficiency in math. If you think logically and enjoy exacting, analytical work, you're on the right track.

While most hardware engineers and PC technical support specialists are tinkerers, programmers tend to think of themselves as craftspeople applying the same blend of judgment and precision to writing a line of code as a woodworker would to carving a table. A bug can affect the operation of entire tasks within the application. The process of debugging an application involves painstaking detective work. It takes patience, persistence, and plenty of stamina to complete development projects that tend to be long and complex. To meet impossible release dates, programmer/analysts often work long hours.

A technical background alone is not enough to get the best jobs. Business skills or experience working in the financial sector or marketing are well rewarded. Other nontechnical skills employers and recruiters look for are project management and communication skills. It's becoming increasingly essential for technical people to become proficient in translating technical concepts into nontechnical language. Project managers should have demonstrated leadership skills and people management experience. Consultants, project managers, and programmers/analysts especially need to be able to listen to and communicate with a wide range of different types of people. Working the help desk requires excellent people skills and nerves of steel.

Education and training

Computer engineers earn a B.S. in electrical or materials engineering. Most specialize in materials used in building computers, such as silicon and plastics.

About half go on to earn a master's degree or doctorate. However, there are no universal requirements for systems programmers/analysts because applications tend to vary widely according the needs of an industry. Companies using scientific or engineering applications prefer programmers/analysts with a B.S. in computer or information science, mathematics, engineering, or the physical sciences. Companies that use computers for business prefer people with some experience in accounting, management, and other business skills. All programmers/analysts and consultants should have a detailed knowledge of the most up-to-date languages, networking, and database management systems. What's hot today may not be tomorrow. It's important to stay up-to-date on today's A-list skills. For example, hiring has recently been extremely strong for software professionals with knowledge of C++ or Java. Other key areas are: Windows, Windows NT, Visual Basic, Hypertext Markup Language (HTML), Microsoft Office, Oracle, and/or SQL technologies.

PC technical support specialists should have a stellar understanding of PC hardware and software, including a thorough familiarity with Intel/Windows operating systems, Microsoft Office, and/or Lotus Notes. They should also have basic knowledge of computer networks, including local area networks (LANs), wide area networks (WANs), and intranets.

Project managers should have a working knowledge of development methodologies as well as project life cycles and technologies. They should have experience in every phase of systems development—including analysis, design, constructions and unit and systems testing activities.

According to *ComputerWorld* magazine, an M.B.A. is the degree of choice for anyone who wants to advance to project management or to go into consulting. There is a growing demand for "renaissance" engineers who have a head for business as well as technology. In fact, some top business schools—Stanford and the University of Pennsylvania's Wharton School among them—now offer specialized M.B.A. programs combining business and high-tech courses to give graduates the tools they need to solve real business problems. Geographic information systems practitioners typically need a master's degree to move ahead.

Technical writers should have a bachelor's degree in English or technical communications, or a specialized knowledge of engineering, business, or one of the physical sciences. In many cases, people with good writing skills can pick up specialized knowledge on the job. Technical trainers can have a B.S. in computer science or business, coupled with experience working with the technology they teach.

Most companies require instructors to complete an intensive training program to ensure they are able to communicate key points effectively. Information archivists need a master's degree in science and information, with an emphasis on archives and records management. You can enter the field with a B.A. and a systems or records management background, but if you want to move into the management ranks, a master's degree will work in your favor. Archivists should also stay current on technology storage systems and techniques. It should go without saying that career-long continuing education will be essential for everyone employed in this dynamic industry.

Professional licensing and certification

Some companies require their training staff to become certified technical trainers (CTTs). Many consultants also earn this designation.

Tips on breaking in

Don't get typecast. Beware of earning a reputation for being a miracle worker. You may be stalling your own advancement. Very small companies may find technical professionals too essential to promote. In a large firm, you may become stuck at a certain level of the bureaucracy. Your best bet is to find a small to medium-sized company that's growing quickly. Growing companies need to fill new roles constantly and are more likely to promote from within.

Try a different path. Some engineers transfer their skills to technical writing. They may move into their company's marketing department or to an advertising or public relations agency. Agencies with high-tech customers are always looking for good writers with technical knowledge.

Get some experience. Many employers will only consider applicants with previous experience. Students should seek out part-time or summer jobs as well as internships in the data processing department of a local company.

Practice creativity. Software companies like to evaluate the creative intelligence of prospective programmers. If you're stumped by questions such as "Why are manhole covers round?," bone up on brainteasers. *A Kick in the Seat of the Pants,* by Roger von Oech (Harper & Row) is a good book for loosening up your problem-solving skills and breaking out of logic ruts.

Get the write stuff. If you're going to pursue a technical career, give yourself an edge and invest in a business writing course. Technical "geeks" are a dime a dozen. But technical pros who can write an intelligible proposal are few and far between.

Career path

The computer industry is less linear than other fields. People tend to drop in and out of jobs, moving back and forth between consulting and corporations. Some take time off to start their own companies. With less certainty about where you'll wind up, you can typically find more opportunity.

Beginning programmer/analysts may enter a training program before working alone on simple assignments, or be put on a team under the supervision of more experienced programmers. The career path for engineers and programmers is usually into management. In large organizations, you may be promoted to lead programmer and supervise other programmers. With general business experience, programmers may become project managers.

In recent years, more companies have seen the value of creating parallel career ladders that allow engineers and programmers to receive substantial promotions and raises without having to move into management.

What can you earn?

Youth is valued—and well rewarded—in the computer industry. Currently, three of every four workers are between the ages of 25 and 44. Stock options (the opportunity to purchase a specified number of shares at a predetermined price below market value) have become a key part of the compensation package for many in the computer industry. Smaller companies and startups often make up in stock options what they cannot afford to pay in salary. This method of compensation has made millionaires of many engineers and programmers working in boom areas, such as California's Silicon Valley.

However, before you put a down payment on a boat, realize that one in 10 startups will have an initial public offering (IPO) of its stock. And one in 10 IPOs become a "Microsoft" or a "Yahoo."

Cultural perks can be an essential part of your compensation package. Many progressive software companies reward long hours and hard work by hosting regular Friday afternoon beer busts and parties to mark project milestones. Some offer sabbaticals after a certain number of years of service, free latte, permission to take the dog to work, yoga classes, and other perks.

Entry-level engineers can begin at salaries from $30,000 to $40,000. Salary growth thereafter can be sluggish. The median salary for engineers with a master's degree and 10 years of experience is $53,400. With 25 years of experience, it is only $65,000. Engineers with no managerial responsibilities rarely earn more than $100,000 a year.

Programmer/analyst salaries vary dramatically depending on where they work. In New York, entry-level programmer/analysts are paid about $50,000. With four-plus years of experience, the average salary increases to $69,000. In Chicago, entry-level programmers/analysts earn about $38,000, jumping to $48,000 in four years.

Project managers earn between $55,000 and 90,000 per year. The more experience, the more money one can make. Senior project managers (those with five years under their belts) make from $70,000 to $130,000 or higher.

Entry-level technical writers earn about $35,000. Mid-career, they can be earning $41,300, topping out at $65,500.

Geographic information systems practitioners start out earning from $20,000 to $30,000. Five to eight years down the road, after they have earned a master's degree, they can earn from $30,000 to $40,000. Top salaries in the public sector reach $50,000. In the private sector, GIS practitioners can double that, making approximately $100,000.

Salaries for PC technical support specialists range from $25,000 to $45,000. Becoming technical support managers can raise compensation to $55,000 or higher. Game developers can earn from $30,000 to $120,000 per year.

Where will you work?

Technology affects every industry mentioned in this book. The best prospects can be found in health care and pharmaceuticals, financial services, utilities, and insurance companies. Although most of the leading computer companies are located in California's Silicon Valley and outside of Boston, new centers have sprung up in Seattle, Atlanta, and Dallas. Software companies exist across the country.

Job Profile

Gary Copeland, senior applications engineer

What general job responsibilities does your title encompass?

System enhancements of the internal version control system written in Microsoft FoxPro and Visual FoxPro.

How many years have you been in this business?

Six years.

How many years of education do you have?

High school plus three years of college. Recent college classes focused on software development using the latest technologies for database, user interfaces, and Web applications.

How many hours do you typically work per week?

50 or more.

What hours do you work on a typical day?

9:00 a.m. to 7:00 p.m. daily.

How big is the company you work for?

700+ employees.

Have you earned professional certification?

I'm a Novell Certified Network Engineer (CNE) and I have a Sun Netdynamics application programming certificate.

What is your annual salary?

Base salary of $87,500. Undetermined performance bonuses and additional contract work could add up to an additional $15,000 or more.

How did you get your job?

Through a job recruiter.

Please describe one of your "typical" days.

Other than the weekly "all hands meeting," meetings vary from day to day.

Hour 1: Catch up on company e-mail.

Hour 2: Review project priorities.

Hours 3-7: Software development.

Hours 8+: Respond to e-mail, plan for next projects.

What are your career aspirations?

To work in a dynamic field with a group of motivated, progressive, and dedicated individuals. Now that e-commerce is such a big field it would be in my plans to gain the skills to be able to work with this fast-paced area.

What kind of people do really well at this business?

People who really love what they do. They can take a problem and give it a working solution.

What do you really like about your job?

The challenge of making some piece of code work in the best way it can.

What do you dislike?

Corporate politics.

What is the biggest misconception about this job?

That it requires a nerd to do it.

How can someone get a job like yours?

Prove they can do the job. (Having a little luck doesn't hurt either.)

Resources

Top systems integration/computer services companies

Andersen Consulting
www.ac.com

Control Data Systems, Inc.
Corporate Headquarters
4201 Lexington Avenue N
Arden Hills, MN 55126-6198
(888)742-5864
Fax: (651)415-3000
www.cdc.com

American Management Systems (AMS)
4050 Legato Road
Fairfax, VA 22033
(703)267-8000
Fax: (703)267-5073
www.amsinc.com

Electronic Data Systems Corp.
5400 Legacy Drive
Plano, TX 75024-3199
(972)604-6000
E-mail: info@eds.com
www.eds.com

Shared Medical Systems Corp.
51 Valley Stream Parkway
Malvern, PA 19355
(610)219-6300
Fax: (610)219-8266
www.smed.com

TRW Communications
1900 Richmond Road
Cleveland, OH 44124
(216)291-7000
Literature Request Line: (216)291-7755
www.trw.com

Top computer hardware companies

Apple Computer, Inc.
1 Infinite Loop
Cupertino, CA 95014
(408)996-1010
www.apple.com

International Business Machines (IBM)
Old Orchard Road
Armonk, NY 10504
(914)765-1900
www.ibm.com

AST Research Inc.
16215 Alton Parkway
Irvine, CA 92713
(714)727-4141
Fax: (714)727-8584
www.ast.com

Compaq Computer Corp.
P.O. Box 692000
Houston, TX 77269-2000
(281)370-0670
Fax: (281)514-1740
www.compaq.com

Sun Microsystems, Inc.
901 San Antonio Road
Palo Alto, CA 94303
(800)555-9SUN
www.sun.com

Digital Equipment Corp
111 Powdermill Road
Maynard, MA 01754-1418
(978)493-5111
www.digital.com

Tandem Computers, Inc.
Atalla Product Group
Compaq Computer Corporation
19191 Vallco Parkway   Loc. 4-28
Cupertino, CA 95014-2594
(408)285-2000 or (800)523-9981
Fax: (408)285-2044
www.tandem.com

Hewlett-Packard Company
3000 Hanover Street
Palo Alto, CA 94304-1185
(650)857-1501
Fax: (650)857-5518
www.hp.com

Top computer software companies

Computer Associates International, Inc.
One Computer Associates Plaza
Islandia, NY 11749
(516)342-5224
www.cai.com

Lotus Development Corp.
55 Cambridge Parkway
Cambridge, MA 02142
(617)577-8500
www.lotus.com

Microsoft Corp.
One Microsoft Way
Redmond, WA 98052-6399
(425)882-8080
www.microsoft.com

Silicon Graphics, Inc.
1600 Amphitheatre Parkway
Mountain View, CA 94043
(650)960-1980
www.sgi.com

Oracle Corp.
500 Oracle Parkway
Redwood Shores, CA 90465
(415)506-7000
www.oracle.com

Computer industry associations

**Association of
Computer Professionals**
P.O. Box 172
Maple Plain, MN 55359
(612)479-6273
Fax: (612)479-3804
E-mail: info@acomputerpro.org
www.acomputerpro.org

**Association for Women
in Computing**
41 Sutter Street
Suite 1006
San Francisco, CA 94104
(415)905-4663
E-mail: awc@awc-hq.org
www.awc-hq.org

**Computer & Communications Industry
Association**
666 Eleventh Street NW, Suite 600
Washington, DC 20001
(202)783-0070
Fax: (202)783-0534
www.ccia.org

**Information Technology Association
of America**
1616 N. Ft. Meyer Drive, Suite 1300
Arlington, VA 22209
(703)522-5055
Fax: (703)525-2279
www.itaa.org

**The Institute for Women
and Technology**
3333 Coyote Hill Road
Palo Alto, CA 94304
(650)812-4496
Fax: (650)812-4969
E-mail: info@iwt.org
www.iwt.org

Webgrrls International
50 Broad Street, Suite 1614
New York, NY 10004
(212)785-1276 ext 504
Fax: (212)785-1383
www.webgrrls.com

Computer industry magazines

Datamation
250 Summer Street
Boston, MA 02210
(212)605-0400
www.datamation.com

Wired News
660 3rd Street 4th Floor
San Francisco, CA 94107
(415)276-8400
Fax: (415)276-8500
www.wired.com

ComputerWorld
CW Publishing Company
500 Old Connecticut Path
Framingham, MA 01701
(508)879-0700
www.computerworld.com

Chapter 5

Education & Training

Teachers and trainers go to the head of the class

Adult education teacher
Childcare center director
Childcare provider
Corporate trainer
K-12 teacher
Language teacher
School administrator
Special education teacher
Development director
Planned giving officer
Best Bet for Entrepreneurs: *Independent trainer*

Forecast

Experts predict that, as current teachers begin to retire and the population of school-age children continues to grow, there will be a shortage of more than 300,000 teachers by the year 2001. Renewed commitment to education should point to better conditions and higher pay in the long term. Corporations spend almost as much as public education does to train and retrain workers in a wide variety of areas. Yet, there is plenty of room for growth.

Growth

Employment is expected to grow as fast as the average for primary and secondary school teachers, librarians, and administrators. Expect faster than average growth for corporate trainers, childcare workers, and secondary school, special education, and adult education teachers. There continue to be shortages in several key areas at the primary and secondary levels, including mathematics, science, and foreign languages.

Overview

Pop quiz: What is the most important asset for the United States to remain competitive in a high-stakes, global marketplace? *Answer:* A well-educated, well-trained work force.

This is simple logic. Yet an estimated 23 million Americans are functionally illiterate. Forty percent of one high school class in a major city couldn't identify the United States on a map. Funding cuts have resulted in declining enrollments in colleges and universities.

Government officials have been slow to get serious about improving the quality of education in America. In addition to administrative actions, such as mandating smaller classes, there has been a renewed commitment to attracting and retaining the best and brightest teachers and administrators.

A master's degree is the minimum price of entry for most careers and standards for professional certification are becoming stricter. The demand for specialized on-the-job technical training and adult education is also on the rise. Education has become nearly a cradle-to-grave business—beginning with preschool, continuing throughout our careers, and going far into retirement—spelling opportunity for job seekers with a range of career goals.

From the basics to business

There are two basic categories of schools in the United States: public and private. Public schools—from local PS 182 to UCLA—receive the bulk of their operating funds from the local, state, and federal governments (read: *your* tax dollars). Private schools are funded entirely by tuition fees and private donations. Criticism of American students' standardized test scores and the sorry financial and physical state of schools in some parts of the U.S. have prompted some local governments to award vouchers to parents, which they can use to pay for sending their children to private schools. In other areas, charter schools are emerging. (These are private schools that are awarded charters to operate as public schools.)

No matter what kind of school you attend and how many degrees we have when you graduate, a lifetime of continuing education awaits. Ten percent of all U.S. employees now receive training on the job, yet an estimated 50 million need it. This will keep *corporate trainers* and *adult education teachers* busy by providing a wide range of training and retraining programs that cover everything from how to speak French to how to operate the most up-to-date technology.

Industry snapshot

The Baby Boomers' babies are boosting school enrollments from the preschool through secondary school levels. Mix in a growing number of students from immigrant families. However, crowded classrooms are just part of the reason that national attention and funding is being funneled back into education. It is no longer possible to ignore the appalling studies that show America is graduating a workforce often lacking the science and math skills needed to compete in important areas of future growth.

Corporations were the first to see the writing on the wall. Today, business spends almost as much as public education does to train and retrain its workers. According to a survey by the American Society of Training and Development (ASTD), 93 percent of all major American companies have also stepped in to teach employees reading, writing, and arithmetic!

Trends to track

Recruiting a "real world" perspective. Fortunately, there is a renewed interest in teaching among college students—as well as professionals who have already pursued other careers. At Columbia Teachers College, 15 percent of the entering class came from jobs in finance, publishing, and other fields. Colleges and universities facing shortages of capable teachers in key areas such as computers and marketing are inviting experienced professionals to bring a valuable real-world perspective into the classroom.

Meanwhile, there's nothing preventing already-certified teachers from dreaming up creative ways to bring real-world relevance into the classroom setting. For example, one enterprising teacher created an interactive Web site designed to transport students on a virtual journey around the world. Between 25,000 and 40,000 students log on to the site to follow the progress of five young travelers through their regular dispatches on the society, culture, and geography of places like Peru, Guatemala, and South Africa. The travel team also answers messages from students, hosts live chats from different regions, and broadcasts live interviews with prominent international figures such as Mary Burton of South Africa's Truth and Reconciliation Commission as well as 1992 Nobel Peace Prize Winner Adolfo Perez of Argentina.

High-tech teaching credentials. Faced with an unexpected wave of teacher retirements, bulging enrollments, and new programs, such as mandatory class size reduction, California has been issuing "emergency" teaching permits to fill teaching ranks. Rather than wait up to five years for these teachers to earn the proper credentials, the state developed an innovative new program. CalStateTEACH is an electronic curriculum delivered via the Internet, e-mail, videos, and books, making it easier—and cheaper—for the state's 30,000 "emergency" teachers to earn their teaching certificates in as little as eight months. At least 26 other states have alternative certification programs for people with a bachelor's degree who would like to teach in their area of expertise.

Power to the people. With government attention comes the possibility of better salaries, better conditions, and professional recognition for teachers and school administrators. Unions are bargaining for more control. New "management team" administrative structures are already changing the face of education. As standards raise the quality of teaching, mentoring programs will help teachers learn teaching skills and support one another.

Business alliances. It is in the interest of every employer to reach out to students while they are still in school. More and more companies will develop programs that prepare today's students to become tomorrow's managers. More emphasis will be placed on developing marketable job skills from technical expertise to problem solving. For example, Polaroid Corporation's "Project Bridge" invites teachers into the corporation for hands-on training in their specialties.

An education charter. The Learner Centered School, Creative Arts Elementary, Leadership High. Although each has the ring of exclusive private schools, these are the names of public, charter schools. As their names imply, charter schools are highly specialized schools, customized to the needs of their pupils. With 1,200 schools going strong in 27 states, President Clinton earmarked $95 million in 1999 for the development another 3,000-plus charter schools within three years. Charter schools cannot charge tuition, discriminate, or promote religion and must administer the same standardized exams that public schools do. However, that's where the similarities end. Charter schools set their own rules and hire their own employees, some of them parents of the students to teach students a nontraditional curricula that may combine math and science with black history, jazz, and Japanese.

Going online to learn. International Data Corporation (IDC), a Framingham, MA-based high tech research and marketing firm, predicts that the market for adult education delivered via the Internet will take off, growing from $1.1 billion in sales at the end of 1999 to $9.3 billion in sales by 2003. Fueled by the corporate training market, Internet-based courses allow employees to learn at their own desks. This not only saves transportation costs, but lets each individual learn at his or her own pace, during the hours that complement individual work schedules. One issue yet to be tackled: accreditation.

Old standards...and still winners

Childcare providers. Most households are dual-income. The majority of these families are turning to formal childcare arrangements. Many employers are increasing childcare benefits to their employees in the form of direct childcare assistance.

Primary and secondary teachers. From the first day of kindergarten to high school graduation, these educators cover every subject area from math to music. More than 1.6 million people work as teachers at the primary level (grades K-8) and another 1.2 million teach in high schools.

Language teachers. As many professions become more international, enrollment should continue to rise in foreign language courses. Japanese and German are the most popular. But beware: Many school systems pay lip service to foreign language programs. Pay tends to be low and the positions are often some of the first to go during a budget cut.

Special education teachers. Social worker, parent, psychologist, and friend, this special breed of educators works closely with students with special needs. There are 7.4 million exceptional students in the United States. Many schools are piloting innovative programs and community integration for these gifted, developmentally disabled, or physically impaired students, as well as students with emotional or behavioral disorders. The BLS expects new jobs to increase at a rate of more than 20,000 per year.

Administrators. Currently, there are about 300,000 of these educational "general managers," ranging from primary school principals to district superintendents. Demand will be higher in areas where trends promise increased enrollment.

Technical trainers. Prospects are especially promising for *technical trainers* as rapidly changing technology becomes more integral to our jobs. These technical experts provide hands-on instruction on the latest technology designed to quickly build comprehension and hasten productivity on the job. Hands-on training can take place in a classroom, via interactive television, or through guided video- or computer-based training courses that can be consulted for future reference.

Development directors. Universities and colleges have traditionally survived on the gifts and donations of wealthy alumni and corporate patrons. *Development directors* design the fundraising strategies that persuade these benefactors to make gifts and donations. They may appeal to the special interests of one party, and the ego of another. For a $1 million donation, a school might name a professorship for the contributor; for $5 million, an entire building. This relationship-building process can take several years.

A new generation of opportunities

Independent trainers. Fortune 500 firms are increasingly hiring *independent trainers* or training firms to handle many aspects of corporate training. Bank training programs farm out accounting and finance modules to local university professors on a consulting basis. This area has bright prospects for teachers, human resources professionals, and technical people with an entrepreneurial bent.

Planned giving officers. A cousin of the development director, the *planned giving officer* helps coordinate charitable gift giving with personal financial planning. Under the guidance of the planned giving officer, a patron may make a donation in the form of a tax-free annuity or trust. This will generate a larger donation for the college or university while providing income to the patron. Since the mid-1980s, when major tax law changes went into effect, planned giving has become the fastest growing area of fundraising. It is a key service for nonprofits, such as colleges and universities.

Adult education teachers. Over the years, there has been a rising demand for courses focused on upgrading specific professional skills, as well as building personal enrichment.

Childcare center director. Many parents want guarantees of safety inspections and some academic work for their toddlers, so they're shifting from family day care to centers that must answer to accrediting bodies.

Do you have what it takes?

Even with the promise of more equitable pay, you're not likely to get rich as a teacher. You *must* be in it for the satisfaction of positively influencing the people you teach.

Childcare providers should be sensitive, compassionate, creative, and patient to care for the emotional, intellectual, and creative needs of many young children.

In addition to being knowledgeable about their subject, primary and secondary school teachers should be able to communicate effectively, inspire trust and confidence, and motivate their students to perform at their best. They should also be organized, creative, patient, and enthusiastic about participating in extracurricular school activities (such as directing a school play or coaching an athletic team).

Special education tends to be a high-stress field, so teachers need to be able to balance their professional and personal lives to prevent burnout.

School administrators should be excellent business managers, with leadership and interpersonal skills to guide and motivate individual teachers and students.

Because development directors and planned giving officers spend a great deal of time calling on senior-level corporate executives and wealthy alumni and patrons, they should present a highly polished image. It helps to be well connected socially; however, creativity and assertiveness are most important in the long run.

In addition to skill or expertise in one or more technical or professional areas, corporate trainers should have excellent presentation skills to effectively reach a broad spectrum of adult audiences. Good organizational, writing, and interpersonal skills are essential.

Independent trainers should be assertive enough to sell themselves and their programs to key corporate decision-makers.

Education and training

Many states regulate training for preschool workers. Although some need only a high school diploma, many earn college degrees in child development or early childhood education. Montessori preschool teachers must complete an additional year of training after receiving their bachelor's degree in early childhood education or a related field.

Primary and secondary teachers need a bachelor's degree in education from an approved teacher training program. This always includes experience working as a student teacher. Many states require teachers to have a Master of Arts in Teaching (M.A.T.) or Master's in Special Education. Administrators who work in public schools need a master's degree in educational administration. At the college and university level, most go on to earn a doctorate. It is common to enter the field with a bachelor's degree and earn one or more graduate degrees while on the job.

Corporate trainers should have a B.S. or extensive work experience in the areas they teach. Most companies require full-time instructors to complete an intensive training program to ensure they are able to effectively communicate key points.

Development directors usually earn a bachelor's degree, although exceptions are sometimes made for people with extensive experience in the field. Planned giving officers may couple a degree in finance or law with fundraising experience. After that, ongoing training is essential for them to stay current with changing tax laws.

Professional licensing and certification

Each state has its own certification programs for public teachers and school administrators. Information about specific licensure or certification requirements and approved teacher training institutions is available from local school systems and state departments of education. Private schools don't require certification.

Many states offer alternative teacher licensure programs for people who have bachelor's degrees in the subject they teach. In recent years, the National Board for Professional Teaching Standards has begun offering voluntary national certification for teachers. Nationally certified teachers may find it easier to get a job in another state. In some states, they may earn higher salaries and be eligible for more bonuses.

Many states and public schools require preschool teachers to earn the certification as a Child Development Associate (CDA) offered by the Council for Early Childhood Professional Recognition. The CDA is recognized as a credential for childcare teachers and directors in 46 states and the District of Columbia. If you don't have any childcare experience, you can earn your CDA by completing the Council's one-year training program.

Tips on breaking in

Consult job resources. Job lines, lists, and online resources abound for the education graduate. *The Job Information List of the Modern Language Association*, for example, lists hundreds of jobs by geographic region, as well as by college, university, and specialty. Related jobs ranging from comparative literature to linguistics are also included. Teach for America places new graduates in schools across the nation. Recruiting New Teachers operates a referral service.

If you're already teaching, you can find out about opportunities in your area by contacting the local superintendent of schools or the state department of education.

Jobs for development directors are advertised in *The Chronicle of Higher Education* and are posted on the bulletin board outside the college or university personnel office.

Career path

With experience, preschool teachers and childcare providers may advance to supervisory positions in large childcare centers or preschools. These positions often require a bachelor's or master's degree, however. Other childcare providers workers work in resource and referral agencies, consulting with parents on childcare services. Some become involved in policy or advocacy work related to childcare and early childhood education. With a bachelor's degree, preschool teachers may become certified to teach grades K-12 in public schools.

Most primary and secondary teachers choose to stay with what they love: teaching. Many special education teachers welcome the opportunity to get involved in developing innovative new programs.

With a master's degree, some teachers move into administration. Some leave teaching to become human resource professionals or corporate trainers.

Development directors usually begin their careers as the second- or third-level person in a college or university development office. Many progress more quickly by moving from institution to institution. In 10 to 12 years, a development officer may be managing the function for a school within the university. The top development job, supervising the activities of eight to 15 development officers, typically opens up 15 to 20 years into a career.

Some planned giving officers move up to manage a development office and then progress to vice president of a college or university. Others move into financial services to assist high net-worth clients.

How much can you earn?

The average salary for entry-level childcare providers is $18,500. With five years of experience, you can earn $25,000. With 10 years of experience, you can earn $40,000.

Public school teachers earn significantly more than private school teachers (approximately $35,000, compared to $22,000). Salaries for elementary and secondary school teachers range from $18,000 to $55,000. Salaries for special education teachers follow the same scale as for general education teachers. In some schools, teachers receive extra pay for coaching sports and participating in extracurricular activities.

In 1996, more than half of all public school teachers belonged to unions—primarily the American Federation of Teachers and the National Education Association. Both bargain with school systems over wages, and hours, along with terms and conditions of employment.

School administrators at the primary level average $62,900. At the secondary level, administrators average $72,400.

Earnings for adult education teachers vary widely by the subject they teach, their academic credentials, experience, and the region of the country where they teach. According to the Bureau of Labor Statistics (BLS), salaried adult education teachers working full-time had median earnings of approximately $31,300 in 1996.

Development directors begin at $25,000 to $30,000. With five years experience, they can make from $38,000 to $45,000 at a small school and from $75,000 to $95,000 at a larger institution.

Salaries for planned giving officers range from between $30,000 to $40,000 at the entry level to an average top salary of $85,000.

According to *Training Magazine,* corporate trainers make an average of $45,000 to $60,000, depending on their subject and the professional level of their audiences. Most independent trainers charge a daily rate ranging from $600 to $2,000. Some charge $100 or more per trainee. Annual revenues can range from $31,000 to $230,000.

Where will you work?

Childcare providers work in daycare centers, nursery schools, preschools, and as nannies in private homes. Primary and secondary teachers and administrators can work in any city or town. Currently, job openings are growing fastest in Arizona, California, Florida, Georgia, Hawaii, Maryland, Nevada, New Hampshire, Virginia, and Washington.

Job Profile

Trina Johnson, training consultant, internal applications

What are your general responsibilities?
I am responsible for the ongoing development and delivery of our corporate training program.

How many years have you been in this business?
I've spent the last year in miscellaneous training roles. I accepted the full-time training position (reporting to HR) in April of this year.

How many years of education do you have?
I have a B.S. in business, with an emphasis in accounting.

How many hours a week do you typically work?
I work 45 to 50 hours.

What are your hours on a typical workday?
7 a.m. to 5:30 p.m.

How big is the company you work for?
We have more than 900 employees.

In what general range does your annual salary fall?
There are many levels of training within the company. The salary range is dependent upon the individual's experience, qualifications, and education. Salaries within the training department range anywhere between $40,000 to $70,000 or more, depending on the position.

How did you get your current job?
I was contacted by a recruiting agency for a completely different position within the company. After working in that position for three years it was apparent to me that I would like to pursue a training career. Due to the software application experience I had acquired over the past several years, the training position was an ideal career move.

What's your typical day like?
In this position there is no such thing as a "typical day." Our corporate training program is offered quarterly and the duration of the training program is three weeks. During these times I am training from 9 a.m. to 4 p.m. each day. I use the time in between the training hours to prepare additional materials, book training rooms, schedule external consultants and order material for the next quarterly session. When I am not training, I am developing or enhancing the existing program to accommodate ongoing technology changes.

What are your career aspirations?
Although I enjoy training and do not plan to change my career path at this time, I will eventually continue my education with a focus in the area of writing. Instead of sharing my knowledge in the classroom, I intend to

educate through books.

What kinds of people do you think would do especially well in your job role?
Someone who is highly motivated, creative, energetic, patient, detailed-oriented, and a team player would enjoy a career in application training.

What do you like most about your job?
I am often one of the first people to work with our new employees. It is very satisfying to know that I am shaping their impression of the company, as well as setting the stage for their success in their new roles.

What do you like least?
There are very few things that I do not enjoy in regard to my training role. However, my least favorite tasks would have to be the administrative items. I find that scheduling, ordering materials, and sending reminders takes much of the time I would prefer to use enhancing the current training program.

What are some common misconceptions about your job/profession/ industry?
How difficult can it be to produce a paycheck? Not very. How difficult can it be to produce a *correct* paycheck? Now that's a challenge. With the changing tax laws, reciprocal state agreements, garnishments, third parties, and group term life, it is amazing that anyone's paycheck is correct. Before working for a payroll company, I never realized the amount of work that it takes to create a paycheck and to ensure that it is correct. I will never be able to look at a paycheck without truly appreciating the time spent on producing it. This is not too exciting, but when it comes to payroll, it can't be wrong—that is what makes my job challenging.

What would you say is the best way to going about landing a job?
There are several ways to pursue a career in training. For individuals who have a background and education in the field of training, contacting a recruiter or applying directly to a company may be the best approach.

I found that working directly with the application first and then transitioning into the training department worked best for me, due to the amount of product knowledge needed to train people to use the application effectively.

Resources

Associations for teachers and school administrators

American Association of School Administrators
1801 North Moore Street
Arlington, VA 22209
(703)528-0700
Fax: (703)841-1543
E-mail: membership@aasa.org
www.aasa.org

American Association for Adult and Continuing Education
1200 19th Street, NW
Suite 300
Washington, DC 20036
(202)429-5131
Fax: (202)223-4579
www.albany.edu

Council for the Advancement and Support of Education
1307 New York Avenue NW
Suite 1000
Washington, DC 20005-4701
(202)328-5900
Fax: (202)387-4973
www.case.org

American Council on Education
One Dupont Circle NW
Washington, DC 20036
(202)939-9300
Fax: (202)833-4760
www.acenet.edu

Modern Language Association
10 Astor Place
New York, NY 10003-6981
(212)475-9500
Fax: (212)477-9863
www.mla.org

American Federation of Teachers
California Federation of Teachers
One Kaiser Plaza Suite 1440
Oakland, CA 94612
(510)832-8812
Fax:(510)832-5044
www.cft.org

National Association for the Education of Young Children
1509 16th Street, NW
Washington, DC 20036

Association for Childhood Education International
11141 Georgia Ave.
Wheaton, MD 20902
(301)942-2443
E-Mail: naeyc@naeyc.org
www.naeyc.org

National Association for Women in Education
1325 18th Street, NW Suite 210
Washington, DC 20036
(202)659-9330
Fax: (202)457-0946
www.nawe.org

National Board for Professional Teaching Standards
26555 Evergreen Road Suite 400
Southfield, MI 48076
(248)351-4444
Fax: (248)351-4170
www.nbpts.org

National Committee on Planned Giving
233 McCrea Street Suite 400
Indianapolis, IN 46225
(317)269-6274
Fax: (317)269-6276
E-mail: ncpg@iupui.edu
www.ncpg.org

National Education Association
1201 16th St., NW
Washington, DC 20036
(202)833-4000
www.nea.org

National School Boards Association
1680 Duke Street
Alexandria, VA 22314
(703)683-7590
www.nsba.org

The Council for Exceptional Children
1920 Association Drive
Reston, VA 20191-1589
(888)CEC-SPED or (703)620-3660
TTY (text only) (703)264-9446
Fax: (703)264-9494
www.cec.sped.org

Recruiting New Teachers, Inc.
385 Concord Avenue, Suite 103
Belmont, MA 02478
(617)489-6000
www.rnt.org

Teach for America
P.O. Box 5114
New York, NY 10185
(800)832-1230
www.teachforamerica.org

**The National Association
of Elementary School Principals**
1615 Duke Street
Alexandria, VA 22314
(800)38-NAESP or (703) 684-3345
www.naesp.org

**The National Association
of Secondary School Principals**
1904 Association Drive
Reston, VA 20191-1537
(703)860-0200
Fax: (703)476-5432
www.nassp.org

Charter Schooling
US Department of Education
www.uscharterschools.org

*Magazines for teachers
and administrators*

The International Educator
P.O. Box 513
Cummaquid, MA 02637
(508)362-1414
Fax: (508)362-1411
E-mail: tie@capecod.net
www.tieonline.com

NEA Today
National Education Association
1201 16th St., NW
Washington, DC 20036
(202)833-4000
www.nea.org

*Current Openings in Education
in the USA*
Education Information Service
P.O. Box 662D
Newton, MA 02161
(617)237-0887

Resources for corporate trainers

**American Society for Training
and Development**
1640 King Street
Box 1443
Alexandria, VA 22313-2043
(703)683-8100
Fax: (703)683-8103
www.astd.org

Directory of leading private companies
121 Chanlon Road
New Providence, NJ 07974
(800)521-8110
www.reedref.com

Chapter 6

Engineering

At the frontlines
in a global marketplace

Biomedical engineer
Chemical engineer
Civil engineer
Electrical engineer
Mechanical engineer
Materials engineer
Safety engineer
Best Bet for Entrepreneurs: *Consulting engineer*

Forecast

Demand will vary by specialty. While the economy and cutbacks in the nation's defense budget will affect opportunities in some areas, the long-term outlook is bright for engineers in all fields, except for mining, nuclear, and petroleum.

Growth

Better than the overall average. Some areas will see short-term growth. Others will bloom later. Civil engineers, needed to revamp and add to the nation's aging highways, will be able to progress at the rate of the government agencies they serve.

Overview

Almost every innovation in our society has required the input of an engineer. These born tinkerers and problem solvers develop and refine products and equipment as varied as stereo systems and artificial hearts. Others design and rehabilitate the roads and bridges we travel upon.

What's your specialty?

Engineering is a field of specialties, and, increasingly, of subspecialties. Some engineering specialties thrive on innovation. *Biomedical engineers* are already fashioning artificial organs. *Materials engineers* develop new types of metal alloys, ceramics, plastics, composites and other materials. Their uses range from the sleek but mighty graphite golf club to the ceramic tiles that protect the space shuttle from burning up upon re-entry to the earth's atmosphere.

Other engineers solve complex problems. *Chemical engineers* apply the principles of chemistry and engineering to solve problems involving the production or use of chemicals. *Electrical engineers* specialize in designing and producing a range of electrical and electronic equipment such as microwave transmission systems and stereo systems. *Mechanical engineers* concentrate on the moving parts that make everything from rocket engines to refrigerators work. *Safety engineers* focus on maximizing worker productivity on the manufacturing floor. *Civil engineers are* the architects of the highways and bridges that make up our nation's infrastructure.

Independent *consulting engineers* work closely with these professionals to carry out specialized projects.

Industry snapshot

The number of engineering graduates has been declining since 1987. In 1990, less than 9 percent of all bachelor's degrees went to engineers, and college ranks continued to fall throughout the 90s. This is bad news for companies in need of more new talent—but good news indeed for new graduates. According to the College Placement Council, engineering graduates receive more than 40 percent of all the job offers made to undergraduates. Most have received at least one offer before graduation.

Trends to track

Concurrent engineering. In the old days, the design process was long and tedious and expensive, involving low-tech tools such as T-squares, triangles, and clay, wood, or metal models. Now, using digital prototyping software—a blend of computer-aided design (CAD), distributed databases, animation, and prototyping software—engineers create a three-dimensional simulated model in far less time and work on correcting problems concurrently. For example, this can cut the time it takes to design a new car, for example, from 28 to 24 months.

Mastery through apprenticeship. Sound like a throwback to the Middle Ages? So be it. Today, 2 percent of U.S. high school graduates have gotten started as apprentices. This trend is likely to develop with the support of federal grants and corporations who must regularly turn away job applicants who lack sufficient skills and experience.

A team approach. As increasingly thorny problems are served up to engineers, companies have begun to foster ad hoc research teams. The theory is simple: Put your smartest engineers in a room and let them brainstorm—and sometimes argue—their way to a brilliant solution.

Biomedical engineers are accustomed to working on multidisciplinary teams with scientists, chemists, and physicians. In other industries, engineers regularly emerge from research and development labs to talk with salespeople and listen to customers.

Women and minorities: Welcome to the ranks. Until now, engineering has not been a fertile field for either women or minorities. The number of women entering high-tech fields peaked in 1986 and has since leveled off. Only 15 percent of all high-tech professionals are women. And while pay is roughly equal, many women who are frustrated by slow—or no—advancement are leaving the field. The story is similar for minorities. However, groups, such as The National Action Council for Minorities in Engineering, have begun to actively campaign for increased minority enrollment in engineering programs to bolster the shrinking pool of entry-level engineers.

Old standards...and still winners

Chemical engineers. As chemical companies research and develop new chemicals and more efficient processes to increase the production of existing chemicals, chemical engineers will find more opportunities opening up—particularly in specialty chemicals, pharmaceuticals, and plastics materials.

Civil engineers. The government has allocated an enormous amount of funding for highway reconstruction across the nation. But you have plenty of time to earn your degree while these funds filter through the creaking machinery of bureaucracy.

Electrical engineers. Consumer demand for new gadgets appears to be unending. Businesses will always welcome time- and money-saving innovations. This should create 34 percent more new jobs by 2005, according to the U.S. Bureau of Labor Statistics.

Materials engineers. Experts in developing new metals, alloys, and materials, as well as new applications for existing materials, materials engineers face a range of opportunities. They may work with environmental engineers in developing new ways to recycle solid waste, or with other mechanical engineers in the production of fuel-efficient ceramic car engines.

Mechanical engineers. Thousands of mechanical devices have been patented by these inventors. The need for more complex and custom-designed equipment, machinery, and tools should open up 24 percent more new jobs by 2005. One of the broadest fields within engineering, this specialty lends itself to further specialization in the areas of automotive, energy, heating, ventilation, or air conditioning.

A new generation of opportunities

Biomedical engineers. Biomedical engineers created the pacemaker and the surgical laser. Others specialize in creating systems to increase the efficiency of laboratories, hospitals, and clinics. As the general population continues to grow older, openings for this hybrid health professional/engineer should follow suit.

Consulting engineers. Even nontechnical businesses need technical solutions to a range of problems. Consulting engineers work independently or represent small consulting firms.

Safety engineers. More complex business operations and increased automation are only part of overall productivity. Safety engineers focus on the rest of the equation: worker productivity. By observing workers performing their jobs, safety engineers are often able to remove steps that drain overall efficiency from key tasks. Safety engineers may also be called upon to help a company locate and equip a new manufacturing facility for maximum production.

Do you have what it takes?

If you love math and science and have always been fascinated by "tinkering" or solving specific problems, you're probably on the right track.

Creativity is as important as having an analytical mind and the capacity for detail.

Engineers should feel comfortable working alone as well as on a team. Interpersonal skills are becoming increasingly important for engineers in all specialties. Industrial and safety engineers in particular should be good listeners and tactful when recommending changes in task, production flow, and/or work styles to line workers.

As a future engineer, you should feel comfortable with technology such as digital prototyping software and computer-aided design (CAD) systems. These tools allow engineers to produce or modify designs much more rapidly so they can analyze more design variations before selecting the best one.

Education and training

An undergraduate degree in an engineering specialty is required for virtually every entry-level position. Although an advanced degree isn't always required for success, about half of all engineers go on to pursue a master's degree in an engineering specialty in order to learn a new technology. Some specialties, such as nuclear engineering, are only taught at the graduate level.

A master's degree or Ph.D. in engineering is required to teach at the university level. An M.B.A. is useful if you want to advance into management or become a consultant. There is a growing demand for "renaissance" engineers who can easily combine business sense with technical expertise. Some mechanical engineers earn law degrees and become patent attorneys.

The pace of change varies by specialty and industry, but the need for continuing education is a common denominator. Larger companies may offer formal classroom or seminar training.

Professional licensing and certification

All 50 states and Washington, D.C., require engineers whose work affects the public's life, health, or property, or who offer their services to the public, to register. Engineers who have earned a bachelor's degree and have four years of experience can be granted the Professional Engineer (P.E.) license with a passing grade on a state-administered licensing exam.

Tips on breaking in

Know your interviewer. If you're just starting out, you'll probably get a job offer while you're still on campus. Job openings are well publicized through college or university placement offices. And recruiters are everywhere. It's always a good idea to ask the placement director about each interviewer's background. If you sit down with an engineer from a company, great. But if you find yourself face to face with a representative of the company's human resources department, you will want to emphasize interpersonal skills rather than engineering lingo. If your interpersonal skills could use a little fine-tuning, have someone in the placement office or a friend videotape you in a mock interview.

Get a recommendation. Some companies contact professors directly for their recommendations, so it's a good idea to let your professors know what your career interests are and how well you've done.

Think small. Women often find better opportunities for advancement in small companies that value technical expertise. Advancement tends to be slow in large corporations.

Career path

Beginning engineering graduates usually do research and routine work for three to five years under the supervision of more experienced engineers. With experience, they begin to take on more difficult tasks and are allowed more independence in developing designs and solving problems.

Some engineers become technical specialists and may supervise a staff of engineers and technicians. Others become engineering managers as a prelude to entering other areas of management or sales.

Relatively few engineers are interested in advancing into management, however, and in recent years more engineering-oriented companies have created parallel career paths that allow engineers to receive substantial promotions and raises without moving into management. Sadly, however, most American CEOs don't understand engineers. Only a third of top CEOs have technical or science backgrounds, compared to two-thirds in Japan.

Other career paths for engineers lead to consulting or the academic world, both more conducive to research or project work they enjoy.

If you do choose a management track, you may begin as a project leader supervising three to five engineers. A group manager supervises the activities of three to five project managers. A department manager is often responsible for 50 to 100 engineers and a budget of more than $1 million.

The vice president of engineering is responsible for overall management functions and normally reports directly to the president or CEO. The position requires 20 years of experience.

How much can you earn?

Engineering majors continue to command the highest salary offers among undergraduates—and starting salaries inch up every year. Average starting salaries range from $35,000 to $45,000. Electrical and biomedical engineers command the highest salaries; civil engineers, the lowest.

This inflated entrance places pressure on internal salary levels in companies that recruit many engineers. Often an experienced engineer makes only a few thousand dollars more than a recent graduate and salary growth tends to remain sluggish after that.

Five to eight years into your career, for example, your compensation as a project manager is usually in the $45,000 to $55,000 range. Lab engineers and senior managers top out around $80,000. Even at best-paying companies, engineers with no management responsibilities rarely earn more than $100,000 a year.

Partners in engineering, architectural, or consulting firms earn from $75,000 to $100,000 or more.

Engineers who pursue a management track can earn considerably more. A corporate vice president of engineering can make more than $150,000 at a technical company.

Where will you work?

About half of all engineers work for companies that design and manufacture electronics, scientific instruments, automobiles, aircraft, chemicals, and petroleum products.

Biomedical engineers work at universities that are affiliated with hospitals or medical complexes.

The remaining group is divided between public utilities and federal, state, and local government departments and agencies, from NASA to the state highway department.

More than 40 percent of all civil engineers work for the government. Another 33 percent join private engineering or architectural firms. Opportunities tend to vary by geographic area and with the health of the economy.

Biomedical engineers are being hired by research organizations and especially medical and pharmaceutical companies.

About two-thirds of all chemical engineers are employed in manufacturing industries such as chemical, petroleum refining, and paper. Most others work for engineering services, research, and testing services, or consulting forms that design chemical plants. Some work for government agencies or as independent consultants.

Job Profile

Lisa M. Alvis, senior manufacturing engineer

What general job responsibilities does that encompass?
I support existing chemical processes and equipment in making automotive brake components in the plant. I troubleshoot problems, work with maintenance to guide them on repairs, with analytical people to determine the correct chemical mixtures, with quality personnel to insure that parts are to spec, and look for ways to improve existing processes and reduce costs.

How many years have you been in this business?
I've been in it for 13 years.

How many years of education do you have?
I have a B.S. in Chemical Engineering and a master's in materials engineering.

How many hours do you typically work per week?
I work 45 to 50 hours per week. Occasionally, I will work a weekend when it is required.

What hours do you work on a typical workday?
I typically work from 6:30 a.m. to 4 p.m.

How big is the company you work for?
I work for Delphi Chassis Systems (there are 2,000 people at my location). Delphi Chassis is a division of Delphi Automotive, which was recently spun off from General Motors (GM). Delphi Automotive is a 200,000-plus-person company, with locations in most countries.

Do you have professional certification (and do you need it)?
No. A professional certificate is required to be an independent contractor in the engineering field in Ohio.

In what general range does your annual salary fall? (Include bonuses, stock options and any other financial perks.)
$50,000 to $100,000.

How did you get your current job?
I was a senior at the University of Dayton working at the UD Research Institute. One of my bosses told me of a job opening he'd heard about from someone at General Motors. I sent a resume to that person and was granted an interview. I received an offer a couple of days later.
At the time, I had no other outstanding offers and was very interested in staying in the Dayton/Cincinnati, OH area. The thought of working for GM

was very appealing and impressive in my mind (even though I had no idea what they did or what I would be doing).

Please describe one of your "typical" days.

6:30 to 8 a.m.: I listen to voice mail, read e-mail and make rounds of my areas. Who—or what—I run in to usually determines how long it takes to complete my rounds. For example, maintenance folks will stop me to show me a problem or ask me to order parts. Supervisors may stop to show me quality issues or equipment problems.

8 to 11 a.m.: I work at my desk, answering phone messages, writing specifications or purchase orders, calling suppliers inquiring about parts or how something works and talking with other engineers about electrical problems or changes needed. I may also work with lab analysts on chemical issues and write memos about subjects that have come up recently. I'm always ready to jump up to go and look at something the minute there is a problem on the plant floor.

11 to 11:30 a.m: I have lunch, usually at my desk while I'm working—sometimes while I run errands.

11:30 a.m. to 4 p.m.: Could be anything. Probably a continuation of the morning: making sure that everything is running well and answering calls about issues that come up.

What are your career aspirations?

In my 13 years with this company, I've advanced two times up the manufacturing engineering ladder. These advances have resulted in more responsibility due to my increased level of experience, but have been along the same lines.

Further movement up the same ladder would move me into managing engineers and doing less actual hands-on engineering work. I don't see myself moving up for some time because I value my free time too much. I don't wish to spend any more time at work. I've expressed this to my superiors and they seem to be okay with it.

I've told my superiors that I will let them know when I want to move, but so far I haven't had that urge. It is also nice being known as an "expert" in the few areas I cover. I really like the job I do. It's never the same two days in a row.

What types of people would do especially well in your job role?

You must be able to get along with your fellow workers (inquiring about your coworkers' outside interests and families as polite conversation). I have seen others in the same environment who are "all work and no play" and the people out in the plant find this to be rude and unfriendly.

I think that you must be open-minded and willing to listen to others' ideas and suggestions. There are many ways to solve a problem and people will often approach things from different angles. If you try to tell everyone that your way is the only way every time, people stop helping you when you need it.

You must be technically competent and resourceful. It's great to know the answer to every problem/question, but it's also acceptable to know how to go about finding the right answer (asking experienced people, call manufacturers or suppliers, and so forth). Credibility is established at any early age. It is almost impossible to survive without it.

Problem-solving skills are very useful. The ability to visualize how things are supposed to be or were is also good. Being able to read a blueprint and any other technical document is necessary. Knowledge of chemicals and how they react in this industry is not only important, but sometimes lifesaving.

What do you like most about your job?
I like the plant environment and the daily variety in the job. It is definitely not monotonous. Also, there are lots of short-term goals that can be accomplished. Every time a piece of equipment stops working, for whatever reason, it really feels great when I can help get it back up and running. Sometimes this takes five minutes, sometimes five days. But it is definitely not five months or years.

What do you like least?
I dislike the bureaucracy of the union and of our own upper management. This is a large company and the many levels of upper management can be exasperating and cumbersome. Also, we have a very strong union at this facility and it seems management and the union are often butting heads and do not have the same goals. I also get frustrated with people who do not work as hard as I do during the nine hours I am at work. We have a lot of "fat" in certain areas.

What are some misconceptions about your job/profession/industry?

That engineers make more money than we do. Also that you should be able to do any type of engineering work if you have an engineering degree, no matter what degree you have. (For example, a chemical engineer typically can't do the job of an electrical engineer). Having an engineering degree won't guarantee you'll be good at every aspect of engineering. In fact, you use very little of what you learn in college.

What is the best way to going about landing a job like yours?
Most companies recruit on college campuses. Interview with everyone for experience and possible connections. Later, headhunters are very good at

placing people. Keeping in touch with fellow engineers may also lead to contacts.

Presently, the market is great for folks looking for this type of job. Around 15 years ago, the market was tight and engineers were having difficulties landing their "dream job."

Cooperative experience in college also lends a big hand, not only because of the exposure to the actual field, but also the possible after-college contacts.

Resources

Engineering industry associations

**American Institute
of Chemical Engineers**
3 Park Avenue
New York, NY 10016-5991
(212)591-7338 or (800)242-4363
www.aiche.org

ASME International
Three Park Avenue
New York, NY 10016-5990
(800)THE-ASME
www.asme.org

American Chemical Society
Department of Career Services
1155 16th Street NW
Washington DC 20036
(202)872-4600 or 800/ 227-5558
www.acs.org

American Society for Engineering Education
1818 N Street, NW, Suite 600
Washington, DC 20036-2479
(202)331-3500
Fax: (202)265-8504
www.asee.org

American Consulting Engineers Council
1015 15th St, NW, Suite 802
Washington, DC 20005
(202)347-7474
Fax: (202)898-0068
E-mail: acec@acec.org
www.acec.org

American Institute of Industrial Engineers
25 Technology Park
Norcross, GA 30092
(404)449-0460
Fax: 770/441-3295
www.iienet.org

American Society of Civil Engineers,
ASCE - Washington Office
1015 15th St. NW, Suite 600
Washington, D.C. 20005
(202)789-2200
Fax: (202)289-6797
www.asce.org

Biomedical Engineering Society
8401 Corporate Drive, Suite 110
Landover, MD 20785-2224
(301)459-1999
Fax: (301)459-2444
mecca.org/BME/BMES/society

NACME,Inc.
The Empire State Building
350 Fifth Acenue, Suite 2212
New York, NY 10118-2299
(212)279-2626
Fax: (212)629-5178
www.nacme.org

National Society of Professional Engineers
1420 King Street
Alexandria, VA 22314
(703)684-2800
Fax: (703)836-4875
www.nspe.org

The Society of Hispanic Professional Engineers
5400 E. Olympic Blvd., Suite 210
Los Angeles, CA 90022
(323)725-3970
Fax: (323)725-0316
E-mail: shpenational@shpe.org
www.shpe.org

Society of Women Engineers
120 Wall Street
Eleventh Floor
New York, NY 10005-3902
(212)509-9577
E-Mail: hq@swe.org
www.swe.org

Engineering industry publications

Engineering News-Record
McGraw-Hill, Inc.
Two Penn Plaza, 9th Floor
New York, NY 10121
(212)512-2000
www.enr.com

Civil Engineering
345 E. 47th Street
New York, NY 10017
(212)705-7514

Electronic Products News
645 Stewart Avenue
Garden City, NY 11530
(516)227-1383
electronicproducts.com

Graduating Engineer
Peterson's/COG Publishing
16030 Ventura Blvd., Suite 560
Encino, CA 91436
(818)789-5371

IEEE Spectrum
345 E. 47th St.
New York, NY 10017
(212)705-7016
www.spectrum.ieee.org

Chapter 7

Entertainment & Sports
The view from behind the scenes

Animation artist
Director
Distribution executive
Producer
Special events marketer
Sports agent
Sports facility manager
Story editor
Talent agent
Unit publicist
Best Bet for Entrepreneurs: *Script reader*

Forecast

Rising foreign demand for American movies, television, and sports, combined with a growing domestic market, points to plenty of opportunities for entertainment and leisure professionals. Cable television, video, and regional and industrial productions will increase the demand for movies and television shows. Sports alone is estimated to be a $180 billion business, 5 percent annual growth. Franchises and sports agents will continue to reap the rewards of corporate sponsorship and "commoditization" of national teams. Women's sports teams are also attracting record numbers of viewers.

Growth

Employment in film and television production, marketing, and distribution, as well as sports facility management and marketing, should faster than the average into the year 2006.

Overview

Blockbusters. Slam dunks. The language describing the multibillion-dollar entertainment business has a kind of exuberance, a bravado that is right in line with its prospects for growth. These days "It's all about synergy," says the president of the California chapter of the National Association of Theater Owners. Theater attendance is up because, "Theaters are no longer theaters, but entertainment destinations."

Add regional theater productions, luxury suite-ballparks, every flavor of cable television, an avalanche of home videos, computer games, and online entertainment and it seems clear that there will be room for any number of leisure pursuits in the lives of American consumers.

While becoming a Julia Roberts or a Tiger Woods is a one-in-a-million shot, there are many parts to play behind the scenes in a growing number of companies in the entertainment industry. But with no formal point of entry in most cases, you'll be facing some pretty tough competition.

Movies or sports?

The number of jobs is increasing in new movie and video productions, national and regional theater, cable television, commercials, as well as industrial films and trade shows.

The number of venues has increased for performers, leading to promising opportunities for the *talent agents* who represent them. On the production side, *script readers* and *story editors* find the best screenplays for *producers,* who obtain financing and hire the principal members of the crew, including the director. *Directors* direct all the on- and off-screen action necessary to complete the final production, typically a movie or television show.

While production and post-production is going on, *unit publicists* begin to prime the public. Their goal is to stir up enough interest to create a ready audience when the movie or show is released. The promotional blitz before the opening weekend can be ripe with sales of movie-related toys. Video games that promise to keep the action going for hard core fans require the specialized talents of *computer animators. Distribution executives* make sure the movies come to every neighborhood by negotiating with the nation's theater owners.

Meanwhile, just try to separate sport fans from their game. Our national passion for sports has become a mighty sector of the American economy. Now sports' "endless season" is played out on network and cable television, as well as in more luxurious stadiums managed by *facility managers*.

Jobs with professional franchises are considered some of the best in the sports industry. As major and minor league teams continue to expand and new leagues are formed, opportunities with the franchises are also expected to expand. A growing international interest in national teams and a new spotlight on women's involvement assures clients for *sports agents* and promises bright prospects for *special events marketers* who create profitable media opportunities for corporate sponsors.

Industry snapshot

Today, there are six major entertainment companies: News Corp., AOL/Time-Warner, Seagrams, Sony, Viacom, and Walt Disney. Each one of the Big Six has its fingers in multiple media "pies." For example, Viacom owns CBS, Paramount, MTV, VH1, Nickelodeon, and Simon & Schuster Publishing Co. Time-Warner, Disney, ABC, and News Corp., all now own sports teams.

And the mergers continue. In the next few years, cable television and telephone companies will bring consumers a range of entertainment and services via expanded cable, wireless, and fiber-optic communications networks. (See Telecommunications & the Internet on page 259.)

In the sports world, licensing is king. It's all about state-of-the-art, luxury-suite-studded stadiums, product endorsements, corporate sponsorships, and media relationships promising billions in revenues. So even if you can't make it on the gridiron or the pitcher's mound, your employment options extend well beyond one team or sport. Working on the sidelines you could represent athletes, plan events, and manage colossal revenue-sharing deals.

Trends to track

The Internet effect. The 1996 Telecommunications Act has loosened restrictions on the convergence of digital TV, PCs, and the Internet. NBC was the first to launch an Internet portal, NBCi, combining news and entertainment content such as video clips from "Must See TV" shows, with breaking financial news, free e-mail, and chat rooms. And the day is not far off when movies will be delivered over the Internet. Once American homes are equipped with high-speed Internet hookups and people are routinely tuning into DVD, the boom will be on. Meanwhile, job seekers can gain entrance to the entertainment industry—and make important contacts—by learning the technology. Working in the digital TV or convergence development group at Pacific Telesis, Intel, or Compaq will school you in three industries and put more money in your pocket than going the traditional route as a production assistant.

Marketing margins. Publicity and creative marketing methods are becoming more important than ever to enable sports teams to fill seats and blockbuster movies to recoup costs.

Sometimes all it takes a little data and a dash of ingenuity. When seats went empty at Oakland Raiders' home games after the team's return from Los Angeles, the Oakland Football Marketing Association launched a campaign to change the team's image. To counter its long-held image as a "cult" for zealot fans, the team put up billboards picturing average people whose eyes are covered with black patches for anonymity. One couple confesses, "Yeah, we go. But the in-laws think we're at church." A man holding his toddler son says, "We never miss a game, but mom thinks we're at the playground." The implicit message is that, contrary to what you may believe, there are fans just like you in the stands at every game. Ticket sales tripled.

Hollywood sheepishly lauded Artisan Entertainment for being the first to draw audiences into the theater using the Internet. A year before *The Blair Witch Project*—a $40,000 mock-documentary horror film—hit theaters, Artisan introduced the "Blair Witch" Web site. The was designed to build interest in the film by introducing the elaborate mythology that serves as the film's back story. To drive traffic to the site, Artisan launched a grassroots campaign on college campuses, published a book, disseminated "Wanted" posters depicting the three actors who play doomed filmmakers, and produced a Sci Fi Channel documentary called *Curse of the Blair Witch*. The result: 75 million hits and $100 million in ticket sales.

The sports commodity. Thanks to franchises, the sports business is ripe with commercial opportunities. The scoreboard, the game clock—even the uniforms worn by ball boys—provide a background for selling. The game itself has been repackaged to accommodate media coverage. The two-minute warning in professional football halts play for advertising. And the players? One agent calls the athletes he represents "specialists in the entertainment business." Dozens of sports stars pitch products. Michael Jordan is as well known for his commercials as he is for his game-winning baskets. And don't forget Mark McGwire's first media message after beating Roger Maris' longstanding record with a record-exploding 70 home runs: "I'm going to

Disney World!" Special events marketers will link corporations and sports figures to generate the interest of diverse groups, from kids to senior citizens.

A love affair with animation. The global animation industry will more than double by 2001 according to Canadian-based 1998 "Roncerelli Report." The most visible example of this boom in animation is in prime-time television. Almost every broadcast network has at least one nighttime cartoon. Some of the most successful shows on cable (aside from sports) are the Nicktoons along with Comedy Central's adult-oriented *South Park*. Those TV successes are spreading to the big screen. Nickelodeon's *Rugrats* grossed more than $100 million in the movies. Needless to say, the powers that be are hiring talent to develop new characters and work on sequels to high-grossing films such as Disney's *Beauty and the Beast* and *The Lion King*. Nickelodeon now has more than 500 animators working at their new animation studio. That doesn't even begin to take into account an explosion of direct-to-video projects along with video and computer games.

See Jane win. The Women's National Basketball Association (WNBA) set an attendance record for women's professional team sports by drawing nearly 2 million fans in its third regular season. After America won the Women's World Soccer Cup, Brandi Chastain and Mia Hamm became household names and role models for a new generation of young girls. All of this sports action only expands opportunities for sports agents, publicists, and special events marketers.

Lucrative licensing. Licensing toys associated with hit movies is nothing new, but its growth has been phenomenal. Thanks to licensing, Lucasfilm didn't need to sell a single ticket to the much-anticipated *Star Wars: Episode I—Phantom Menace* in order to recoup $115 million cost of the production. Before it hit box offices, toy manufacturers such as Hasbro were lining up to pay the production company $400 million for the privilege of making movie-based toys. And Hasbro is just one of 75 licensees making hundreds of products!

Old standards...and still winners

Story editors. In the movies or television, it all begins with the story. Story editors try to find the best stories for their studios by evaluating hundreds of publications, scripts, and screenplays. A large part of the job is developing relationships with the publishers and agents who submit the manuscripts. Prospects are bright as more productions are sought by cable networks.

Producers. Producers select scripts or screenplays for television or movie production. If they are successful in getting the necessary financing, they hire directors and other principal members of the production cast and crew. They must negotiate contracts with artistic personnel in accordance with collective bargaining agreements. Once the production is underway, producers coordinate writers, directors, managers, and other production and marketing personnel, making sure the project stays on budget and on schedule. The best part: You don't need to be one of the Hollywood glitterati to make a contribution. For example, one 24-hour cable TV channel covering nothing but computers is a hit with computer geeks. ZDTV's *Screen Savers* is just one in a lineup of computer advice shows with hosts direct from the IS department. In addition, 2,500 viewers are equipped with tiny desktop "netcams" in order to participate live during the show.

Directors. In order to interpret a movie or television screenplay, directors audition and select cast members. They begin by conducting rehearsals, directing every aspect of each scene—from performances to camera movement. They must approve scenery, costumes, choreography, and music. Most directors hire casting directors to supply supporting "extras."

Unit publicists. Priming the movie-going public for a movie long before it will appear on the screen is the challenge of the unit publicist. This is done through a carefully designed publicity campaign that includes a tantalizing movie trailer, as well as a package of information about the movie and its cast and crew for the media. A key part of the campaign involves setting up interviews with television and print media. Publicists and marketers will have the challenge of reaching out to a highly fragmented mass market through various niches. (See Marketing, Advertising, & Public Relations on page 195 for more information about database and direct marketing. Look at Telecommunications & the Internet on page 259 for details on online delivery.)

Distribution executives. To bring a finished film to a nationwide audience, distribution executives, and theater owners negotiate the terms under which it will be shown. Two key parts of the negotiation involve the percentage of the box office receipts the theater owner will keep and how long the theater agrees to run the film.

Talent agents. A stepping stone to executive positions in the movie industry, this career provides a broad business perspective. Talent agents act as brokers, answering the needs of film studios with a particular actor or actress they represent. They also review scripts in search of the right roles for their clients. Although the talent agent's role is indispensable, the reality is that their careers rise and fall with the success or failure of the performers they represent.

Sports agents. Most top athletes are represented by a sports agent working for a large firm. Like a movie talent agent, a sports agent signs promising talent—such as ball players, skaters, or swimmers—and then acts as a business manager. The key to the success of these relationships lies in negotiating the most lucrative deals with franchise teams and corporations seeking endorsements. Reputation is everything to a sports agent. Word tends to spread quickly among professional athletes about the agents and agencies that make the best deals.

Sports facility managers. Revenues from state-of-the-art stadiums can be a bigger part of the overall value and profitability of a franchise rather than media revenues. Professionals with experience in facilities management oversee the maintenance and security in diverse areas such as luxury suites, concessions, and advertising.

Script readers. There are lot of talented people—and a lot more wannabes—writing screenplays and TV pilots. When it comes to separating the wheat from the chaff, script readers are the first line of defense. Their synopsis of each script determines whether it's passed along to a second reader or returned with a polite "thanks, but..." letter. This is the perfect work for would-be screenplay writers who want the inside line on what studios are most likely to buy along with the direct connection with second readers.

A new generation of opportunities

Special events marketers. Special events add visibility and hefty profits for corporations and sports management companies that employ special events marketers. For example, look at the Adidas Soccer Lab, a mobile interactive soccer park inviting Women's World Cup fans to participate in soccer skills testing and coaching clinics. Special event marketers do everything from selling a concept to making sure the beer is cold.

Animation artists. The days of veteran production artists hand-drawing frames for storyboards is gone. Today's artist is young and tech-savvy. More studios are taking chances on young filmmakers who are closer to the age of the audiences. Television is a lucrative way to get a foot in the door of this well-paying profession. In fact, many promising students are being hired to adapt their student work into TV shows.

Do you have what it takes?

As soon as a studio "green lights" a project, the competition for jobs begins. There may be 100 applicants for even the most menial slots. Personal relationships are critical of you want to make it. Patience and a thick skin will also serve you well. Every position requires excellent communication and interpersonal skills.

Producers should have a knowledge and aptitude for business in order to obtain financing, manage productions, and resolve personnel problems. Directors should be creative and able to motivate people—from performers to producers.

Unit publicists and special events marketers need to be creative to develop innovative marketing plans for new movies and special events. They should also be comfortable interacting with a range of people—from actors and athletes to corporate executives—and should be excellent project managers.

Distribution executives must be top-notch negotiators to gain agreement on terms (such as percentages).

Talent and sports agents should have an innate ability to spot and identify new talent. To court a variety of prospective clients, talent and sports agents need to be assertive yet tactful enough to ensure that their clients stay happy. Self-motivation is essential for these professionals, who can never afford to rest on their laurels.

Script readers and story editors should enjoy reading and have a knowledge of current market interests so that they can determine which stories will make successful movies for their studios. Like sports and talent agents, they need people skills to negotiate with publishers, literary agents, and writers and then sell selected stories to their studios.

Sports facility managers need general management skills with an emphasis on cost-control and planning.

Ideally, animators are imaginative and exceptionally artistic—both on paper and on screen. Where special effects houses such as George Lucas's Industrial Light and Magic will train people who can draw to use software, technical proficiency is truly the ideal. The bottom line, however, is this: You need a serious artist's portfolio showing life drawings and animal studies.

Education and training

There are no hard and fast degree requirements for most professionals in entertainment. Success depends more on talent and experience, as well as knowing the right people and grabbing opportunities as they present themselves.

Many sports and talent agents find that legal training helps in negotiating complex contracts for their clients.

Unit publicists and special events marketers may earn a bachelor's degree in public relations, business, or marketing. Experience in direct mail or in one of the many database analysis software packages is becoming increasingly useful.

Script readers and story editors (who may also be aspiring screenplay writers themselves) can enter the field with a bachelor's degree in English literature, journalism, or communications.

Directors and producers may come from many backgrounds. Formal training in theater arts, including directing and producing, is available at some colleges and universities. The Directors Guild offers a formal training program for assistant directors with a B.A. or a minimum of three-years experience. Applicants must take an all-day written test and pass an oral exam. Approximately one percent pass. Contact the Assistant Directors Training Program, Directors Guild of America. (See "Resources" at the end of this chapter.)

The best degree for sports facility managers is a B.A. in facilities management and an M.B.A. Fewer than 25 schools offer degrees in facilities management. These include Massachusetts Institute of Technology (MIT), University of Iowa, University of North Dakota, and Brigham Young University.

Some animators are hired right out of high school. If you want the best job prospects, head for the Rhode Island School of Design, California Institute of the Arts (Cal Arts), the Ringling School of Art and Design, or UCLA. If you're exceptionally talented, you may just be able to squeeze in a solid education in drawing, color theory, composition, and design before you're recruited. Cal Arts was founded by Walt Disney in 1961 to train animators for his studio. For every 400 applications, about 30 are accepted.

Tips on breaking in

Be an intern. Internships are easier to obtain than you might imagine. Even if you aren't paid for your efforts, you'll have an opportunity to make contacts and acquire valuable experience. For example, the American Film Institute sponsors an internship program. The American Association of

Independent Producers supports on-the-job training and apprentice programs. (See "Resources" at the end of this chapter.) Of course, aspiring directors should take part in high school and college plays and work in small theaters to gain experience.

Go where the action is. In the movie business, that's New York or Los Angeles—the entertainment industry's capitals. Plan to move to one of these two cities if you're really serious about breaking into the business. However, regional centers have also sprung up in other locations. (See "Where will you work?" for more information).

Do *anything*. Especially in the early stages of your career, don't reject any job as being "beneath you" if it can open doors or teach you about the inner workings of the business. Regardless of where you start, take advantage of every opportunity to learn. Work hard to establish relationships with people who can help you today or in the future.

Use your special skills. While most sports agents break into the field by representing a particular college athlete, a knowledge of contracts or a creative marketing idea for athletes during the off-season can also pave the way into an agency.

Make—and nourish—your contacts. If you don't have any personal friends already in the business, begin by surveying your family and personal acquaintances. People have broken into the business because an uncle was a partner with a Cleveland public accounting firm that happened to audit one of the movie studios. One call from your uncle may just open the right door.

Get behind a "good" sport. Sports agents agree that the most difficult athletes to represent are football players. Relatively few players are recruited into the professional ranks each year. The average football player's playing career is very brief, usually spanning less than five years. On the other hand, look at the season-free popularity of the pro golfers on the PGA Seniors Professional Tour.

Get funding. Foundations can often advance new work by producers and directors. Contact foundations listed in *Foundation Grants to Individuals, Foundation Directory,* and *Corporate Foundation Profiles* to obtain their application procedures. (See "Resources" at the end of this chapter.) You may find the best route is to approach a local foundation familiar with your work to apply on your behalf.

Career path

With experience, producers and directors develop a reputation that allows them to work on larger productions or in more prestigious theaters. Skill, versatility, and perseverance can be the makings of a lifelong career.

Many unit publicists start out working for one of the public relations firms in Los Angeles and then use their specialized area of expertise to move into one of the studios.

For talent agents, the route to success hasn't changed much in 50 years. True to the cliche, it begins in the mail room at a talent agency (such as the venerable William Morris Agency). There, you'll learn about deals and personalities and develop an in-depth understanding of the way things get done.

The most common route out of the mail room is by establishing a relationship with a talent agent and eventually becoming his or her assistant. Many top studio executives started out in talent agencies.

A story editor may start as a script reader in a studio. Script readers typically start out doing freelance work first and then go to work full-time for the studios or agencies they freelanced for. Some script readers enter the field from publishing houses and literary agencies. Many use the position to support their own writing.

Sports agents generally don't have their sights set as much on management as on negotiating increasingly larger contracts for more prominent, higher paid athletes. A sports agent who starts out representing one athlete earning $100,000 can eventually represent 20, each earning $1 million or more.

Career progression is relatively informal within most professional sports franchises. You may take on several different assignments before moving into general management after 10 to 15 years.

Most animators enter the field by working in television, where there is such a huge demand for talent that producers are willing to try new blood. The biggest opportunities are in cable. However, all of the networks are seeking young artists for support jobs

How much can you earn?

Studio employees in the publicity and distribution areas are often covered by union contracts. Annual earnings at the entry level range from $15,000 to $35,000. After five years, you can earn from $45,000 to $60,000. Pay tends to top out at $75,000 to $85,000.

A talent or sports agent's compensation is based on a percentage of what his or her clients earn. Rookie agents consider themselves lucky to be offered $25,000 to $30,000 to start. In five to eight years, an agent who builds a client base should earn from $75,000 to $100,000. With 10 years of experience, salaries can reach $150,000 to $300,000. An agent representing prominent clientele can earn a compensation package totaling more than $1 million. Remember that earnings are always directly tied to the earnings of the talent you represent. Thus, an agent's earnings can fluctuate dramatically from year to year.

Sports facility managers who start their careers with a sports franchise can earn from $14,000 to $50,000 in the early years. M.B.A. graduates earn more. In 10 to 15 years, you may head a department, earning $30,000 to $90,000. General managers earn $100,000 or more.

A special events marketer who starts at $20,000 can be making $40,000 at midcareer. Depending on your creativity and contacts, however, the field is wide open—some earn up to $200,000.

Script readers for major studios earn an average of $40,000—or about $50 per script working freelance. Story editors earn an average of $100,000.

Producers take a percentage of a movie's or television show's earnings. A successful movie or show can make them multimillionaires. Producers negotiate fees for directors with the Society of Stage Directors and Choreographers or the Directors Guild of America. Well-known directors—think Steven Spielberg and James Cameron—can also earn in the millions.

Animation artists start in the range of $35,000 to $50,000 at networks like Nickelodeon. A top visual effects animator for Industrial Light and Magic can make approximately $200,000 a year. This is on par with salaries for the young creators of Cartoon Network and Nickelodeon shows before merchandising, overseas sales, and syndication begin to kick in.

Where will you work?

Movie studios, independent companies, specialized production companies, and talent agencies tend to be clustered around Hollywood and New York. However, regional centers have sprung up in cities such as San Francisco and Minneapolis, as well as in states such as Texas, Florida, and Georgia. In fact, Florida is number three in film production outside of New York and Hollywood. The best venues for television commercials are New York, Los Angeles and Chicago. However, Florida and Atlanta are the fastest-growing regional centers.

On a different bend, professional sports franchises are located in virtually every major city in the United States.

Job Profile

Milton O. Thompson, president and CEO, Grand Slam Companies

What are your general responsibilities?

I act as the general supervisor of all operating companies in our group of companies. That means I appropriately manage day-to-day details relating to the needs of our clients (professional athletes), handle all public disclosures, and perform all presentations to future clients.

How many years of education do you have?

I have a B.A. with a double major in political science and philosophy. I also have a J.D. (Doctor of Jurisprudence).

How many hours a week do you typically work?

I am never off the clock. I remain constantly responsive to clients and am willing to work within their schedules. For example, many athletes can only meet on Sunday, so I often have meetings on Sunday evening.

What are your hours on a typical workday?

Again, I work around the clock. But typically, I put in a 10-hour day.

How big is the company you work for?

We have a group of several companies set up in a very atypical way. That makes it difficult to measure size using a conventional corporate scale. I supervise approximately 20 people.

Do you have (or need) professional certification?

To be a sports agent, you must be certified by the Players Association of the sports league you work within (such as the National Basketball Association [NBA] or the National Football League [NFL]).

In what general range does your annual salary fall?

It can be six figures or more if I do my job right. It could be nothing at all if I don't.

How did you get your current job?

I founded the company in 1981.

What's your typical day like?

There is no typical day. Most days my activities consist of making presentations, participating in meetings, visiting clients, and attending to my civic responsibilities. When in the office, I'm usually on the phone with clients.

What are your career aspirations?

I feel that I have essentially fulfilled my career aspirations. But I would like to have the company grow to be not only more efficient, but more profitable.

What kinds of people do you think would do well in your job role?

In this line of work, I think that you, first and foremost, must be a "people person." Having the ability to deal with a diverse group of people, maintaining your patience, and being firm—but fair—are important attributes. You should also have a "cast-iron" stomach in order to deal with stresses that come with the job. A law degree (J.D.) is key in dealing with the various quasilegal, legal, and regulatory issues which are part of serving clients.

What do you like most about your job?

I love the ability to work with all kinds of people and the freedom to be diverse among our group of companies.

What do you like least?

General administrative responsibilities.

What are some misconceptions about your job/profession/industry?

People think that, because of its high level of exposure, this job is glamorous—and easy—but it's not.

What is the best way to going about landing a job like yours?

It is important to creatively search for your niche in whatever you do. That way, you have great potential to be the best. You must also be willing to take risks.

Resources

Film and production companies

Castle Rock Entertainment
335 N. Maple Dr.
No. 135
Beverly Hills, CA 90210
(213)285-2300

HBO
1100 Avenue of the Americas
New York, NY 10036
(212)512-1000

Columbia Pictures-TV
3400 W. Riverside Dr.
Burbank, CA 91505
(818)972-8512

Lorimar Productions
4000 Warner Blvd.
Burbank, CA 91522
(818)954-6000

Hanna Barbera Production, Inc.
3400 W. Caheunga Blvd.
Los Angeles, CA 90068
(213)851-5000

Lucasfilm Ltd.
5858 Lucas Valley Rd.
Nicasio, CA 94946
(415)662-1700

New Line Cinema Corp.
575 8th Ave.
New York, NY 10018
(212)239-8880

Orion Pictures Corp.
1325 Avenue of the Americas
New York, NY 10019
(212)956-3800

Paramount Pictures Corp.
5555 Melrose Ave.
Hollywood, CA 90038
(213)956-5000

The Walt Disney Company
500 South Buena Vista St.
Burbank, CA 91521
(818)560-1000

Twentieth Century-Fox Film
10201 W. Pico Blvd.
Los Angeles, CA 90035
(213)277-2211

Universal City Studios, Inc.
100 Universal City Plaza
North Hollywood, CA 91608
(818)777-1000

Talent agencies

Creative Artists Agency, Inc.
9830 Wilshire Blvd.
Beverly Hills, CA 90212
(310)288-4545

William Morris Agency
151 E1 Camino Dr.
Beverly Hills, CA 90212
(310)274-7451

Movie industry associations

Academy of Motion Picture Arts & Sciences
8949 Wilshire Blvd.
Beverly Hills, CA 90211
(213)859-9619

American Film Institute
John F. Kennedy Center
 for the Performing Arts
Washington, DC 20566
(202)828-4000

American Film Marketing Association
12424 Wilshire Blvd.
Los Angeles, CA 90025
(213)447-1555

Association for Independent Video and Film
625 Broadway
New York, NY 10012
(212)473-3400

Director's Guild of America
(Assistant Director's Training Program)
14144 Ventura Blvd.
Sherman Oaks, CA 91423
(213)289-2000

Educational Theatre Association
3368 Central Pkwy.
Cincinnati, OH 45225
(513)559-1996

International Association of Independent Producers
P.O. Box 2801
Washington, DC 20013
(202)775-1113

Motion Picture Association of America
1133 Avenue of the Americas
New York, NY 10036
(212)840-6161

Show Business Association
1510 Broadway
New York, NY 10036
(212)354-7600

Writer's Guild of America, West
8955 Beverly Blvd.
Los Angeles, CA 90048

Entertainment Industry Referral and Assistance Center
11132 Ventura Blvd.
Studio City, CA 91604
(818)848-9997

Movie industry directories

International Film Guide
Zoetrope, Inc.
80 E. 11th St.
NewYork, NY 10013
(212)254-8235

International Motion Picture Almanac, International Television and Video Almanac
Quigley Publishing Co.
159 W. 53rd St.
New York, NY 10019
(212)247-3100

Literary Market Place
B.B. Bowker
245 W. 17th St.
NewYork, NY 10011
(212)645-9700

Ross Reports Television
Television Index, Inc.
40-29 27th St.
Long Island City, NY 11101
(748)937-3900

Who's Who in the Motion Picture Industry
Packard Publishing
P.O. Box 2187
Beverly Hills, CA 90213
(213)854-0276

Movie industry magazines

Back Stage
303 West 42nd St.
NewYork, NY 10001
(212)947-0020

Box Office
1800 N. Highland Ave.
Hollywood, CA 90028
(213)465-1186

Daily Variety
5700 Wilshire Blvd.
Los Angeles, CA 90036
(213)857-6600

Hollywood Reporter
6715 W. Sunset Blvd.
Hollywood, CA 90028
(213)464-7411

Show Business
1501 Broadway, Penthouse
New York, NY 10036
(212)345-7600

The Writer
120 Boylston St.
Boston, MA 022116
(617)423-3157

Sports industry associations

International Facility Management Association
One Greenway Plaza
11th Floor
Houston, TX 77046
(713)623-IFMA

National League of Professional Baseball Clubs
350 Park Ave., 18th Floor
New York, NY 10022
(212)826-7700

National Football League
410 Park Ave.
New York, NY 10022
(212)758-1500

Sporting Goods Manufacturers Association
200 Castlewood Rd.
North Palm Beach, FL 33408
(407)842-4100

National Basketball Association
645 5th Ave., 15th Floor
New York, NY 10022
(212)826-7000

Sports magazines

Sports Illustrated
1271 Avenue of the Americas
New York, NY 10020
(212)522-1212

The Sporting News
1212 North Lindbergh Blvd.
St Louis, MO 63132
(314)997-7111

Sport Magazine
8490 Sunset Blvd.
Los Angeles, CA 90069
(213)854-2250

Entertainment Web sites

www.skillsnet.net/core.cfm
A guide that includes information about jobs in animation, visual effects, and interactive digital media.

www.film.com
A good independent source for film clips, upcoming movie bizz, Oscar winners, and industry information, all with an edgy tone.

www.script-o-rama.com
A library of TV and movie scripts.

Chapter 8

Heath Care
& Heath Care Services
A healthy choice for the long term

Advanced practice nurse (nurse practitioner)
Audiologist
Certified registered nurse anesthetist (C.R.N.A.)
Certified nurse midwife (C.N.M.)
Chiropractor
Dental assistant
Dental hygienist
EEG technologist
Geriatrician
Health services manager
Home health aide
Licensed practical nurse (L.P.N.)
Medical assistant
Medical secretary
Medical technicians/technologists
Occupational therapist
Physician assistant
Physical therapist
Primary care physician
Registered nurse (R.N.)
Respiratory therapist
Speech pathologist
Surgical technologist
Veterinarian
Best Bets for Entrepreneurs: *Chiropractor, Veterinarian*

Forecast

According to the latest BLS employment projections, three of the 10 fastest growing occupations between 1998 and 2009 are in this field. The increased demand for health care services, fed by the growing proportion of elderly in the population, is expected to continue for a full 50 years. Here's how growth breaks down in these fastest growing occupations: personal and home care aides, 58 percent; medical assistants, 58 percent; and physician assistants, 42 percent. As hospitals continue to change the way they operate and open more subsidiary outpatient clinics, surgicenters, and treatment programs. A nationwide shortage of primary care professionals will promise continued work for physicians and physician assistants.

Growth

Although employment growth will slow down a bit in this industry, expect continued and steady growth in most health-related occupations through 2008.

Overview

The baby boom generation is maturing into a still-youthful middle age. More senior citizens are remaining healthy and active through their "golden years" thanks to advances in technology. Meanwhile, a new, mini-baby boom is underway.

Whatever emerges from Washington in the way of national health care reform, one thing is certain: the demand for health care services won't suffer in the decade ahead. Americans spent more than $1 trillion on health care in 1997. That adds up to over 13 percent of the entire U.S. gross national product and points to a wealth of job opportunities. Hundreds of thousands of new jobs will open up for nurses, home heath care aides, and physical therapists through the year 2006.

In the hospital, the clinic, and at home

Shortages of qualified health care professionals should result in better salaries and working conditions, often beyond hospital walls. You can find job possibilities in managed care networks, group medical practices, community and rural outpatient clinics, and surgicenters, long-term nursing facilities, and in patients' homes.

Although the shortage of *registered nurses* (R.N.s) and *licensed practical nurses (L.P.N.s)* has been well publicized, health maintenance organizations (HMOs) and preferred provider organizations (PPOs) continue to court *primary care physicians*. The foundation of managed care networks, these general practitioners, pediatricians, and internists screen and treat patients and refer those who need extensive testing or surgery to a specialist within an HMO or PPO network of providers. Rural and inner-city hospitals and clinics are also courting residents with sign-on bonuses. These busy doctors also welcome assistance from *physician assistants* and *advanced practice nurses* (also known as nurse practitioners) who are trained to perform many of the tasks physicians have traditionally handled. As group medical practices become larger and more complex, *medical secretaries* and *medical assistants* will continue to be in demand.

Middle-aged baby boomers who require health screening tests such as mammograms, advanced testing such as magnetic resonance imaging (MRI), and other such routine surgical procedures will visit a range of *medical technicians* and *technologists* at outpatient clinics run by *health services managers*. Advances in medical technology are saving lives that were once lost to serious injuries and strokes. Patients facing a lengthy and challenging recovery period will be in the hands of *physical, occupational,* and *respiratory therapists,* as well as *speech pathologists/audiologists* who can help them regain movement and begin to function independently. Regardless of illness or accident, more people will seek out preventive medicine by regularly visiting health professionals as diverse as *chiropractors*, *dental hygienists,* and *dental assistants*.

Senior citizens will require specialized care from a new breed of physician: the *geriatrician*. These doctors who specialize in caring for the elderly may arrange for assistance from a *home health aide*. Changing demographics also point to more pet owners, meaning increased demand for the *veterinarians* who treat them.

Industry snapshot

The days when physicians had free rein to prescribe care, medical tests, procedures, and even lengthy hospital stays are nearly gone. Most Americans are now under the care of an HMO or a PPO. These managed care programs have trimmed health care costs using practical business methods, either by staffing their own facilities or paying salaries to physicians who represent a network of providers.

With annual health care expenses spiraling higher and higher each year, most of us inside and outside the industry agreed that a revolution in cost-containment was long overdue. Large managed care providers applied business logic across the board, turning patients into customers.

In some case, this approach has met with phenomenal success. Doctors are off-loading more routine procedures to skilled support professionals. Hospitals have turned to firms that specialize in everything—from nursing homes to diabetes treatment. Clinics focusing on special treatments are on the rise (including chemotherapy, MRIs, and physical therapy). Technology advances have also made it possible for nurses and other health care workers to administer complex treatments to the elderly and severely disabled in the comfort of their own homes.

However, doctors who have grown weary of having their medical decisions routinely second-guessed contend that a bottom-line view of medicine seriously diminishes the quality of health care we receive. Meanwhile, the health care industry is holding its collective breath as reform continues to be debated in Washington.

Trends to track

The revolution continues. In 1996 and 1997, there were close to 1,400 managed care mergers. Hospital ownership, in some cases, changed almost daily. Look for more job cuts in hospitals along with general uncertainty inspired by most transition periods. Industry insiders are hopeful that the next stage of development is likely to bring about comprehensive, integrated health management systems that provide physicians and other health professionals the data, technology, and back-office support they need to provide quality care.

Geriatric gold. The number of Americans aged 85 and over will grow more than three times as fast as the total population by 2005. This points to the need for specialized health care focused on the unique health and living needs of the elderly in hospitals and nursing homes as well as through hospice, home health care, and personal care services.

Elective income. Up until five years go, physicians' incomes were increasing faster than any other career category. However, HMOs have put a considerable dent in doctors' earning power. Some doctors are taking steps to increasing their revenues by performing elective procedures—which are paid for out-of-pocket by patients. LASIK (Laser-Assisted In-Situ Keratomileusis), laser surgery to repair nearsightedness or farsightedness, is especially popular. More than 800,000 procedures were conducted in the United States in 1999, double that of the previous year. The cost: a cool $2,200 per cornea. Other doctors who speak a foreign language or have crosscultural connections are courting non-American patients who have the means to pay in full for treatment.

Union do's? Lower payment is the driving force behind a movement to unionize. The Union of American Physicians and Dentists is one of half a dozen unions trying to organize the nation's 737,000 licensed physicians. Still in the early stages, unions represent 40,000 doctors (approximately 5.4 percent of the total physician workforce).

Old standards...and still winners

Primary care physicians. About a third of the nation's half-million physicians are primary care physicians. These family practice physicians, pediatricians, and internists provide the first level of general care most of us need throughout our lives. If tests or surgery are needed, the primary care physician has the expertise to recommend the appropriate specialist.

Although graduating residents will not want for job opportunities, there is a severe shortage of primary care physicians particularly in rural towns and cities of 25,000 or less. In areas where this shortage is blocking the growth of cost-effective managed care programs, hospitals, state governments, and local communities are beginning to offer signing bonuses, income guarantees, and low-interest loans to lure primary care physicians away from the cities and suburbs.

Registered nurses (R.N.s). R.N.s work in hospitals, clinics, physicians' offices, community health programs, or schools. The myriad of nursely duties include providing bedside care, performing difficult procedures, such as starting intravenous fluids, and generally carrying out medical regimens prescribed by attending physicians. Registered nurses may also manage *licensed practical nurses* (L.P.N.s), aides, and hospital orderlies. However, in some cases, pressure to reduce costs has led hospitals to replace R.N.s with L.P.N.s or even medical assistants.

Licensed practical nurses (L.P.N.s). Prospects for L.P.N.s, who provide basic bedside care to patients under the direction of physicians and R.N.s, are well-suited to work in nursing homes, thanks to recent state and federal regulations that require nursing homes to employ more L.P.N.s. Medical centers, ambulatory surgicenters, specialized outpatient clinics, and home health care services also offer abundant opportunities.

L.P.N.s check vital signs, give injections, and apply dressings. They also help patients with bathing, dressing, personal hygiene, and eating. In some states, they can administer prescribed medicines or start intravenous fluids. Some L.P.N.s help deliver and care for infants. L.P.N.s in nursing homes may develop care plans for residents and supervise nursing aides. In doctors' offices and clinics, they may also make appointments, keep records, and perform other clerical duties. L.P.N.s who work in home health care may also prepare meals and teach family members simple nursing tasks.

Advanced practice nurses (nurse practitioners). With advanced education and clinical training, these registered nurses diagnose and treat many illnesses and chronic conditions. In 45 states, they can write prescriptions. For example, *certified registered nurse anesthetists* (C.R.N.A.s) perform the same work as anesthetists do prior to minor surgeries in hospitals or outpatient clinics. C.R.N.A.s are the sole providers of anesthetics in 85 percent of hospitals in rural areas. Even in larger hospitals, they are not always closely supervised by doctors. *Certified nurse midwives* (C.N.M.s) give gynecological exams and perform routine prenatal care, counsel women and families about family planning, and deliver babies. Some become mothers' advocates or policymakers in the public health arena.

According to the American Nurses Association, nurse practitioners already provide 60 to 80 percent of the care for which people normally see a physician. Graduations of nurse practitioners increased about 16 percent in 1998 over the previous year, according to the American Association of Colleges of Nursing and the National Organization of Nurse Practitioner Faculties.

Physical therapists. After a stroke, a sports injury, or a nasty auto accident, patients often need therapy to regain lost mobility. Physical therapists often specialize in a particular group of problems, such as sports injuries, geriatrics, or cardiopulmonary disease. Working closely with a physician, therapists develop treatment programs that include exercises to increase strength, coordination, and range of motion. They may use tools—such as heat, massage, and water, for example—to reduce pain and improve physical capabilities. Some estimate that every licensed physical therapist has five job offers upon certification. Physical therapists can work in hospitals, nursing homes, outpatient clinics, schools, or home health care. More than 20 percent are in private practice.

Occupational therapists. Occupational therapists recommend activities that will help patients who are mentally, physically, or emotionally disabled learn to regain physical capabilities, function independently, or return to work. Working in a hospital, nursing home, or rehabilitation center, therapists use a variety of activities and exercises to increase motor skills, strength, endurance, concentration, or motivation. Some therapists concentrate on working with children, while others work primarily with the elderly.

Respiratory therapists. Respiratory therapists evaluate, treat, and care for all types of patients who have breathing disorders—ranging from premature infants to elderly people. To evaluate patients, therapists test the capacity of their lungs and analyze the levels of oxygen and carbon dioxide concentration in the blood. In home care, therapists teach patients and their families to use ventilators and other life support systems. They visit several times a month to inspect and clean equipment, ensuring its proper use, and make emergency visits if equipment problems arise. Respiratory therapists are increasingly working under the supervision of nurses. Some are expanding into cardiopulmonary procedures, such as electrocardiograms and stress testing.

Medical technicians/technologists. As the baby boom generation ages, the incidence of disease will increase. Medical technicians/technologists will provide physicians with the results of specific tests so the physician can make a diagnosis and prescribe treatment. In the future, they should be more in demand in physicians' offices and outpatient clinics, rather than simply in hospitals. *EEG technologists* operate the electroencephalograph (EEG) machines that record electrical impulses transmitted by the brain. They also keep records and maintain their equipment. As the volume of surgery increases and operating room staff patterns change, some employers prefer to use *surgical technologists* rather than operating room nurses to cut costs. Surgical technologists assist in operations under the supervision of surgeons or registered nurses. They help set up the operating room with surgical instruments and other materials. They may also prepare patients for surgery. During the operation, they pass sterile instruments to surgeons and assistants and may care for and diagnose specimens taken for laboratory analysis.

Medical secretaries. An essential part of every doctor's office, clinic, outpatient center, and hospital, medical secretaries answer the phones, schedule new appointments, and juggle canceled and emergency appointments. The position needs a unique combination of personal skills and sophisticated computer and record-keeping skills.

Medical assistants. These nurses' aides and administrators ensure the smooth operation of physicians' offices, hospitals, and outpatient clinics. They make and confirm appointments, locate medical records, and show patients to examining rooms. They may also handle payments and maintain examining rooms and equipment.

Physician assistants. Like advanced practice nurses, physician assistants perform many tasks that normally fall to a physician, such as taking medical histories or making preliminary diagnoses. Physician assistants may also treat minor injuries, suture a wound, or cast a broken limb. Some make house calls, go on hospital rounds, or supervise other medical staff members.

A growing emphasis on cost containment should lead to more jobs for physician assistants in all areas of health care. However, opportunities are especially good in inner-city and rural clinics that have difficulty attracting primary care physicians.

Health services managers. As the health care industry expands and diversifies, more *health services managers* will bring business skills to the operation of a wide range of outpatient facilities created by large hospitals, such as clinics, substance abuse treatment centers, and home health care services. This often entails responsibility for millions of dollars in facilities and equipment, as well as hundreds of employees.

While opportunities are dwindling in hospitals and HMOs, health services managers will still find bright prospects in home health care, nursing homes, and clinics.

Chiropractors. As alternative forms of medicine get the nod from the medical community, *chiropractors* will gain a more prominent profile. The chiropractic approach to health care is holistic, stressing the patient's overall well-being through exercise, diet, and rest. Although chiropractors are best known for their manual manipulations or adjustments of the spinal column, they also employ other forms of treatment including water, light, massage, ultrasound, electric, and heat therapy.

Chiropractors hold that misalignment of spinal vertebrae or irritation of the spinal nerves can alter many important body functions by affecting the nervous system. Chiropractors do not prescribe drugs or perform surgery. Some chiropractors specialize in areas related to athletic injuries, neurology, orthopedics, nutrition, and internal disorders. All chiropractors are solo or group practitioners who also have the administrative responsibilities of running a practice. In larger offices, chiropractors delegate these tasks to office managers and chiropractic assistants. Chiropractors in private practice are ultimately responsible for developing a clientele, hiring employees, and keeping records.

Dental assistants. An aging population means more root canals and other dental services. It's the savvy dentist who takes on dental assistants to perform routine tasks. This leaves the dentist with more time to perform profitable procedures. *Dental assistants* perform a variety of patient care, office, and laboratory duties. They prepare patients for treatment and assist the dentist during the procedure by handing him or her instruments and materials.

Some dental assistants prepare materials for making impressions and restorations, expose radiographs, and process dental x-ray film as directed by a dentist. They may also remove sutures, apply anesthetics and cavity preventive agents on teeth and gums, remove excess cement used in the filling process, and place rubber dams on the teeth to isolate them for individual treatment.

Some dental assistants have laboratory duties, such as making casts of the teeth and mouth from impressions taken by dentists, and office duties such as ordering dental supplies and materials.

Dental hygienists. *Dental hygienists* clean teeth and provide other preventive dental care. They begin by examining patients' teeth and gums and recording the presence of diseases or abnormalities. They remove calcium deposits, stains, and plaque from the teeth, take and develop dental x-rays, and apply cavity preventive agents (such as fluorides and pit and fissure sealants). In some states, hygienists administer local anesthetics and anesthetic gas; place and carve filling materials, temporary fillings, and periodontal dressings; remove sutures; and smooth and polish metal restorations.

Speech pathologist/audiologists. Speech and language problems can result from hearing loss, brain injury or deterioration, cerebral palsy, stroke, cleft palate, voice pathology, mental retardation, or emotional problems. Problems can be congenital, developmental, or acquired. *Speech pathologists* use written and oral tests, as well as special instruments, to diagnose the nature and extent of impairment. They develop a plan of care tailored to each patient's needs. Working in speech and language clinics, they may independently develop and carry out treatment programs. In medical facilities, they may work with physicians, social workers, psychologists, and other therapists to develop and execute treatment plans.

Audiologists work with people who have hearing, balance, and related problems resulting from trauma at birth, viral infections, genetic disorders, or exposure to loud noise. They use audiometers and other testing devices to measure the loudness at which a person begins to hear sounds, the ability to distinguish between sounds, and the nature and extent of hearing loss. Audiologists interpret these results and may coordinate them with medical, educational, and psychological information to make a diagnosis and determine a course of treatment. Audiologists work in a variety of settings and as members of interdisciplinary professional teams.

Veterinarians. This special breed of doctor treats patients who can only bark, meow, or chirp to describe their ailments. Most *veterinarians* are in private practice where they treat a growing population of household pets. Prospects for veterinarians who specialize in farm animals are above average because there is less competition in this area.

A new generation of opportunities

Geriatricians. By 2005, almost 36 million people in the United States will be 65 or older. The number of Americans aged 85 and over will grow more than three times as fast as the total population in this time. These facts point to the need for physicians with specialized knowledge of diseases and medical problems common in the elderly (such as Alzheimer's disease and osteoporosis).

Home health aides. Elderly, disabled, and ill people need the services of *home health aides* in order to live comfortably in their homes rather than in institutions like nursing homes. Home health aides travel to visit clients according to a schedule set by a physician, nurse, or therapist. Detailed instructions guide them in performing a range of medical and personal services—from administering medication to preparing meals. Daily personal care may include bathing, helping with prescribed exercises, and changing dressings. Aides report changes in the patient's condition and participate in reviewing cases with a team of health professionals.

Do you have what it takes?

Health care professionals need physical stamina and emotional stability to care for a range of patients. Some must stand and concentrate for long periods of time during surgeries. Others have to lift patients and move equipment regularly. Even the most emotionally stable people in the field are prone to burnout from dealing with ill and dying patients.

All health care professionals should be patient, compassionate, and have a sincere interest in their patients' welfare. Most need manual dexterity and good vision, as well as excellent communication skills, to gain the trust of ill or frightened patients. They must be able to accept responsibility, direct or supervise others, follow orders precisely, and determine when consultation is required. Medical technicians and technologists should have an aptitude for working with electronic equipment.

Veterinarians should have an affinity for animals and the ability to get along with animal owners. They must also be able to make decisions in emergencies.

To make effective business decisions, health services managers should be open minded and good at sifting through conflicting information. Like their counterparts in other fields, health services managers need to be self-starters. To create the positive atmosphere so important to quality patient care, they must work well with all kinds of people. Strong leadership and interpersonal skills are critical. In medical group practices, success depends on having a good working relationship with the physician-owners. Public speaking skills are a plus. These are the jobs where an M.B.A. comes in handy and a background in cost-cutting, marketing, and information management will give you an edge over the competition.

Education and training

As a rule of thumb, the more training you have, the better your job prospects will be in the health care field. Employers also tend to look for applicants who have clinical experience.

Physicians need a bachelor's degree before entering a three-year medical school program. A minimum of six additional years of internship and residency is required to practice as a physician. Geriatricians should select a residency program with a geriatrics specialty.

Registered nurses must graduate from an approved school of nursing. A four-year bachelor's degree will enhance your career options and is usually required for supervisory and administrative positions.

Most programs for licensed practical nurses last about one year and include both classroom study and clinical practice.

The two most popular educational paths to registered nursing are earning an associate degree (A.D.N.) or a bachelor of science degree in nursing (B.S.N.). A.D.N. programs, offered by community and junior colleges, take about two years to complete. B.S.N. programs, offered by colleges and universities, take four to five years, but offer much better potential for advancement. A bachelor's degree is generally necessary for administrative positions and is a prerequisite for admission to graduate nursing programs in research, consulting, teaching, or a clinical specialization. A growing number of programs include clinical experience in nursing homes, public health departments, home health agencies, and ambulatory clinics. Increasingly, management-level nursing positions require completion of a one- to two-year graduate degree program in nursing or health services administration.

Advanced practice nurses need additional training and education. In addition to being an R.N., a nurse practitioner should have an M.S. in nursing. A certified nurse midwife should have an M.S. and complete a one-and-a-half year certificate program. Boston University offers a unique dual master's in nurse midwifery and public health. A certified registered nurse anesthetist should complete two to three years of additional training before passing national board exams.

Physician assistants should complete an accredited training program and have the work experience to receive a certificate, associate's, or bachelor's degree.

Medical assistants can enter the field with no formal education, but many employers prefer a one-year certificate from a vocational-technical school or a two-year associates degree from a community college. Computer expertise is also a plus.

Medical secretaries should complete a specialized training program through a community or business college. Many temporary help agencies provide formal training in computer and office skills.

Most EEG technologists complete a certificate training program in a hospital or receive an associate degree from a two-year community college. Radiologic technologists can attend one- to four-year programs leading to a certificate, associate, or bachelor's degree. Two-year programs are most prevalent. A master's or bachelor's may be necessary for supervisory, administrative, and teaching positions. Surgical technologists attend formal programs that combine classroom study and clinical supervision. One- or two-year programs offered by community and junior colleges, vocational-technical institutes, and hospitals lead to a certificate or associate degree. Hospital programs last from six months to a year.

Occupational and physical therapists should have a certificate, B.S., or M.S. from an accredited training program. Some states require continuing education.

Most accredited programs for respiratory therapists last two years and lead to an associate degree. Some are four-year bachelor's degree programs. Increasingly, respiratory therapists receive on-the-job training, so that they can administer electrocardiograms and stress tests and draw blood samples from patients.

Educational requirements for chiropractors vary from state to state. In general, state licensing boards require chiropractors to complete a four-year chiropractic college course earning the degree of Doctor of Chiropractic (D.C.) following at least two years of undergraduate education. All state boards recognize academic training in chiropractic colleges accredited by the Council on Chiropractic Education.

Health services managers should have a degree in hospital administration or business with courses or experience in marketing and finance. A graduate degree in health services administration, nursing administration, or an M.B.A. is required for many upper-level administrative positions with hospitals and their subsidiaries. A Ph.D. is required for positions in teaching, consulting, or research. Nursing service administrators are usually chosen from among registered nurses with administrative abilities and advanced education.

Training requirements for home health aides are changing with federal guidelines. Those whose employers receive reimbursement from Medicare must complete at least 75 hours of classroom and practical training supervised by a registered nurse and pass a competency test covering 12 different areas.

Many states now require home health aides to complete brief formal training programs.

Programs for dental assistants are offered by community and junior colleges, trade schools, and technical institutes. Most programs approved by the American Dental Association's Commission on Dental Accreditation take a year or less to complete and lead to a certificate or diploma. Two-year programs offered in community and junior colleges lead to an associate degree. Some private vocational schools offer four- to six-month courses in dental assisting, but these are not accredited by the Commission on Dental Accreditation.

Dental hygienists must graduate from a program approved by the Commission on Dental Accreditation. An associate's degree is sufficient for practice in a private dental office. A bachelor's or master's degree in dental hygiene is usually required for research, teaching, or clinical practice in public or school health programs. Twelve universities offer master's degree programs in dental hygiene. About half of the dental hygiene programs prefer applicants who have completed at least one year of college. Some of the bachelor's degree programs require applicants to have completed two years.

Most states that license speech pathologists and audiologists require a master's degree or equivalent.

Veterinarians must complete a four-year program at a college of veterinary medicine approved by the Council on Education of the American Veterinary Medical Association to earn a Doctor of Veterinary Medicine (D.V.M. or V.M.D.) degree. Many colleges do not require a bachelor's degree for entrance, but all require 45 to 60 credit hours in science, math, and liberal arts at the undergraduate level. Competition for admission to veterinary school is keen. Applicants must have a higher than average grade point average (GPA) and passing test scores from the Graduate Record Examination (GRE), the Veterinary College Admission Test (VCAT), or the Medical College Admission Test (MCAT).

Formal experience, such as work with veterinarians or scientists in clinics, agribusiness, research, or in some area of health science, is particularly advantageous. Veterinary graduates who plan to work with specific types of animals or specialize in a clinical area, such as pathology, surgery, radiology, or laboratory animal medicine, usually complete a one-year internship. Veterinarians who seek board certification in a specialty must also complete a two- to three-year residency program that provides intensive training in one of the following areas: internal medicine, oncology, radiology, surgery, dermatology, anesthesiology, neurology, cardiology, ophthalmology, or exotic small animal medicine.

Training and testing programs may be offered by the employing agency and may vary depending on state regulations. Some states require aides to pass a physical examination.

All health care professionals study throughout their careers to keep up with health practices and medical advances.

Professional licensing and certification

All states require L.P.N.s and R.N.s to pass a licensing examination after completing an accredited nursing program. Nurses may be licensed in more than one state, either by taking an examination or through reciprocal endorsement. Continuing education is a requirement for license renewal in some states.

Advanced practice nurses need to be certified by the American Nurses Association to work in more than half the states in the United States. With a license and one year of experience working in acute care, an R.N. can enter a two- to three-year program to become a certified registered nurse anesthetist (C.R.N.A.). Graduates must pass a pass a certifying exam after completing the program.

Increasingly, employers seek medical assistants who are certified by the American Association of Medical Technologists.

In 45 states, physician assistants must pass a certifying exam. In some states their duties are determined by his or her supervising physician. In others, the state regulatory agency sets standards.

The American Board of Registration of Electroencephalographic Technologists awards the Registered EEG Technologist certification.

Many states require radiologic technologists to be licensed by the American Registry of Radiologic Technologists. Voluntary registration is seen as a plus by many employers. To become registered, technologists must graduate from a school accredited by the Committee of Allied Health Education and Accreditation or meet other prerequisites, and they must pass a written exam.

Many employers prefer to hire surgical technologists who have earned voluntary certification from the Liaison Council on Certification. Candidates must have graduated from a formal training program and pass a written examination. Continuing education and reexamination are required to renew certification every six years.

The National Home Caring Council, part of the Foundation for Hospice and Home Care, offers a voluntary National Homemaker/Home Health Care certification.

All states require physical therapists to be licensed. Graduates of an accredited physical therapy program must pass an examination. Most states require occupational therapists to be licensed. Candidates must pass a national certification examination given by the American Occupational Therapy Certification Board.

Respiratory care professionals are licensed in 42 states. Two credentials are awarded to respiratory care practitioners who satisfy the requirements of the National Board for Respiratory Care: Certified respiratory therapy technician (C.R.T.T.) and registered respiratory therapist (R.R.T.). Most employers require that applicants for entry-level or generalist positions hold the C.R.T.T. or are eligible to take the certification examination. Those in supervisory positions and working in intensive care specialties usually require the R.R.T. (or R.R.T. eligibility). Graduates of two- and four-year programs in respiratory therapy, as well as those of one-year technician programs—are eligible to take the C.R.T.T. examination first. C.R.T.T.s who meet education and experience requirements can take a separate examination, leading to R.R.T. certification.

All states require health services managers of nursing homes to pass a licensing exam, to complete a state-approved training program, and to pursue continuing education. State requirements change, so contact the appropriate state agency for the most up-to-date requirements.

State laws and regulations specify the types of services chiropractors may provide. All 50 states and the District of Columbia grant licenses to chiropractors who meet educational requirements and pass a state board examination. Many states have reciprocity agreements that permit chiropractors licensed in another state to obtain a license without further examination. To become licensed, chiropractors in most states must pass all or part of the three-part test administered by the National Board of Chiropractic Examiners. Additional state examinations may be required to supplement National Board tests.

In order to maintain their license, chiropractors must complete a state-specified number of hours of continuing education each year. Continuing education programs are offered by chiropractic colleges, the American Chiropractic Association (ACA), the International Chiropractors Association (ICA), and state chiropractic associations. Special councils within the ACA and ICA also offer programs leading to clinical specialty certification, called "diplomata certification," in areas such as orthopedics, neurology, sports injuries, occupational and industrial health, nutrition, radiology, thermography, and internal disorders.

Several states have adopted standards for dental assistants who perform radiologic procedures. Completion of a voluntary certification exam, available through the Dental Assisting National Board, satisfies those standards. Graduates of accredited training programs or dental assistants with two years of full-time experience and who are certified in cardiopulmonary resuscitation may qualify to take the board certification exam.

Dental hygienists must be licensed by the state in which they practice and pass both a written examination administered by the American Dental Association Joint Commission on National Dental Examinations, as well as a clinical examination administered by state or regional testing agencies. Most states also require dental hygienists to pass an examination on legal aspects of dental hygiene practice.

Most states that license speech pathologists and audiologists require a master's degree or equivalent, as well as 300 to 375 hours of supervised clinical experience, a passing score on a national examination, and nine months of postgraduate professional clinical experience. There are continuing education requirements for licensure renewal in 34 states.

Medicaid, Medicare, and private health insurers generally require speech pathologists and audiologists to be licensed to qualify for reimbursement. Speech pathologists can also earn the Certificate of Clinical Competence in Speech-Language Pathology (CCC-SLP) offered by the American Speech-Language-Hearing Association. Audiologists can earn the Certificate of Clinical Competence in Audiology (CCC-A).

All 50 states and the District of Columbia require that veterinarians be licensed before they can practice. The only exemptions are for veterinarians working for some federal agencies as well as some state governments. Licensing is controlled by the states and is not strictly uniform, although all states require successful completion of the D.V.M. degree or its equivalent and a passing score on a national board examination. The Educational Commission for Foreign Veterinary Graduates (ECFVG) grants certification to individuals trained outside the United States who demonstrate that they meet specified English language and clinical proficiency requirements. ECFVG certification fulfills the educational requirement for licensure in all states except Nebraska.

The majority of states also require candidates to pass a state jurisprudence examination, covering state laws and regulations. Some states also do additional testing on clinical competency. There are very few reciprocal agreements between states, making it difficult for a veterinarian to practice in a new state without first taking another examination.

Tips on breaking in

Go to school on the government. If you can't afford the cost of medical school, the Department of Defense offers a free medical education to qualified college graduates between the ages of 18 and 27. A successful applicant must agree to serve seven years as a commissioned officer in the Army, Navy, Air Force, or Public Health Service at a salary in the mid-$20,000s.

For details, write to:

Director of Admissions Dept. 9RD
F.E. Hebert School of Medicine
Uniformed Services University of the Health Sciences
4301 Jones Bridge Road
Bethesda, MD 20814

Career path

Registered nurses can be promoted to head nurse, then to assistant director of nursing services, director, and ultimately vice president. With additional education and training, nurses can become advanced practice nurses.

Some nurses move into the business side of health care. Their nursing expertise and experience on a health care team equip them to manage ambulatory, acute, home health, and chronic-care services. Some are employed by health care corporations in health planning and development, marketing, and quality assurance.

Advancement is limited for medical assistants and medical secretaries. With further education and training, they may become nurses, physician assistants, or medical technologists.

As physician assistants gain experience, they work with less supervision. Some supervise other health care workers in a hospital, group practice, or outpatient clinic.

Most surgical technologists are employed by hospitals, physicians' offices, and clinics. A few, known as "private scrubs," are employed by surgeons who work with special teams that perform such surgical procedures as organ transplants. Career advancement is limited. With additional training, surgical technologists can work with lasers and assist in more complex procedures, such as open-heart surgery. Some take positions with insurance companies or sterile supply services or become instructors in surgical technology training programs.

Most EEG technologists work in EEG or neurology laboratories in hospitals, where they can advance to chief technologist by performing more difficult tests. EEG technologists also work in clinics and for neurologists and neurosurgeons. An increasing number are taking jobs with HMOs. Some decide to teach or conduct research.

More than half of all radiologic technologists work in hospitals. Others work in clinics, such as diagnostic imaging centers. With experience and additional training, they may begin to take on special procedures.

Advancement is limited for home health aides working for home health agencies, visiting nurse associations, hospitals, public health and welfare departments, or temporary help firms. The most experienced aides assist with medical equipment. Many find the emotional demands and low pay reasons to move into a related field. Some choose self-employment and accept clients, set fees, and arrange their own schedules.

Occupational and physical therapists generally remain therapists for the duration of their careers. Many have little interest in traditional career progression. Many work part-time and enjoy the flexibility that the job allows. Some therapists go into private practice. Others continue their education and eventually pursue careers in hospital administration.

Health services managers with a bachelor's degree usually begin as an administrative assistant or assistant department head in a large hospital, or as department head or assistant administrator in a small hospital or nursing home. With a master's degree, new graduates can enter as assistant administrator or manage a nonhealth-related department, such as finance.

Over the next five to seven years, managers often rotate through a series of assignments in order to gain exposure to the variety of business functions within a hospital. Some health services managers advance by moving into more responsible and higher-paying jobs within the same institution. Following this path, you will manage increasingly larger and more complex departments. In time, you may be promoted to the number two person in charge of the facility. In this position, your duties may include overall responsibilities during late evening shifts. In addition, you'll function as the general manager when the head administrator is away.

Other health services managers benefit from holding general management positions at increasingly larger facilities. This career path often requires relocation.

Health services managers in hospitals and HMOs will face very keen competition for upper-level management. It typically takes about 10 years to be promoted to CEO of a small- to medium-sized hospital. It can take 20 years in a large hospital or management company.

In nursing homes and long-term care facilities where a graduate degree in health administration is not ordinarily required, job opportunities are better for people with strong business and management skills. Without further education, advancement opportunities are limited.

Some dental assistants working the front office may become office managers. Others, working "chairside" with dentists, may go back to school to become dental hygienists.

Newly licensed chiropractors have a number of options. They can apply for a residency program, set up a new practice, purchase an established practice, partner with an established practitioner, or take a salaried position with an established chiropractor to acquire the experience.

Most veterinarians begin as employees or partners in established practices. With experience, most set up their own practice or purchase an established practice.

Respiratory therapists advance in clinical practice by moving from caring for "general" to "critical" patients who have significant problems in other organ systems, such as the heart or kidneys. Respiratory therapists with four-year degrees may also advance to supervisory or managerial positions in a respiratory therapy department. Respiratory therapists in home care and equipment rental firms may move into a branch manager position.

How much can I earn?

The type and size of the health facility affects the salaries of health care professionals. Primary care physicians can start at $80,000 plus bonuses in some rural areas that are desperate for medical expertise. Starting salaries can be as low as $32,000. Most family practice physicians, pediatricians, and internists average $50,000 to $80,000 per year. Specialists—geriatricians—can make $100,000 to $180,000.

L.P.Ns earn an average of $21,000 to $36,400.

The salary range for R.N.s is $45,000 to $70,000. An advanced practice nurse who has training in a specialized area of clinical practice can earn up to $80,000.

Medical assistants earn an average of $17,000 to $24,000. The salary range for medical secretaries is $25,000 to $40,000.

Physician assistants working full-time in hospitals and medical schools earn an average $45,000 to $65,000. Earnings are slightly less for those working for the federal government.

Physical and occupational therapists earn an average $45,000 to $80,000, although self-employed physical therapists working full-time can earn more than $100,000.

According to a 1997 survey by the American Speech-Language-Hearing Association, the median annual salary for full-time certified speech pathologists was $44,000; for audiologists, $43,000. Certified speech pathologists with one to three years of experience earned a median annual salary of $38,000. With 22 years of experience, they earned a median annual salary of $52,000.

Licensed audiologists with one to three years of experience earned $32,000. With 20 or more years of experience, audiologists earned about $55,000.

EEG technologists working in hospitals earn an average of $25,000. Laboratory supervisors and training program directors earn more. Surgical technologists earn from $22,000 to $30,000. Radiologic technologists earn from $25,000 to $35,000 a year.

According to a Hay Group survey of acute care hospitals, the median annual base salary of full-time respiratory therapists was $32,500 in January 1997. The middle 50 percent earned between $29,300 and $35,000.

Many home health aides earn minimum wage. Most earn six to 10 dollars per hour. In larger cities, they may earn up to $15 an hour, but only for time worked in the home. They are not paid for time spent traveling from patient to patient.

Health services managers of group medical practices earn an average of $58,000. Managers of very large group practices with net revenues over $10 million can $96,000 or more. According to the American Hospital Association, hospital CEO salaries range from $100,000 to $300,000.

According to the ACA, in 1995 the median income for chiropractors was about $80,000 after expenses. In chiropractic, as in other types of independent practice, earnings are relatively low in the beginning, and increase as the practice grows. Earnings are also influenced by the characteristics and qualifications of the practitioner, and geographic location.

Veterinarians average $32,000 for entry-level jobs. After five years, they can earn $60,000 and after 10 years, $80,000

In 1996, median earnings for dental assistants working full-time were $19,000. The middle 50 percent earned between $15,000 and $24,000. The lowest 10 percent earned less than $11,000; the top 10 percent, more than $27,000.

According to the American Dental Association, experienced dental hygienists who worked 32 hours a week or more in a private practice averaged about $39,500 a year in 1995.

Where will you work?

Hospitals, outpatient clinics, nursing homes, group medical practices, and home health agencies are located in almost every city. However, opportunities for health care professionals are particularly plentiful in smaller cities and towns in the Southeast and Midwest.

Many chiropractors are located in small communities, but the proportion in larger communities is increasing. Western and southwestern states have a higher concentration of chiropractors relative to the population than the Middle Atlantic states.

Some speech-language pathologists and audiologists work in schools.

Health care professionals may also work as clinical supervisors for student clinicians, researchers, or university and college professors.

Job Profile

Susan James, respiratory care practitioner

What general job responsibilities does your title encompass?
I provide pulmonary and cardiac respiratory care to patients of all ages in many different care settings—outpatient, general/medical, emergency room (ER), critical care, trauma, intensive care (ICU), surgery, labor and delivery, neonatal ICU, and rehabilitation. I operate all aspects of respiratory equipment and administer medications. I also educate patients and their family members on how patient's disease is progressing and monitor their condition at home.

How many years have you been in this business?
I've been working for almost eight years.

How many years of education do you have?
I have a B.S. in chemistry with an A.S. in respiratory care.

How many hours do you typically work per week?
Approximately 36 hours. Usually I work three 12-hour shifts and I'm on duty every other weekend.

What hours do you work on a typical day?
Either 7 a.m. to 7 p.m., or 7 p.m. to 7 a.m.

Have you earned professional certification?
Yes. I am a Certified Respiratory Therapy Technician (C.R.T.T.) and Registered Respiratory Therapist (R.R.T.). I am also licensed to practice in the state of California as a Respiratory Care Practitioner (R.C.P.).

What is your annual salary?
$30,000-$40,000.

How did you get your job?
I walked in and spoke to a human resources manager at the hospital.

Please describe one of your "typical" days?
That would be too hard—they're never the same. Basically, I take care of patients in the hospital while I'm on-call to ER, outpatient, labor and delivery, and so forth.

What are your career aspirations?
More community-based education. I'm starting a series of asthma education workshops for the community. I started the Pediatric Task Force to education health care providers within this hospital last year and set up protocols for providing care to pediatric patients.
We held the first Children's Health Fair on the hospital grounds. I'm working to bring standardized protocols to care of asthma patients from the emergency room through discharge from the hospital.
I'm just starting to write a proposal to bring ongoing pulmonary rehab and cardiac rehab classes to the community, in conjunction with physical therapy, the hospital, and local doctors. I've also obtained a grant from the American Lung Association's "Open Always" programs to education public school and day care teachers and students about asthma and emergency care.

What kind of people do really well at this business?
People who are independent and able to make quick decisions (often in life-or-death situations). You have to be adaptable and able to work in high-stress and high-emotion situations.

What do you really like about your job?
I really like to work with people and at the same time have a job I care about and one which "fills" me. I like using knowledge gained at school. I don't know if I make a difference in peoples' lives, but they make a difference in mine.

What do you dislike?
The pay is not commensurate with the responsibility.

What is the biggest misconception about this job?
Most people outside of health care don't know what a respiratory care practitioner is or does.

How can someone get a job like yours?
After you finish school and are licensed, work in a large urban hospital where you can get experience through exposure to a wide variety of patients and conditions.

Resources

Health care associations

American Academy of Audiology
8300 Greensboro Drive, Suite 750
McLean, VA 22102
(703)790-8466
Fax: (703)790-8631
www.audiology.org

**American Academy
of Physician Assistants**
950 N. Washington Street
Alexandria, VA 22314-1552
(703)836-2272
Fax: (703)684-1924
www.aapa.org

**American Association of Colleges
of Nursing**
One Dupont Circle, NW, Suite 530
Washington, DC 20036
(202)463-6930
Fax: (202)785-8320
www.aacn.nche.edu

**American Association
of Critical-Care Nurses**
101 Columbia
Aliso Viejo CA 92656
(949)362-2000
E-mail: info@aacn.org
www.aacn.org
(Publishes: *Critical Care Nurse* and
American Journal of Critical Care)

**American Association of Homes
for the Aging**
901 E Street, NW, Suite 500
Washington, DC 20004-2011
(202)783-2242
Fax: (202)783-2255
www.aahsa.org

**American Association
of Nurse Anesthetists**
222 South Prospect Ave.
Park Ridge, IL 60068-4001
(847)692-7050
Fax: (847)692-6968
E-mail: info@aana.com
www.aana.com

**American Association
for Respiratory Care**
11030 Ables Lane
Dallas, TX 75229
(972)243-2272
Fax: (972)484-2720
E-mail: info@aarc.org
www.aarc.org

**American College
of Healthcare Executives**
One North Franklin, Suite 1700
Chicago, IL 60606-3491
(312)424-2800
Fax: (312)424-0023

American Health Care Association
1201 L Street, NW
Washington, DC 20005
(202)842-4444
Fax: (202)842-3860
www.ahca.org

**American Health Information
Management Association**
233 N. Michigan Ave., Suite 2150
Chicago, IL 60601-5519
(312)233-1100
Fax: (312)233-1090
E-mail: info@ahima.org
www.ahima.org

American Medical Association
Allied Health Education and Accreditation
515 N. State Street
Chicago, IL 60610
(312)464-0183
www.ama-assn.org

American Medical Technologists
710 Higgins Road
Park Ridge, IL 60068-5765
(847)823-5169
Fax: (847)823-0458
www.amt1.com

American Nurses Association
600 Maryland Avenue, SW, Suite 100 West
Washington, DC 20024
(800)274-4ANA
www.nursingworld.org
(Publishes *The American Nurse* and
American Journal of Nursing)

American Chiropractic Association
1701 Clarendon Boulevard
Arlington, VA 22209
(703)276-8800 or (800)986-INFO
Fax: (703)243-2593
E-mail: memberinfo@amerchiro.org
www.americhiro.org

American Dental Association
211 E. Chicago Avenue
Chicago, IL 60611
(312)440-2500
Fax: (312)440-2800
www.ada.org

American Dental Hygienists' Association
Division of Professional Development
444 N. Michigan Ave, Suite 3400
Chicago, IL 60611
(312)440-8900
www.adha.org

American Hospital Association
One North Franklin
Chicago, IL 60606
(312)422-3000
Fax: (312)422-4796
www.aha.org

American Nurses Association
600 Maryland Avenue, SW, Suite 100 West
Washington, DC 20024
(800)274-4ANA
www.nursingworld.org

**American Occupational
Therapy Association**
4720 Montgomery Lane
P.O. Box 31220
Bethesda, MD 20824-1220
(301)652-2682
TDD: (800)377-8555
Fax: (301)652-7711
www.aota.org

**American Registry of
Diagnostic Medical Songographers**
600 Jefferson Plaza, Suite 360
Rockville, MD 20852-1150
(301)738-8401 or (800)541-9754
www.ardms.org

**American Registry
of Radiologic Technologists**
1255 Northland Drive
St. Paul, MN 55120-1155
(651)687-0048
www.arrt.org

**American Society of
Electroneurodiagnostic
Technologists, Inc.**
204 West 7th Street
Carroll, IA 51401-2317
(712)792-2978
Fax: (712)792-6962
www.aset.org

**American Society
of Radiologic Technologists**
15000 Central Ave. SE
Albuquerque, NM 87123-3917
(505)298-4500 or (800)444-2778
Fax: (505)298-5063
FaxBack: (505)298-4500, Ext. 298

**American Speech-Language-Hearing
Association**
10801 Rockville Pike
Rockville, MD 20852
(301)897-0157 or (888)321-ASHA
TTY: (301)571-0457
www.asha.org

Association of Operating Room Nurses
2170 South Parker Road, Suite 300
Denver, CO 80231-5711
(303)755-6300 or (800)755-2676
www.aorn.org

Association of Surgical Technologists
7108-C South Alton Way
Englewood, CO 80112-2106
(303)694-9130
Fax: (303)694-9169
Faxback: (888)627-8018
www.ast.org

Gerontological Society of America
1030 15th Street, NW, Suite 250
Washington, DC 20005
www.geron.org

**Medical Group
Management Association**
104 Inverness Terrace East
Englewood, CO 80112
(303)799-1111 or (888)608-5601
Fax: (303)643-4439
Faxback: (877)329-6462
www.mgma.com

National Association of Home Care
228 Seventh Street, SE
Washington, DC 20003
(202)547-7424
Fax: (202)547-3540
www.nahc.org

**National Federation
of Licensed Practical Nurses**
1418 Aversboro Road
Garner, NC 27529
(919)779-0046
Fax: (919)779-5642
(Publishes *American Journal
of Practical Nursing*)

The National League for Nursing
61 Broadway
New York, NY 10006
(212)363-5555 or (800)669-9656
Fax: (607)723-8408

National Rehabilitation Association
1625 Massachusetts Ave., NW, Suite 601
Washington, DC 20036-2244
(202)939-1750
www.housingonline.com

National Rural Health Association
One West Armour Blvd., Suite 203
Kansas City, MO 64111
(816)756-3140
Fax: (816)756-3144
E-mail: mail@nrharural.org
www.nrharural.org

Health care industry publications

AHA Guide to the Health Care Field
American Hospital Association
325 7th Street, NW
Washington, DC 20004
www.aha.org

American Journal of Critical Care
American Association of Critical-Care Nurses
101 Columbia
Aliso Viejo CA 92656
(949)362-2000
www.aacn.org

American Journal of Nursing
American Nurses Association
600 Maryland Ave., SW, Suite 100 West
Washington, DC 20024
(800)274-4ANA
www.nursingworld.org

American Journal of Occupational Therapy
1383 Piccard Drive, Box 1725
Rockville, MD 20850
(301)948-9626

American Journal of Practical Nursing
National Federation
of Licensed Practical Nurses
1418 Aversboro Road
Garner, NC 27529
(919)779-0046
Fax: (919)779-5642

The American Nurse
American Nurses Association
600 Maryland Avenue, SW, Suite 100 West
Washington, DC 20024
(800)274-4ANA
www.nursingworld.org

Critical Care Nurse
American Association
of Critical-Care Nurses
101 Columbia
Aliso Viejo CA 92656
(949)362-2000
www.aacn.org

Contemporary Long Term Care
(212)592-6265
www.cltcmag.com

Hospital Phone Book
Reed Reference Publishing
121 Chanlon Road
New Providence, NJ 07974
(800)521-8110
www.reedref.com

Nursing Career Directory
Springhouse Corp.
1111 Bethlehem Pike
P.O. Box 908
Springhouse, PA 19477-0908
(215)646-8700
Fax: (215)646-4508
www.springnet.com

Chapter 9

Human Resources & Employee Services
From personnel to employee empowerment

Benefits specialist
Compensation specialist
Employee Assistance Program (EAP) counselor
Human resources manager
Management development specialist
Outplacement services marketer
Outplacement services counselor
Best Bets for Entrepreneurs:
Career counselor, Recruiter, International HR consultant

Forecast

According to the U.S. Bureau of Labor Statistics, most new jobs will stem from increasing efforts by companies to recruit and retain quality employees. Employers are expected to earmark more resources for job-specific training programs, especially where advances in technology directly affect job performance. While there continues to be demand for specialists able to handle highly technical areas of the human resources, as well as managers able to advise top executives, self-service technology is beginning to phase out lower-level positions. Corporate downsizing and voluntary job-hopping will continue, providing plenty of work for outplacement services specialists, recruiters, and career counselors.

Growth

Growth is faster than the average for recruiters, career counselors, and outplacement specialists.

Overview

Approximately 20 years ago, you probably made a quick stop in the personnel office on the first day of a new job. After you put your signature on the standard forms, the manager or staff might tell you all about the upcoming company picnic and then send you on your way with a copy of the employee newsletter. That was likely to be the end of your mutual contact.

Today, you're likely to spend a good part of your first day with the human resources manager and staff preparing to choose from a menu of "cafeteria-style" benefits. Afterwards, you may sit through an employee orientation session to get up to speed on everything from corporate culture to sexual harassment policies.

Once a "safe" career choice, human resources (HR) has emerged from its cocoon to become one of the most important and visible departments in any company. In companies like Apple Computer, very few business decisions are made without input from HR. Few companies—of any size—can afford to become entangled in legislation that creates stricter standards for equal opportunity employment and benefits. At the same time, courts continue to set precedents on new workplace issues, such as sexual harassment.

But the bottom line can be found in this function's new name. Companies caught up in a *more* competitive marketplace simply cannot afford to ignore their most precious resource: people. Even in the throes of continued streamlining and restructuring, companies will funnel more resources into employment-assistance programs and comprehensive training and retraining.

In the event of further layoffs, company-paid outplacement services soften the blow by helping displaced workers get back on their feet. Human resources is where it all comes together.

In-house or outplacement

Generally, *human resources managers* oversee three main areas: bringing the best people into the company, retaining current employees, and easing the way for employees displaced by a layoff or reorganization.

In medium- and large-sized companies, human resources managers oversee a staff of specialists as well as outside consultants, such as *recruiters*.

To attract and retain the best and brightest recruits, most companies must focus on offering competitive compensation and benefits packages. *Benefits specialists* and *compensation specialists* handle the highly technical details, such as gathering the necessary data, evaluating new programs, and preparing statutory reports.

Once an employee is on board with a company, *training managers* and *employee assistance program (EAP) counselors* make sure his or her skills and knowledge are updated and provide an outlet for discussing personal problems and finding treatments for addictions that can undermine job performance.

Many human resources managers help their companies maneuver continuing mergers and layoffs by extending a range of outplacement and career counseling resources to displaced employees.

Industry snapshot

Over the past 15 years, corporate America has learned—sometimes the hard way—that issues that affect workers can also significantly affect the bottom line. For better or for worse, these issues go far beyond equal pay to the heart of the corporate culture. A mania for mergers during the 1980s created more than a few cultural mismatches that threatened the ultimate success of the resulting businesses. The changing role of women and the influx of minorities brought to light potentially explosive issues that might bury a company in lawsuits.

Human resources managers who stepped in time and again to successfully deal with potential disasters earned a new kind of credibility with senior executives.

Continued reorganizations and layoffs, as well as government standard-setting, will keep human resource specialists in demand for some time to come.

Trends to track

Retaining employees. Turnover can be expensive. So can burning out your best people. In this current tight labor market, watch for innovative new programs aimed at retaining quality people. For example, computer maker Sun Microsystems hired "get a life" counselors to coach workaholics on setting personal leisure goals as well as business goals. The company also offers employees who may be thinking of prospecting for new career opportunities access to individual career counseling. Each month about 250 people take advantage of the in-house program. Surprisingly, attrition among employees who go through career counseling is 3 percentage points lower than those who don't. Informational workshops and special perks—from telecommuting to sabbaticals—are in practice at other companies.

Self-service HR. Much of the paperwork associated with human resources—such as enrolling in a 401(k) plan or requesting vacation—is now handled online at many midsize to large companies. Self-service resources and transactions via the company intranet give employees greater control over personal information from anywhere in the world while taking the clerical burden off of the HR support staff. In some companies, employees can also log on to view past performance reviews and current work targets, enroll in training, and apply for internal jobs.

International focus. As U.S. companies continue to go multinational, they are recruiting HR professionals with solid experience recruiting multicultural talent and administering human resources for a global workforce. For example, Wang & Li Asia Resources, a San Francisco executive recruiting firm, specializes in matching junior- to mid-level managers with companies doing business in the Pacific Rim and elsewhere abroad. Asian-Americans who have a Western education and training, speak a second language, and have a grasp of how to do business in an Asian culture are especially hot commodities for this recruiting niche.

Outplacement services come of age. Layoffs and reorganizations are a way of life. So more companies are softening the blow by providing outplacement resources for the "victims." More and more, these services are becoming part of a standard severance package for middle managers and hourly employees. Companies wish to paint a sympathetic image, but also depend on outplacement services to reduce the risk of lawsuits brought by displaced workers.

Old standards...and still winners

Human resources managers. The size and type of a company will determine the size and complexity of its human resources department. Small companies may employ one manager and outsource some functions such as recruiting to consultants or firms. HR managers and consultants are often called upon to make presentations on new benefits to employees, listen to individual grievances, handle sensitive issues, such as high turnover, and plan a range of special programs from "brown bag" lunchtime seminars to executive retreats. Many people in companies enter as human resources generalists.

Compensation specialists. By monitoring salary trends, a compensation specialist can help companies or clients bring salaries in line with competitive salaries paid for similar jobs throughout the industry. This area often deals with complex issues that are not easily resolved. For example, if salaries for top M.B.A. students have been increasing at an average annual rate of 6 to 8 percent, while merit raises for current employees have been running at 3 to 5 percent, a newly hired M.B.A. can earn as much—if not more—than an experienced co-worker. Simply raising the salaries of experienced people would create a salary discrepancy between departments. Compensation specialists may suggest developing compensation packages made up of bonuses, commissions, and/or stock options to more closely link compensation to performance.

Benefits specialists. The rising cost of health care and more complex options for retirement are just two of the challenges that benefits specialists handle. In analyzing a wide variety of health care solutions, they may present a range of possibilities from asking for employee contributions to providing more cost-effective options such as managed care programs that provide health care services in exchange for a guaranteed flow of business. Equally complex retirement programs require a specialized knowledge of tax laws and state and federal guidelines. Benefits specialists deal with issues concerning when employees should be able to access their money without tax penalties and how much the company should commit to matching employee contributions.

Management development specialists. Management development specialists concentrate on making the most of a company's employee pool by providing or contracting ongoing training and setting standards for performance reviews. Some teach employees new skills, such as how to operate a word processor or prepare a budget. Others focus on management issues, such as motivating, disciplining, and managing different kinds of people. Performance evaluation is their key area of expertise. Using information supplied by line managers, management development specialists map out career paths that clearly define the skills necessary for advancement. They may also develop standards to guide managers through the evaluation process itself in an effort to eliminate personalities and politics from the promotion process.

Recruiters. In a tight job market, experienced recruiters who are skilled at making appropriate matches are worth their weight in gold to the companies they serve. Sometimes known as "headhunters," recruiters specialize in placing management and technical people in available jobs in specific industries. Much of their prospecting and initial interviewing can be done by telephone, so about 25 percent are self-employed.

A new generation of opportunities

HR consultant. A new generation of human resources specialists and consulting firms are offering their expertise on a contractual basis to companies that can't afford to staff full-time training and development programs or that need help administering complex employee benefits and compensation programs. Long-term temporary workers and contractors—one in 10 workers—may be part of the next wave of employment litigation. If temps or contractors are reclassified as employees, a company could be required to pay retroactive benefits. This is just the type of issue that spurs HR managers into action—by educating managers on how to deal with outside contractors legally. Some are hiring outside staffing agencies to help manage temporary workforces.

Employee assistance program (EAP) counselors. Employee assistance programs provide a safe and confidential resource for employees coping with problems such as debt, substance abuse, difficult family matters, and stress. Working in the human resources department, an agency, or in private practice, an EAP counselor provides individual counseling and can recommend appropriate treatment. By reaching out to valuable employees in this way, a company can limit long-term productivity losses.

Outplacement services counselors. Employees who have been "displaced" by companies turn to outplacement counselors for a listening ear, concrete advice, and the resources necessary to launch and maintain a successful job search. Counselors typically help clients deal with a range of emotions and maintain momentum during what may become a long and lonely job hunt. After a careful review of the client's employment background, counselors develop a comprehensive job search plan, including advice on interviewing and salary negotiations. Senior-level managers may take advantage of personal offices and secretarial support. Middle managers may participate in a group outplacement workshop focused on resume preparation and job-search techniques. Hourly workers work with counselors to write or update their resumes and practice interview skills.

Outplacement services marketers. Of course all of this support comes with a price tag attached. It's up to outplacement services marketers to convince human resources managers or vice presidents to invest from 12 to 15 percent of a displaced employee's salary in his or her job search. Outplacement services can become quite expensive for companies when layoffs happen at the executive level. The challenge for marketers in this field is the same as it is for people who sell any big-ticket product or service.

The difference is that many are introducing the concept and advantages of outplacement services to companies that have never used them. The key to success is developing an overall strategy that fits the needs of individual companies. As the field matures and competition gets tougher, many outplacement services marketers are unbundling their services to offer an array of services tailored to a variety of budgets.

Career counselors. Career counselors do for people what appraisers do for diamonds—they assess an individual's strengths, facets, flaws, and marketable assets. Career counselors administer achievement tests to determine a client's untapped aptitude. By combining test results with an assessment of the individual's education, training, work history, interests, personality, and skills, they can derive a composite of that individual's ideal career. Career counselors may also help people develop job hunting skills, revamp their resumes, and hone their interviewing techniques.

Do you have what it takes?

In general, human resources professionals need a mix of people skills and technical knowledge. Human resources managers must be able to build credibility with employees, line managers, and CEOs by identifying and solving a range of problems. They should be as comfortable discussing issues one-on-one as they are giving formal presentations to introduce new benefits.

Compensation and benefits specialists must blend quantitative skills, such as advanced math and statistics, with the communication skills necessary to present data and offer suggestions.

In addition to being a good judge of character, a successful recruiter should be self-confident and motivated to make many cold calls. It takes a certain blend of tact and tenacity to develop relationships between companies and prospective recruits.

An outplacement services counselor's strong suit is listening. Often clients arrive upset and need to vent their frustrations. Personal experience can be an excellent way to establish initial contact. An interest in helping others manage their careers is essential. Outplacement services marketers should be assertive enough to get in to see a corporate vice president or human resources manager and persuasive enough to close the sale.

Education and training

Human resources managers may start out with a bachelor's degree in business, but a master's degree is the key to executive-level positions. While there are prestigious graduate programs in human resources, recruiters tend to favor M.B.A.s because they give managers a broad-based business perspective in line with other company managers. Graduate study in industrial or labor relations is increasingly important for human resources professionals working for large corporations that employ union workers.

Benefits and compensations specialists often earn a bachelor's degree in math or accounting. But because the benefits area is dominated by finance and tax issues, entry-level applicants might consider going on to earn an M.B.A. or law degree.

Management development specialists should earn a Ph.D. in industrial and organizational psychology. Consulting firms look for experienced individuals with strong writing and presentation skills.

EAP counselors should earn a bachelor's or master's degree in social welfare, as well as having experience as a counselor or licensed therapist. In addition to the ability to assess a range of conditions—from alcoholism to Alzheimer's disease—they should be familiar with appropriate resources for treatment.

Outplacement services marketers should have experience selling expensive products or services to corporate clients. Some former recruiters have successfully stepped into this field.

Outplacement services counselors may have a variety of backgrounds. Many have a master's degree or Ph.D. in psychology, or have held human resources positions. Counselors also need to have an in-depth understanding of many different industries and be knowledgeable about job search strategies.

For many specialized jobs and managerial positions, previous experience is a plus. Even entry-level workers should have some internship experience. Staying up-to-date on management trends and workplace legislation is important as well.

Recruiters should have three or more years of experience working in the field they are recruiting in.

Career counselors should hold a master's degree in career counseling. Most accredited programs require 48 to 60 semester hours of graduate study in addition to supervised clinical experience in counseling.

Professional licensing and certification

The Employee Assistance Professionals Association administers a certification exam.

Contract workers must be certified by the outplacement firm and then complete one or two weeks of training.

Many career counselors are nationally certified by the National Board for Certified Counselors (NBCC), which grants the general practice credential, "National Certified Counselor." Certification requires a master's degree in counseling, at least two years of supervised professional counseling, and a passing grade on NBCC's Examination for Licensure and Certification. To maintain certification, counselors must complete 100 hours of acceptable continuing education credits every five years.

Tips on breaking in

Look for friendly ground. Some companies are more committed to progressive human resources policies than others. Look for companies with a reputation for supporting human resources and that are also financially healthy and expanding.

Use your experience. Professionals with experience in business, government, education, social services administration, and the military often find it easy to move into senior-level human resources management.

Build credibility first. Recent graduates often find it difficult to establish credibility in outplacement services because their clients typically have 20 or more years of experience. Many counselors start as part-time contract workers for outplacement firms, filling in during peak periods. Contract workers are often elevated to full-time status when business expands.

Career path

Human resources managers often enter formal or on-the-job training programs in which they learn how to classify jobs, interview applicants, or administer benefits. With experience, they may advance to managerial positions and oversee a major element in human resources, such as compensation.

The key to career progress for human resources managers is establishing relationships and gaining credibility with line managers throughout the company.

Compensation, benefits, and management development specialists typically start as analysts, assisting human resource or management development supervisors with portions of a project. Three to five years later, they may take on larger portions of a project and begin to supervise other staff.

With 10 to 15 years of experience, supervisors can be promoted to director or vice-president of human resources.

Compensation specialists often start out with human resources consulting firms and then move into larger corporations where opportunities for advancement are better.

Outplacement services counselors and marketers often bring experience from other fields (such as human resources or sales) to their first job at an outplacement services firm.

After beginning as an associate, outplacement services marketers may be promoted to vice president in as little as two years. The title of vice president is meant primarily to establish credibility with high-level corporate prospects.

The title of senior vice president indicates responsibility for a particular function, such as marketing, program development, or administration. The executive vice president almost always comes from the marketing side of the business. A few large firms have regional managers who are responsible for the activities of as many as a dozen offices.

A sizable number of outplacement services professionals leave their firms to go out on their own.

Career counselors can advance to supervisory positions within firms. Some move into consulting, teaching, or start a private practice of their own.

How much can you earn?

Salaries for human resources managers vary with the size of the company, the complexity of the job, and their level of responsibility. The average at a small company is from $50,000 to $72,000. At a medium-size company, the range is from $80,000 to $132,000. Vice presidents at large corporations can earn more than $200,000 a year.

Entry-level salaries for compensation, benefits, and management development specialists range from $25,000 to $48,000, depending on their education. In five to eight years, they can earn from $40,000 to $75,000. Top salaries average $90,000, however, consultants in these areas can earn more than $250,000 a year.

EAP counselors working inside a company earn an average of $42,000 to $60,000. Counselors in private practice or who direct the function for Fortune 500 companies can earn $100,000 or more.

Career and outplacement services counselors start in the $40,000 to $50,000 range. With five years of experience, they can earn $55,000 to $65,000. Few earn more than $75,000.

Contract workers in the outplacement services field are paid a per diem, ranging from $300 to $500.

Outplacement services marketers' incomes depend on their productivity. The average salary range is from $35,000 to $45,000, plus bonuses. However, experienced marketers can earn $65,000 to $80,000. Six-figure incomes are usually restricted to owners and managers of multiple offices within a large firm.

Recruiters charge from 20 to 40 percent of the first-year earnings of the professionals they place. Some work on contingency, others on retainer. They collect 30 percent of their total fee upon acceptance of the search, 30 percent in 30 days, and 30 percent at the end of 60 days. Executive recruiters who conduct an average of 15 searches a year can make more than $100,000.

HR consultants start at $35,000 to $45,000. Senior consultants can earn $150,000 to $250,000 per year.

Where will you work?

Human resources managers, compensation, benefits, and management development specialists, and EAP counselors are employed in consulting firms and companies in virtually every industry, primarily in the private sector.

The outplacement services field is still young and ripe for a growing number of small firms serving local companies. Check your local yellow pages or *Directory of Outplacement Consulting Firms*.

Recruiters may work for an executive search firm. However, many are self-employed.

Career counselors may work for colleges, companies, counseling firms, or in private practice.

Job Profile

Kathleen Armstrong, compensation analyst

What are your general responsibilities?

My official job summary (on my job description) states: "Perform professional-level administrative and analytical duties to maintain and administer company compensation policies." That means that I keep job descriptions and grades up to date by conducting audits to analyze duties and responsibilities. I also write and analyze any new job descriptions the company may need. I maintain, update, and administer DHL's salary program. I help line management on any compensation issues they may have. I participate in and conduct salary surveys as well.

How long have you been in this business?

I've been in HR as a professional for approximately three years. I spent one year as a generalist and two years in compensation.

I also spent three years in college running the HR department of one of the dining facilities on campus. I did all of the HR-type duties for student employees—from hiring to firing, payroll to policy writing and administration—everything. That's what got me interested in HR as a career in the first place. Although it wasn't "professional-level" experience, I usually mention it on resumes and interviews because it was still very valuable experience.

How many years of education do you have?

I have a bachelor's degree in business with two concentrations in finance and management.

How many hours a week do you typically work?

My work week varies, depending on the time of year. During salary planning time (from August through December) I can expect to work anywhere from 40 to 55 hours per week—sometimes more. During the rest of the year (assuming there are no large projects going on) my workweek typically stays between 40 and 45 hours per week.

What are your hours on a typical work day?

I usually work from 7 or 7:30 a.m. until 4:30 or 5 p.m.

How big is the company you work for?

DHL has 10,954 employees across the nation.

Do you have professional certification (and do you need it)?

There is no professional certification required for my position, although I am working towards becoming a Certified Compensation Professional through the American Compensation Association. This certification is recognized throughout the United States by compensation professionals and will benefit my career. Many companies look for it when recruiting, but don't require it for hiring.

How did you get your current job?

My job was listed on the Society for Human Resources Management Web site.

What's your typical day like?

I honestly don't have a typical day. I cannot say that from 8 to 8:30 I do one thing and from 9 to 9:30 a.m. I do another. Many of us have our 15- to 20-minute coffee break together. During that time, I hear more about what is going on in the company then I do the rest of the day! The rest of my day is typically spent in my cube working on surveys, salary planning, job descriptions, or market analysis. If any of these projects need to be communicated, I may have a meeting with line managers.

What are your career aspirations?

In general, I'd like to continue my career in Human Resources. I don't know if that necessarily means that I'll continue in compensation specifically. Within the next few years I'd like to get some more general HR experience. From there I'll probably decide whether or not to stay general or to focus entirely on compensation.

What kind of people do you think would do especially well in your job role?

Any job in Human Resources requires good people skills. This means good communication skills, tactfulness, a concern for people, and also a view of the big picture. Anyone who gets too bogged down in his or her specific job will not do well in HR. In compensation, an individual has to have a logical/analytical mind. One would need to be able to analyze data but also see where that data fits into what their ultimate goal is. Compensation is a great career for someone who likes numbers and analysis, but doesn't want to miss out on the overall impact that will have on a company.

What do you like most about your job?

Using data analysis to back up a theory I may have about how to pay people best.

What do you like least?

Writing job descriptions.

What are some common misconceptions about your job/profession/industry?

Many people who don't know what really goes on in HR believe that the HR group is the "police," here to say no to all requests. In fact, a good HR group is one that can partner up with line management to not only come up with good solutions to problems, but provide programs that will make a company a great place to work.

What is the best way to going about landing a job like yours?

Check out any HR-oriented Web sites for entry-level positions. It's sometimes difficult to get that first job in HR, so many times one must start out as an HR assistant of some sort. A bit of experience in that type of job will go a long way in getting your foot in the door.

Resources

Human resources consulting firms

Hay Group Inc.
Worldwide Headquarters
The Wanamaker Building
100 Penn Square East
Philadelphia, PA 19107-3388
(215)861-2000
Fax: (215)861-2111
www.haygroup.com

William M. Mercer, Inc.
201 3rd Street, NW, Suite 1450
Albuquerque, NM 87102
(505)243-1377
Fax: (505)243-1760
www.wmmercer.com

Hewitt Associates L.L.C.
c/o Orlando Opportunities
100 Half Day Road
Lincolnshire, IL 60069
www.hewittassoc.com

Corporations with excellent reputations for human resources

Apple Computer, Inc.
1 Infinite Loop
Cupertino, CA 95014
(408)996-1010
www.apple.com

Coca-Cola
P.O. Drawer 1734
Atlanta, GA 30301
(404)676-2121
www.thecoca-colacompany.com

NationsBank Corp.
100 N. Tryon St.
Charlotte, NC 28255
(704)386-8200

Procter & Gamble
P.O. Box 599
Cincinnati, OH 45201
(513)983-1100
www.pg.com

Union Carbide
39 Old Ridgebury Rd.
Danbury, CT 06817
(203)794-2000

Human resources industry associations

American Society for Training and Development
1640 King Street
Box 1443
Alexandria, VA, 22313-2043
(703)683-8100
Fax: (703)683-8103
www.astd.org

American Compensation Association
14040 N. Northsight Boulevard
Scottsdale, AZ 85260
(480)951-9191
Fax: (480)483-8352
E-mail: aca@acaonline.org
www.acaonline.org

**International Foundation
of Employee Benefit Plans**
18700 W. Bluemound Rd.
P.O. Box 69
Brookfield, WI 53008-0069
(262)786-6710, ext. 8216
Fax: (262)786-8670
Faxback: (888) 217-5960
www.ifebp.org

**Association of Executive
Search Consultants**
500 Fifth Avenue, Suite 930
New York, NY 10110
(212)398-9556
www.aesc.org

**Society for Human Resource
Management**
1800 Duke Street
Alexandria, VA 22314
(703)548-3440
Fax: (703)535-6490
Email: shrm@shrm.org
www.shrm.org

Employment Management Association
1333 Corporate Drive, Suite 117
Irving, TX 95038
(972)550-9116
www.dfwema.org

Human resource industry magazines

HR Magazine
Society for Human Resources
Management
1800 Duke Street
Alexandria, VA 22314
(703)548-3440
Fax: (703)535-6490
www.shrm.org/docs/HRmagazine.html

Outplacement industry associations

**National Association
of Career Development Consultants**
1707 L St., NW, Suite 333
Washington, DC 20036
(202)452-9102

Outplacement industry directory

*Directory of Outplacement Consulting
Firms*
Kennedy Publications
Templeton Road
Fitzwilliam, NH 03447
(603)585-6544

Chapter 10

Law & Legal Services
The new business of jurisprudence

Corporate counsel
Environmental lawyer
Estate lawyer
Information resource manager
Intellectual property lawyer
Labor/employment lawyer
Law firm administrator
Law firm marketer
Legal public relations specialist
Legal secretary
Paralegal
Mediation/arbitration lawyer

Forecast

According to the U.S. Bureau of Labor Statistics, competition should be intense among an increasing number of law school graduates. Opportunities for lawyers will be concentrated in areas with a growing demand for legal services, such as intellectual property and labor law. The challenge of keeping a cap on court cases and expenses has opened up new opportunities for mediation/arbitration lawyers, as well as legal services professionals, such as paralegals, legal secretaries, and law firm administrators. Prospects continue to be excellent for marketing and public relations specialists with knowledge of the legal profession.

Growth

Employment of paralegals is expected to grow much faster than average—ranking this job among the 10 fastest growing occupations in the economy through the year 2008, according to the latest BLS employment projections.

The number of jobs for paralegals will grow 62 percent by 2008. Employment of lawyers and legal secretaries is expected to grow about as fast as the average.

Bankruptcies and white collar crime are on the rise. Sexual harassment settlements are awarded in the millions of dollars. Disputes over the protection of the local water supply and intellectual property are defining new areas of law. Indeed, we have become a litigious society, at least in part because our personal and professional lives continue to grow more complex.

Law often reflects our changing social mores and business practices. Verdicts break ground and send messages about important issues—from employment practices to environmental concerns. And despite all those bad lawyer jokes we love to snicker at, many of us can't get enough of courtroom drama—be it on *The Practice* or real-life Court TV.

The practice of law promises to remain prestigious and high-paying over the long term—but look for a new twist. Law firms once able to rise above common business practices, such as marketing and cost containment, are waking up to the fact that they need to act more like the businesses they represent to operate in a more competitive world.

Firm, corporation, private practice, and government work

About seven out of 10 of the country's 622,000 practicing *lawyers* work in law firms or in private practice. Only about 2 percent choose to go it alone. Law is too complex and competitive to make that feasible for most. The remaining lawyers work in government and for companies as in-house counsel.

Private-sector lawyers can be either *transactional lawyers* or *litigators*. Transactional lawyers deal with a wide range of business issues, such as corporate financing, contracts, acquisitions, bankruptcy, among others. Litigators wade into the situations that could land their clients in court—from breach of contract to employment-related problems.

If you've got your sights set on pulling down a six-figure salary working for blue chip clients at one of the country's prestige firms, get ready for intense competition. The hiring process is intense. And once inside, you'll be wrestling for a partnership with 150 to 2,000 other lawyers. At a middle-tier firm, you're more likely to find opportunities to specialize in a certain type of client or practice, such as intellectual property, environmental, or labor law. With several years of experience, you may want to move into the ranks of a client company as *in-house counsel* or do a stint in city government as a *prosecutor* or *public defender*. Salaries are lower, but not as low as many people think. And despite the low compensation, competition for these jobs is intense.

Lawyers may be the most visible members of the profession, but it is *paralegals* who will have the brightest prospects. Working in newly cost-conscious law firms, paralegals help lawyers conduct time-consuming research and prepare court cases. Because they are also trained to draft a wide variety of legal documents at rates far lower than a law firm would charge, paralegals are also in demand in corporate legal departments, insurance companies, real estate and title insurance firms, government agencies, consumer groups, and courts.

Like paralegals, *legal secretaries* are coming into their own as right arms to busy lawyers. Many specialize in preparing legal papers under the supervision of an attorney, including summonses, complaints, motions, responses, and subpoenas. As law firms continue to display a new business sense, doors are also opening to *marketing* and *public relations specialists* and *administrators*.

An alarmingly high tide of pending court cases is bringing more mediation/arbitration lawyers forward to help companies, government agencies, and families reach a settlement, often outside of the judge's operation.

Industry snapshot

While new laws and judicial interpretations of existing laws promise a steady stream of business for most lawyers and paralegals, the economy is bound to have a dampening effect in some areas of law and legal services.

The demand for discretionary legal services, such as drafting wills and handling real estate transactions, tends to decline during a recession. Corporations tighten their belts and are less inclined to sue. On the other hand, the excesses of the 1980s prompted a rise in bankruptcies and real estate "workouts" to help real estate developers dispose of office complexes and other misguided ventures. Meanwhile, cutbacks at large firms have made it more difficult to become a partner. As a result, more lawyers are building careers at smaller "boutique" firms that specialize in one or more areas, such as small business, tax, or family law.

In addition, corporations have begun to recognize the cost advantages of employing in-house counsel to handle much of the work that was previously given to law firms. As a result, billings have leveled off for law firms. Hence there is a new business sense that includes a sharper focus on the productivity of individual lawyers, even partners.

Trends to track

Don't litigate, mediate. State and federal courts in California now require that parties to civil litigation first go through some type of alternative dispute resolution (ADR). Many companies stipulate that employees, customers, or business partners must agree to mediation or arbitration. A study by Cornell University and PricewaterhouseCoopers found that 88 percent of the top 1,000 companies have encouraged disputing parties to try to reach a compromise through an independent agent or mediator. Out of these, 79 percent used arbitration, where parties agree to present their cases to a private judge or panel and live by the resulting decision. The economic benefits are evident. For mediation cases, the filing fee is $150 per party and the hourly charge is $190 to $450 per hour. For arbitration, the filing fee is $500 for settlements up to $10,000 and $7,000 for cases involving settlements from $1 million to $5 million.

Temporary lawyers. Some recent law school graduates who are unable to find permanent positions are turning to the growing number of legal temporary staffing firms, which place attorneys in short-term jobs until they are able to secure full-time positions. This service allows companies to hire lawyers on an "as needed" basis and allows beginning lawyers to develop practical skills while looking for permanent positions.

The lawyer-sleuth. When employee complaints of sexual harassment or discrimination surfaced in companies in the past, human resource managers typically followed up with an investigation. However, a landmark ruling by the California Supreme Court in 1998 brought the quality of these internal investigations into question. The bottom line: Even if a company comes to the wrong conclusion in responding to harassment charges, it can defend itself by showing the conclusion came out of a reasonable and good-faith investigation. As result, many companies are looking beyond their own payrolls for investigative help. But when a complaint could mushroom into a several-million-dollar lawsuit, not just any investigator will do. Employment lawyers have the legal expertise to interview all parties and witnesses and examine relevant documents, submitting a report with a range of possible actions.

Old standards...and still winners

Paralegals. Paralegals help lawyers prepare cases for court by researching facts and precedents, obtaining records, summarizing depositions, and preparing legal arguments. They also draft agreements and prepare corporate tax returns. The majority of paralegals work for private law firms. However, many new opportunities are opening up in government-funded legal services for the poor and elderly. Insurance companies and other businesses have a consistent need for paralegal services as well.

Corporate counsel. According to a major consulting company quoted in *The Wall Street Journal,* it is more difficult to become a partner at a law firm these days. The corporate track is luring more law firm associates with three to six years of experience to handle a range of legal responsibilities— from fighting lawsuits to translating complex labor law for human resources managers. Lawyers with experience in securities and transactions are in high demand as mergers and acquisitions continue to dominate.

Estate lawyers. Helping clients preserve their money by creating and managing trusts and estates lacks the glamour of litigation. However, this area offers less competition than most.

Labor/employment lawyers. New legislation, coupled with an increasing public awareness of issues such as sexual harassment, workplace violence, and labor management conflicts, brought work-related litigation to the forefront in the 1990s. In the new millennium, employers will face a staggering number of rules and regulations and will need the help of lawyers who are up-to-date on far-reaching labor and employment laws.

A new generation of opportunities

Environmental lawyer. Environmental law challenges lawyers to prosecute or defend companies accused of noncompliance with federal environmental standards, such as those for asbestos removal, waste disposal, land acquisition, and pollution. Currently there is an acute shortage of lawyers in this area. And with Congress continuing to tinker with regulations, it will become essential for lawyers to have up-to-the-minute knowledge. For example, the influence of the North American Free Trade Agreement (NAFTA) and the European Community has already given environmental law a big push.

Intellectual property lawyers. The boom in software sales underlined the monetary value of intellectual property, throwing this field wide open to lawyers with expertise in laws concerning patents, trademarks, copyrights, trade secrets, and false advertising. For example, online systems have recently introduced electronic publication rights and multimedia products have given creative people, such as musicians and their publishers, claims to additional royalty revenues.

Legal secretaries. With highly specialized knowledge of legal terminology and procedures, these professionals are equipped to do much more than take a letter and fetch coffee. Most legal secretaries specialize in preparing correspondence and legal papers, such as summonses, complaints, motions, responses, and subpoenas under the supervision of a lawyer. They also may review legal journals and assist in other ways with legal research, such as verifying quotes and citations in legal briefs.

Law firm marketers. These days law firms find themselves in the uncomfortable position of competing for the same clients, as well as for a small pool of top law school graduates. According to an expert quoted in *The Wall Street Journal,* up to 75 percent of all law firms use public relations consultants. And as the regulations governing how lawyers can market their services relax, in-house marketing experts are soft-selling a firm's image and legal services to prospective clients. As clients become more sophisticated and corporations rely increasingly on in-house counsel, large law firms and specialized boutiques find themselves prospecting for clients. Working in-house, legal marketers sell a firm's image through printed materials, informational seminars, and special events such as speaking engagements for prominent partners.

Information resources manager. A growing number of paralegals will combine computer and legal research skills to significantly increase their efficiency.

Law firm administrators. Lawyers who looked down their noses at business administrators in the past are welcoming them with open arms as cost cutting and more efficient operations become top priority. Most administrators set up and manage accounting or database functions. In a day when it's more difficult for associates to become partners, administrators are being offered partnerships in some top firms.

Public relations specialists. Law firms are squeamish about advertising, so they prefer to hire agencies to tread the fine line of promoting the law firm or its partners without appearing pushy. Experience in law or a related area is a plus.

Mediation/arbitration lawyers. A growing number of judges and lawyers are brushing up their negotiating skills and turning to alternative dispute resolution (ADR) as a quicker, cheaper, less painful way to come to legal agreement outside of the courtroom. Rather than follow rigid formal procedures, mediation and arbitration lawyers focus on getting results. Best of all, the decision is final. There are no appeals.

Do you have what it takes?

Lawyers, paralegals, information resources managers, and legal secretaries should be detail-oriented and able think logically. They also should have excellent writing and speaking skills.

Paralegals, information resources managers, and legal secretaries should also be skilled researchers and thorough investigators.

Lawyers should be assertive negotiators, as well as tactful counselors. For example, intellectual property lawyers must feel comfortable working with creative clients. Mediation/arbitration lawyers need to move disputing parties to a quick and final resolution in the absence of formal legal procedures.

Marketers and public relations specialists need knowledge of, or ideally, a background in law. (See Marketing, Advertising, & Public Relations, page 195, for more details.)

People who work the law profession often spend 12 to 14 hours a day working under the stress of deadlines, decisions, and billable hours.

Education and training

About 36,000 new lawyers enter the field each year, so competition for the best jobs is tough. Most lawyers enter law school for three years to receive their J.D. (juris doctor) right after receiving an undergraduate degree, usually in English, history, or journalism. A number of law schools have night or part-time divisions that usually require four years of study.

Your career options will be initially determined by which law school you go to and how well you do. The top firms recruit only from the top-ranked law schools and interview only students who graduate near the top 10 percent of their class. All law schools approved by the American Bar Association (ABA), except for those in Puerto Rico, require applicants to take the Law School Admission Test (LSAT). Review classes will help you become familiar with the format and content of the test.

Nearly all law schools require applicants to have certified transcripts sent to the Law School Data Assembly Service, which then sends applicants' LSAT scores and their standardized records of college grades to the law schools of their choice. Both this service and the LSAT are administered by the Law School Admission Council.

Your specialization also may determine which law school you choose. For example, if you want to specialize in intellectual property law, you should investigate the University of Houston, the John Marshall Law School in Chicago, and the Franklin Pierce Law Center in Concord, N.H. Nontechnical lawyers typically learn about technology on the job.

Labor/employment lawyers need to take courses in labor law. Estate lawyers need a knowledge of accounting. A new emphasis on the business of law has resulted in the emergence of joint M.B.A./J.D. graduate programs.

After graduation, lawyers must keep informed about legal and nonlegal developments that affect their practice. Currently, 37 states and jurisdictions mandate Continuing Legal Education (CLE). Many law schools and state and local bar associations provide continuing education courses that help lawyers stay abreast of recent developments. Some states award CLE credits to lawyers who participate in seminars on the Internet.

A bachelor's degree is now a standard prerequisite for paralegals. There are more than 800 formal paralegal training programs offered by four-year colleges and universities, law schools, community and junior colleges, business schools, and proprietary schools. Many paralegal training programs include an internship in a law office, corporate legal department, or government agency.

Contact the National Association of Legal Assistants (NALA) for schools and programs approved by the ABA. The ABA also offers a self-teaching cassette course, seminars, and library facilities. In addition to up-to-date computer skills necessary to conduct legal research, paralegals need continuing education to stay abreast of new developments in the law that affect their area of practice.

Because the field is relatively new, legal marketers tend to cross over from many other professionals backgrounds. Both in-house marketers and public relations specialists should combine knowledge of how law firms work and their knowledge of public relations and marketing practices. (See Marketing, Advertising, & Public Relations, page 195, for more details.)

Legal secretaries should complete a specialized training program through a community or business college. Many temporary help agencies provide formal training in computer and office skills.

Professional licensing and certification

Lawyers must be licensed to practice law or admitted to the bar association for the state in which they practice. Applicants for admission to the bar must pass a written examination. In most jurisdictions, applicants must also pass a separate written ethics examination. Lawyers who have been admitted to the bar in one jurisdiction may occasionally be admitted to the bar in another without taking an examination. Such lawyers can qualify if they meet that jurisdiction's standards of good moral character, and have a specified period of legal experience. Federal courts and agencies set their own qualifications for such certification.

With certain exceptions, graduates of schools that not approved by the ABA can pass the bar and practice only in the state or jurisdiction in which they received their law degree. Although there is no nationwide bar examination, 47 states, the District of Columbia, Guam, the Northern Mariana Islands, and the Virgin Islands require lawyers to pass a six-hour Multistate Bar Examination (MBE) as part of the bar examination. One-time performance examinations to test practical skills of beginning lawyers are required by eight states. (Contact the ABA for complete requirements.)

Although paralegals are not required to be certified, it helps their job prospects. The National Association of Legal Assistants (NALA) administers a two-day qualifying exam. Experienced paralegals who pass are designated a Certified Legal Assistant (CLA). The Paralegal Advanced Competency Exam, established in 1996 and administered through the National Federation of Paralegal Associations, offers professional recognition to paralegals with a bachelor's degree and at least two years of experience. Those who pass this examination may use the designation Registered Paralegal (RP).

Secretaries may become "Accredited Legal Secretaries" (ALS) from the Certifying Board of the National Association of Legal Secretaries. This organization also administers an examination to certify a legal secretary with three years of experience as a "Professional Legal Secretary" (PLS). Legal Secretaries International confers the title, "Board Certified Civil Trial Legal Secretary" in special areas, such as litigation or probate, to those who have five years of law-related experience and who can pass the examination.

Tips on breaking in

If you're not sure, stick a toe in the water. Too many disillusioned lawyers leave the profession after investing years in schooling. If you're even a little bit unsure about a career in law, become a paralegal. You'll quench you knowledge for law and get an insider's view of the legal profession. And if you're a star performer at a big firm, you may even find your law school education paid for.

Go local. If a top-ranked law school is beyond your reach, focus on the best schools near where you'd like to live and work. Local schools are often very effective in placing their graduates.

Join a study group. Because there is an overwhelming amount of reading, writing, and studying required in law school, it pays to hook up with a strong study group. You'll make lasting contacts while you boost your grade point average.

Work. The summer internships or clerkships after your first and second years at law school are very important. They allow you the opportunity to test out different firms and hopefully will result in an offer.

Go for the brass ring. Some firms have the reputation for promoting most of their associates whereas others promote only a few. Ask the recruiter who interviews you about the firm's policy before accepting an offer.

Corporate clout for women. This signals a dramatic shift in the balance in opportunities for female lawyers, who are already well represented.

Career path

A new bottom-line business orientation provides less security than the traditional law firm career track has in the past, but the structure is the same. Lawyers start out in firms doing research before taking on cases as an associate.

The time it takes to grab the brass ring—a partnership—can vary considerably. Few firms make partners of associates with less than eight years of experience. On the other hand, 12 years is considered lengthy. You can increase your odds of becoming a partner in the early years of your career by establishing credibility working with as many partners as you can. After that, bringing in new clients will bolster your chances.

Then again, some lawyers use their legal training in administrative or managerial positions in various departments of large corporations. A transfer from a corporation's legal department to another department often is viewed as a way to gain administrative experience and rise in the ranks of management.

Paralegals gain experience by progressively taking on more responsibility with less supervision. In large law firms, corporate legal departments, and government agencies, experienced paralegals may supervise other paralegals and clerical staff, as well as delegate work assigned by lawyers. Chances for advancement include promotion to managerial and law-related positions within the firm or corporate legal department. However, some paralegals find it easier to move to another law firm when seeking more responsibility or advancement. Some go to work for independent paralegal firms.

Legal secretaries generally advance to a more responsible secretarial position by promotion. Many legal secretaries become paralegals.

How much can you earn?

Lawyers and paralegals can make considerably more in the private sector than in government. Lawyers and partners in large, well-known law firms earn the most. Lawyers working in very small firms or as individual practitioners may start at $30,000, sometimes less.

Average starting salaries for lawyers range from $50,000 to $80,000. The median salary for all lawyers is about $70,000. Five to eight years into your career as a lawyer, you can be making from $70,000 to $120,000. Partners make from $120,000 into the millions at top national firms.

Paralegals start at an average $29,300. With five to eight years of experience they can make $40,000. Supervisors or specialists may earn from $45,000 to $75,000 supervising a large staff of paralegals. In addition to a salary, many paralegals receive an annual bonus, which averaged about $1,900 in 1995 according to the National Federation of Paralegal Associations. Salaries depend on education, training, experience, the type and size of the employer, and the geographic location of the job. Generally, paralegals who work for large law firms or in large metropolitan areas earn more than those who work for smaller firms or in less-populated regions.

Law firm marketers who supervise a staff of one or two can begin at $46,000. In about five years, they may make $50,000 to $55,000; in 10 years, $62,000 to $66,000. Those who supervise a large marketing department in a top firm can make $84,000 a year.

Legal administrators can earn between $35,000 and $100,000 depending on the size of the firm. Accounting managers and data processing managers can earn between $30,000 and $60,000.

Experienced legal secretaries can make $50,000 to $70,000 a year.

Where will you work?

Private law firms will continue to be the largest employers of legal professionals. A growing array of other organizations, such as corporate legal departments, insurance companies, real estate and title insurance firms, and banks, also hire legal staffs.

You can practice law anywhere you choose. Of course, there are a few exceptions. If you have a highly specialized practice, such as entertainment or investments, you may have to work in Los Angeles or New York.

For lawyers who wish to work independently, establishing a new practice will probably be easiest in small towns and expanding suburban areas, as long as an active market for legal services exists.

Job Profile

Matt Armanino, director of business development and legal affairs

What general responsibilities does your job encompass?
Primarily, I'm responsible for business development activities for a fast-growth, startup technology company. This includes developing strategic partnering relationships and indirect-channel distribution partnerships.
I'm also responsible for managing legal function and corporate legal compliance. In this area, my general responsibilities include corporate governance, intellectual property protection, and commercial transactions.

How many years have you been in this business?
I've been here for five years.

How many years of education do you have?
I have a B.A. and a J.D.

How many hours do you typically work per week?
60 to 70 hours per week.

What hours do you work on a typical day?
6 a.m. to 8 p.m.

How big is the company you work for?
Approximately 55 employees.

Have you earned professional certification?
Yes, I'm a member of the California Bar Association.

How did you get your job?
Through a network contact. A former employee of my last company is president of the company I'm working for now.

Please describe one of your "typical" days?
My days are very rarely typical of one another. In fact, my workdays vary greatly depending on whether I am on the road traveling, working from home, or working in the office.
When I'm on the road, I spend the majority of my time meeting with business partners and prospective partners, as well as customers and analysts.

When I work from home, I spend the majority of my time structuring and negotiating legal agreements, attending meetings via telephone, and developing business/market strategies.

When I'm in the office, my work is very similar to the work I do from home except that I spend several hours commuting to and from work and devote more time to in-person meetings with representatives from other companies and with other members of my company's management team.

What are your career aspirations?

To be an instrumental part in building a successful company and developing a new market. Ultimately, I'd like to start my own company or become a CEO or COO of a successful company.

What kind of people do really well at this business?

People who are creative, innovative, determined, well-organized, and focused will do well. You should be able to develop effective business strategies and execute against those strategies. You need to be a good communicator, a good listener, and an effective facilitator. You need to be able to multitask and set priorities. You need to be able to work well with others and be a creative problem-solver. You should also be evangelistic about the products or solutions that your company is commercializing.

What do you really like about your job?

I have the opportunity to make a meaningful impact on making this company a success. I also really enjoy working with and learning from other incredibly bright people in an energetic and fun work environment.

What do you dislike?

The job can be very time-consuming and, at times, the amount of work that needs to be done can become overwhelming. However, the positives far outweigh the negatives.

What is the biggest misconception about this job?

The thought that lawyers do not make good businesspeople because they are too risk-adverse.

How can someone get a job like yours?

Network, network, network. My background as a corporate attorney focusing on commercial transactions and negotiation and structuring strategic transactions helped me get this job. Experience in business development, product strategy, or product marketing is a plus. For me, it came down to hard work, good luck, and a willingness to take a risk with a startup company.

Resources

Legal associations

American Bar Association
750 N. Lake Shore Drive
Chicago, IL 60611
(800)285-2221
www.abanet.org

**American College of Law
Students' Bar Association**
1717 South State College Blvd., Suite 100
Anaheim, CA 92608
www.webedge1.com/sba.htm

The American Law Institute
4025 Chestnut Street
Philadelphia, PA 19104
(215)243-1600
Fax: (215)243-1664
www.ali.org

**The National Association
of Legal Assistants**
1516 S. Boston, Suite 200
Tulsa, OK 74119
(918)587-6828
Fax: (918)582-6772
www.nala.org

National Bar Association
1225 11th Street NW
Washington, DC 20001-4217
(202)842-3900
Fax: (202)289-6170
www.nationalbar.org

The National Lawyers Guild
126 University Place, 5th Floor
New York, N.Y. 10003
(212)627-2656
Fax: (212)627-2404
E-mail: nlgno@nlg.org
www.nlg.org

Legal magazines

ABA Journal
American Bar Association
750 N. Lake Shore Drive
Chicago, IL 60611
(312)988-6003

National Law Journal
105 Madison Ave., 8th Floor
New York, N.Y. 10016
Fax: (212)481-7923

Law directories

Attorney Yellow Pages
820 De La Bosque
Longwood, FL 32779
E-mail: info@ayponline.com
www.ayponline.com

Chapter 11

Marketing, Advertising, & Public Relations

The creative business of influence

Advertising account executive
Advertising copywriter
Technical writer
Direct response marketing specialist
Graphic designer
Marketing manager
Destination marketer
Financial services marketer
Law firm marketer
Outplacement services marketer
Special events marketer
Public relations manager
Law firm PR specialist
Environmental PR specialist
Web producer
Web designer
Web copywriter
Best Bets for Entrepreneurs:
Freelance graphic designer, Web designer, Freelance copywriter

Forecast

Marketing will continue to be a focal point for companies that want to stay competitive in a fast-paced global economy. Although PR budgets tend to rise and fall with the economy, look for overall improvement, along with a boom in opportunities within specialized areas, such as environmental issues and law.

Growth

According to the BLS, the number of jobs for advertising, marketing, and public relations managers will increase 23 percent through the year 2008. Look for explosive growth in Web-related occupations, especially in the short term.

Overview

It's Saturday afternoon and you're standing in an aisle of the local drug store, ready to reach for a new brand of deodorant soap...

Stop! What is compelling you to reach for this particular brand, rather than one of the half-dozen or so deodorant soaps stacked on the shelf beside it? It may be something as practical as price. But more likely, your choice is the end result of a complex marketing strategy that began with demographics and ended with that catchy slogan you can't get out of your head.

Closely related to brand image is public relations. As more companies are forced to deal with thorny issues like·environmental cleanup, as well as unforeseen crises, PR specialists will help them bid for and maintain the trust of a public that is much larger than any company's customer base.

Building brands, diffusing crises

In most companies, the process begins with the *marketing manager*. Using market research and data on customer preferences and buying patterns, marketing managers position their products and/or services in a way that will set them apart from the competition. The more alike the competition is—or the more confusing product technology seems to consumers—the tougher the job becomes.

Take soap again. Soap is soap is soap, right? Let's say that you can prove that your soap contains the most effective deodorant on the market. Now, who is likely to be most interested? People leading stressful lives. People with little time on their hands. People who want—who need—to make a good impression on other people. These are your customers.

Of course this is oversimplifying what is often a very complex process. Developing an effective marketing strategy is serious business, especially now that more products are flooding the marketplace and customer niches are getting smaller and more specialized. In fact, for most companies, an effective marketing strategy—borne out by an equally effective advertising campaign—will be essential to survival.

Once marketing has identified the product's distinctive features and potential customers, it's up to the advertising team to create and deliver a message that convinces them to buy your brand of soap over all the others.

Often, differences are established on an emotional level. Working closely with the marketing manager (or client) and a creative staff, *advertising account executives* and *direct response marketing specialists* try to develop a campaign that is relevant to prospective consumers and that integrates many types of media—especially the Internet.

Copywriters and *graphic designers,* many with specialized experience in Web communications, conspire to attract the attention of prospective customers by pairing humorous, everyday situations with a catchy slogan for radio and banner ads. They also create the theme that will appear on a host of marketing materials, from print brochures to product demos on CD-ROMs. Next season, you're searching for the next big idea. Part analysis and part mystery, marketing and advertising are stressful, but fun!

But what happens if one of the products you sell is tainted? The Tylenol poisoning scandal of 1982 is a case in point. Few consumers have forgotten the horror that accompanied the discovery of bottles of the painkiller tainted with a deadly poison for sale on drugstore shelves. That kind of media awareness could easily drive a company out of business. Public relations experts helped Johnson & Johnson weather the crisis without losing any of its market share.

As soon as the poisoned products were discovered, company executives responded to a panicked public by announcing that every bottle of Tylenol would be removed from store shelves, remanufactured in tablet form, and reissued only in tamper-resistant bottles. Quick and decisive action, as well as detailed, factual information, revealed a corporation intent on doing what was right. That is effective PR in action.

Public relations managers and *specialists* design public relations strategies that are both proactive and reactive. At their foundations is a plan for regularly informing the public of the company's good actions. This means announcing new products, customer service programs, and executive appointments through a variety of media. But it will take more than a barrage of press releases. Public relations managers may also advise CEOs to seek publicity for the company by sponsoring community works or developing info-ads that position the company as a socially responsible "citizen."

Chevron's "People Do" campaign was a powerful example of this kind of proactive public relations. In expensive advertising spots that look more like a National Geographic special than a plug for petroleum products, the company detailed its role in preserving endangered wildlife in the course of doing business.

Of course, in the event of an unforeseen crisis, a plan is also in place for taking quick action to stem the tide of damaging press. By working closely with senior management to develop a public relations strategy that is integrated in a company's mission statement, public relations managers can create a multifaceted campaign that positively affects a company's bottom line. Increasingly, PR specialists working in agencies or companies are addressing the needs of industries or professions facing change, such as law and financial services.

Industry snapshot

After cruising through the 1970s and 80s, many client-dependent advertising and public relations agencies were stopped cold by the recession. Some client companies trimmed marketing and advertising budgets to the bone. Agencies accustomed to an average annual increase in spending of 14 percent in the early 80s had to make do with about 4 percent by the early 90s. Between 1989 and 1991, advertising employment dropped 5.5 percent. As a result many small and medium-size agencies closed while others merged.

A recovering economy has set things back on track. After all, as long as there is a consumer market, there will be a demand for marketing and advertising. But as more products with shorter lifecycles are introduced, worldwide competition will be cutthroat. Quality will be a byword for product development. Customer satisfaction will make or break companies. And all of this will create the need for market-driven companies that can deliver innovative solutions to very specific market segments.

Increasingly sophisticated database technology allows marketing managers to target even more specialized niches of consumers who share not only similar demographics, but also interests and purchasing patterns. With the ability to merge information from various sources—from cash register scanners to Web site "hits"—marketing managers have already seen response rates in the double digits to promotions that once yielded only 2 percent. With more tools at their disposal, marketing and PR professionals are being held accountable for measurable, meaningful results.

Rather than competing themselves out of business, many companies are joining forces to share costs and customers. Alliances have already taken place between international companies, major U.S. competitors, and smaller companies. They range from sharing the costs of research and development to licensing new "co-branded" products, such as regional Friendly's ice cream flavored with York Peppermint Patties.

Finally, technology continues to revolutionize advertising and marketing campaigns. From multimedia to desktop publishing, holography to database marketing, the road ahead is ready to be explored by tech-savvy creative people.

Trends to track

Digital synergy. It is doubtful that the Internet will take the place of direct mail, broadcast, outdoor, or point-of-purchase media—at least not in our lifetime. But advertisers and marketers are finding that integrating digital communications extend, focus, and revitalize advertising and marketing campaigns. (See Entertainment & Sports on page 119 for more detail on how Hollywood is bringing people to theaters using the Internet.) Specialized Web sites, targeted e-mail, and e-newsletters are pushing media messages out further and faster than ever before. The dynamic quality of electronic communications erases much of the time and expense involved in testing and revising campaigns.

Getting closer to customers. The Internet has the power to collect increasingly specific details about millions of consumers. Savvy "e-tailers" are using sophisticated software to mine the data they collect in order to personalize their marketing efforts in unprecedented ways. Although this can be effective, it also raises privacy issues that will continue to be addressed well into the new millennium.

For example, when **Amazon.com** started featuring "bestseller lists" sorted by the ZIP codes of companies and colleges that customers were ordering from, the results made interesting reading in themselves. For example, who would have thought *101 Nights of Grrreat Sex* would be among the top ten most ordered books at National Semiconductor, a computer chip maker? However harmless it seemed at the outset, this particular marketing ploy disturbed some customers. As a result, **Amazon.com** now allows customers to "opt out" of having data about their purchasing patterns collected while they're shopping online.

Meanwhile, high-tech companies continue to look for ways to tap into our buying power. As everyday appliances get smarter and more able to respond to our needs, they may also collect more information about our personal habits and feed it to marketers.

Tapping into kids' buying power. Kids under 13 now spend $25 billion a year—and influence another $200 billion of their parents' spending. This has inspired game and toy manufacturers to adopt creatively aggressive marketing plans that go well beyond traditional TV spots and print ads. Traveling Pokemon Game Boy tournaments can attract 5,000 to 15,000 kids in a single weekend. Toy Craze used its game called *Crazy Bones* to develop a math curriculum based on the U.S. Department of Education national mathematical requirements, which it then distributed to teachers. The company intends to spend 15 to 20 percent of its profits on this type of hands-on approach to marketing. The company also plans to send out teams to teach kids how to play the game at school soccer practices and YMCAs.

Old standards...and still winners

Marketing managers. "Market share" is the mantra for marketing managers working in companies of all sizes in almost every industry. Grabbing and maintaining a bigger piece of the pie means attracting new customers, as well as maintaining the loyalty of existing ones. To do this, marketing managers develop a strategy that will mesh product messages with the corporate mission. Marketing managers must be knowledgeable about direct market research, sales, promotion, and pricing. They also have to keep their eye on trends that could spark the development of a new product.

Working with advertising, direct marketing, and public relations agencies, marketing managers develop a comprehensive marketing strategy that meets customers and prospects on many fronts—from trade publications to trade shows to the Web. They use a wide range of tools, from corporate brochures to online demonstrations to support salespeople in the field. The pressure is on to boost sales. A bad call could cost a marketing manager his or her job.

In small firms, marketing can be the responsibility of one person, whereas large firms often offer enough products and services to warrant an entire marketing team.

See also *financial services marketers,* under Banking & Financial Services; *destination marketers,* under Travel & Hospitality; *law firm marketers,* under Law & Legal Services; *outplacement services marketers,* under Human Resources & Employee Services; and *special events marketers,* under Entertainment & Sports.

Advertising account executives. The most successful account executive does more than bring in new clients. As a liaison between the marketing manager or client company and the creative team within an advertising agency, an account executive should be a marketing expert with a feel for design. Increasingly, agencies are looking for people with broad-based experience in related fields, such as public relations and sales promotion, who can help clients develop and refine their marketing strategies.

Some client companies diversify their advertising accounts by assigning media and creative work to different agencies. Other companies are seeking out full-service marketing/advertising agencies that specialize in "bundling" a single message by using a range of media, from billboards to television to trade shows to the World Wide Web. This brand of one-stop shopping can substantially strengthen the final impact on prospective customers.

Advertising copywriters. These professional wordsmiths craft the sentences and slogans that catch a prospective customer's attention. They also tailor an advertising message to specific types of media as well as target markets. In most advertising agencies, copywriters brainstorm with creative directors to develop a creative concept that fits the company's marketing strategy. They also work closely with designers to refine the layout. Often, writers have to "write to fit" the space allotted by designers.

With more new generations of technical products appearing on the market, there will be an increasing demand for people who can demystify complex concepts for the customer. Technical writers may develop ads, benefits-oriented collateral, or detailed data sheets for agencies or companies. (For more information about opportunities for technical writers, see Computer & Information Systems.)

Graphic designers. With more choices, consumers have become more discriminating. Quality—down to the last detail—must be evident, from sales promotion to packaging. Designers should be talented and resourceful and have up-to-date production skills, including desktop publishing skills. The most successful know how to bring together basic design elements—color, typography, and white space, for example—to develop an original look. The best designs not only command attention, but support the copy or message.

Freelance creatives. Freelance work has traditionally been common for advertising copywriters and designers. But increasingly, companies are also looking outside for marketing consultants and staff to manage projects. Companies will continue to use shadow agencies or design firms not officially assigned to the account to do backup or project work.

Public relations managers. While some companies will always be more vulnerable than others to bad press, more CEOs dealing with a succession of thorny issues, such as environmental cleanup, are finding public relations as necessary as marketing and sales.

Writing press releases is only a small part of a public relations professional's job. In fact, managers often focus most of their efforts on working closely with senior managers to develop a PR strategy they'll use to spin off a creative, multifaceted PR campaign. This campaign might include efforts as diverse as articles in the trade press, a speaker tour for top managers, a company-sponsored "green" campaign, and strategies for quick response in the event of a crisis. PR specialists with experience in highly specialized areas, such as law and environmental concerns, are especially in demand.

Many PR managers work closely with lawyers to anticipate troublesome situations a company may face and construct worst-case scenarios and strategies for damage control.

For most PR managers, the "key to the kingdom" is their extensive network of contacts in business, government, and local, national, and trade media.

A new generation of opportunities

Direct response marketing specialists. This new generation of direct marketing experts uses the Internet not only to reach prospective buyers but also to elicit responses that can be used to qualify leads, verify demographics, and determine purchase preferences. Most of the time, direct response marketing involves creating a relationship with prospects and customers by providing value-added communication via regular e-mail messages, newsletters, or special offers. Prospects will often exchange information about themselves in exchange for entry into a sweepstakes, the promise of more detailed information about a particular product, or discounts on purchases. This is sometimes called "permission marketing" because prospects and customers give advertisers permission to continue contacting them by opting to respond to certain offers. Direct response marketing specialists constantly monitor the performance of a range of offers and make adjustments to boost response.

Web copywriters. These electronic wordsmiths specialize in creating copy for the computer screen. It must be short, sweet, and compelling enough to stop Web surfers. It must also contain clear links to reel them in for more details.

Web designers. These graphic designers who blend technical savvy with knowledge of what works within the constraints of electronic media are especially in demand.

Web producers. Web producers manage all aspects of the production of a Web site—from scheduling creative activities to the launch. In addition to developing production schedules, they delegate work to Web programmers, designers, and writers and manage the workflow throughout the project to ensure that it's completed on time and within budget.

Do you have what it takes?

Whether you join the business side or the creative side, get ready for constant deadline pressure. The pressure to produce results—in the face of fickle markets, customers, and clients—is the common denominator in marketing and advertising.

Marketing managers should be both analytical—familiar with research techniques and emerging market trends—and creative. Like advertising account managers, marketing managers should be polished and articulate enough to communicate at high levels in the corporate world as well as in informal brainstorming sessions in the creative world.

Web producers need excellent project management skills, as well as the ability to multitask in working with a variety of different people to meet deadlines.

By contrast, creative people, such as writers and designers, are often square pegs in the corporate world. This colorful and eclectic group survives on talent and blossoms in the continual state of flux present within most advertising agencies. Most are happiest working odd hours and don't normally object to working frequent evenings and weekends to meet deadlines.

Public relations managers and specialists should be creative, with a natural talent for communicating effectively with a wide range of people, from CEOs to members of the media. Recruiters look for people who are polished and articulate.

Increasingly, managers and specialists must be tough-minded businesspeople who can establish credibility with line managers and be accountable for the results of their campaigns.

Education and training

Marketing managers, direct response specialists, and Web producers should have a bachelor's degree in business, marketing, or a technical field. Marketing managers will go further with an M.B.A. (with an emphasis in marketing, and courses in business law, economics, accounting, finance, mathematics, and statistics). Direct response marketing and Web specialists need extensive knowledge of interactive design and interactive and Internet technologies, as well as a thorough understanding of the design and messaging constraints of the Web.

If you have your sights set on working in a high-tech company, a bachelor's degree in engineering or science, combined with an M.B.A., may help you gain entry.

Advertising account executives usually earn a business degree with an emphasis in marketing. Some go on to earn an M.B.A.

Assembling a good portfolio of creative work to show copy chiefs or creative directors at prospective agencies should be the focus of full-time or freelance advertising copywriters and graphic designers. Typically, this requires training in advertising, communications, or English for writers at a four-year college or university. Graphic designers may earn a bachelor's degree in fine art, commercial art, or graphic design, or they may complete a two-year post-secondary art school program in graphic design, fine arts, or visual communications.

Most programs in art and design also provide training in computer design techniques, a prerequisite for landing many design jobs.

Many backgrounds are suitable for entry into public relations. A bachelor's degree in public relations, communications, or journalism has traditionally been the price of entry for public relations managers. About half of all PR professionals are former journalists, lured to the profession by higher salaries and career advancement.

For new graduates, however, a business degree may be the right ticket. With increasing pressure from management to demonstrate tangible results, some recruiters are courting business graduates.

Depending on your specialty, an M.B.A. can be helpful. So can a background in finance, marketing, international business, law, or science. For example, investor relations specialists should earn a degree in business or finance and an M.B.A.

No matter what degree you earn, it's wise to take courses in psychology, sociology, economics, and public opinion research as well. Experience working in government is essential for PR professionals headed to Washington, D.C.

It goes without saying that experience with database and word processing applications, as well as a familiarity with electronic publishing, graphics, video production, and Web design and development are crucial.

Once you've landed a job, continuing education will be important to your advancement. Many large firms sponsor management training programs. Others pay for attendance at professional seminars and conferences, as well as local and national management training programs sponsored by industry associations.

Tips on breaking in

Write. High school and college newspapers and literary magazines, community newspapers, and radio and TV stations all provide valuable (albeit often unpaid) practical experience.

Get an internship. Internships provide an invaluable way for college students to gain experience. Many companies, magazines, and broadcast stations offer internships to students, who write short stories and conduct research and interviews while learning about public relations, publishing, or broadcasting.

Choose the right school. Some journalism schools, such as Northwestern University's Medill School, specialize in placing students in advertising agencies.

Create a portfolio. Both writers and designers should start early developing a portfolio of their published (or unpublished) work. This can include work done in school, as well as freelance work or projects from a summer job or internship.

If you're dying to show your creative skills in a certain area but lack on-the-job experience, make up a problem and create an original ad or other creative solution.

Career path

Marketing professionals may start as a marketing assistant in a small company or as a management trainee in a large corporation. Most management jobs are filled through promotion. In small firms, you may take on more responsibility earlier in your career, but advancement can be slow after that. It can take from five to 10 years to become a marketing manager supervising up to 10 people. Some marketing trainees who work for manufacturers become product managers. After 10 or 15 years, you can be named marketing director or vice president of sales and marketing. Many CEOs rise through the ranks from a marketing background.

An account executive's career develops with work on progressively larger accounts. With five years of experience, an account executive might supervise the activities of five or 10 junior account executives and ultimately become responsible for the agency's overall relationship with a major client company, such as Frito-Lay. The vice president of account services is responsible for managing a number of client relationships and helps shape the firm's strategic direction.

In small firms, beginning writers work as assistants, writing and editing progressively longer and more important pieces. Most often, advancement comes by moving to other companies or agencies. In larger firms, beginners generally do research, fact-checking, or copyediting. It may take longer to begin writing and editing.

Graphic designers often start out doing relatively routine work and observing at advertising agencies or graphic design studios, while practicing their creative skills on the side.

The career progression for most copywriters and graphic designers comes with work on larger and more prestigious accounts. Many copywriters and graphic designers choose not to pursue a management career. Others go on to become art directors, creative directors, and even agency presidents.

Some writers and many graphic designers do freelance work part-time while they are still in school and even after they begin working full-time. Others have enough talent and confidence to start out freelancing full-time right after graduating from art school. Nearly 40 percent of all graphic designers are self-employed. Freelancers must develop a set of clients—agency creative directors and corporate marketing managers, for example—who regularly contract for work. Some freelancers earn high incomes and recognition, such as local advertising club awards, for their work.

You may begin your public relations career at an agency, writing press releases for a variety of clients. Within the first five years, you'll begin to develop expertise in a particular industry. As your knowledge grows, you will be invited into client strategy sessions.

With seven to nine years of experience, PR managers often handle a medium-sized client account or a significant portion of a major client's account. At this stage, you may be supervising three to five employees.

The next step is director, 15 to 20 years into your career. Directors are responsible for the overall management of a large client. Directors report to vice presidents if the firm is public and to partners if it is private.

In small firms, PR assistants begin by writing press releases and writing and editing progressively longer, more important pieces. Most often, advancement comes by moving to other companies or PR agencies. In larger firms, jobs are usually structured more formally. Beginners may do research, fact-checking, or copyediting and take on writing and editing less rapidly. Advancement comes with the assignment of more important projects.

PR people who specialize in a particular industry or area often move back and forth between companies and agencies.

How much can you earn?

Advertising account executives can increase their compensation by going to work for a competing agency. Salaries in the $50,000 to $60,000 range are common for fast-trackers with five years of experience. The head creative and account person working on a key account can easily earn more than $100,000 a year.

Starting salaries for graphic designers and writers begin in the low to mid-$20,000s. Midway through your career, you may make $30,000 to $50,000. Salaries for writers and designers with 10 or more years of experience—or who have earned a reputation for effective Web copy and design—can be much higher. In general, the best salaries go to graphic designers working in art/design studios and writers working in high-tech companies.

Earnings for self-employed designers vary widely. Those struggling to gain experience and forge a reputation may have to charge less than minimum wage for work. Well-established freelancers may earn more than salaried artists.

Marketing salaries vary widely depending on the company, industry, location, and experience. The average for an entry-level marketing assistant or trainee is $21,000. After several years on the job, salaries can range from $36,000 to $90,000. Top marketing executives can make $130,000 to $170,000. Often bonuses, equal to as much as 10 percent of the base salary, as well as stock options and other non-salary perks, sweeten the deal.

For PR professionals, entry-level salaries range from $18,000 to $24,000. In recent years, PR executives who earned more than $100,000 per year either specialized in investor relations or had risen to the senior management level at a PR agency.

Where will you work?

Traditionally, you had to move to New York, Chicago, or Los Angeles if you were serious about a career with an advertising or public relations agency. These days, innovative "hot shops," the rising stars of advertising and direct response marketing, can be found in many other cities throughout the country. *Advertising Age* magazine publishes an annual directory of agencies and ranks firms according to their business and creative capabilities. While the majority of PR firms are indeed located in New York, Los Angeles, and Chicago, well-respected smaller agencies operate in many mid-sized cities. Most Web services agencies are found in New York, San Francisco, and Silicon Valley.

Freelance copywriters and designers typically find work anywhere they live. It is also becoming much more common to work via e-mail, fax, and overnight mail. Many graphics specialists post evolving designs on Web sites for clients to view and approve.

Marketing managers are found in virtually every industry. The best opportunities are in services and high-tech firms.

Job Profile

Teal Elliott, manager of marketing communications

What are your general responsibilities?
I'm responsible for the development of marketing communication strategy and materials. I drive the creation of communication materials, including packaging, collateral, sales support materials, presentations, and Web content. Also the creation of strategic communication—including print and banner advertising, trade shows, affiliate programs, and other Web programs.

As the first point of contact for projects, I manage client accounts from throughout the company, which include product management, corporate management, professional services, online resources and services, channel marketing, sales, PR, partner programs, and direct marketing. I assist these clients in developing appropriate communications vehicles that meet their goals and objectives. I am responsible for developing and tracking budgets, schedules, and the production of multiple projects. The bulk of our communication efforts are on the Web (e-mail campaigns, banner ads, affiliate marketing programs, etc.), so I need to be apprised of current Web marketing trends, functionality, and technologies.

How long have you been in this business?
I have been working in marketing management since 1991.

How many years of education do you have?
I have a B.A. in speech communications with a minor in marketing.

How many hours a week do you typically work?
Approximately 60 hours a week.

What are your hours on a typical workday?
8 a.m. to 7 p.m. and additional hours after 8 p.m.

How big is the company you work for?
We have 250 employees, with estimated revenues of $25 million.

Do you need to have professional certification?
It's not necessary for this position.

In what general range does your annual salary fall?
$100,000 to $150,000. Typically the range is as follows:
Base salary range: $80,000 to $95,000. Bonus: $5,000 to $15,000.
Stock options: 2,000 to 6,000 shares post-IPO, up to 25,000 shares before the initial public offering.
Silicon Valley software and Internet companies are desperate to hire qualified managers, so they are paying very competitive salaries just to persuade individuals to join their company. I negotiated with all companies I interviewed with because the packages were similar. A good negotiator can easily get a full package worth $150,000 or more as a "marcom" manager—even if you don't manage a staff.

How did you get your current job?
I got this job through a headhunter, who I found through a marketing colleague. She forwarded a marketing e-mail newsletter, which lists available marketing positions and headhunter contacts. The headhunter required a completed profile on my background. After one phone interview with the headhunter, she scheduled an in-person interview with my current manager.

What's your typical day like?
Essentially my typical day is filled with meetings and checking e-mail:
8-8:30 a.m. Listen and reply to phone messages.
8-10 a.m. Read, reply, and create e-mail regarding deliverables on specific projects.
10-Noon Meetings on project status with internal and external managers.
Noon-1 p.m. Lunch break, but still working—reading, replying, writing e-mail.
1-3 p.m. More meetings to discuss new or existing projects.
3-4 p.m. Read, reply, create e-mail.
4-5:30 p.m. More meetings.
5:30-7 p.m. Read, reply, write e-mail.
7-9 p.m. Relax at home.
9-10 p.m. Work on projects at home or review industry publications.

Most employees of high-tech companies communicate through e-mail. Most people do not call to discuss projects. It's amazing I get any work done within the typical day, because this is really what my life at work is about— e-mail and meetings.

What are your career aspirations?

I'd like to be a director of marketing within one to three years, working for a small to midsize software or Internet company in Silicon Valley. In my current position, I am responsible for the execution of projects. In my next position, I expect to be more strategic and focused on the big picture, and employ a staff of individuals who can execute the strategy. I am excited about the opportunity to manage individuals and assist them with their career aspirations.

Of course, then there's the idea of actually having a life outside of work, instead of becoming a director, and changing my career aspirations to something really enjoyable and less stressful, like dog training or becoming a full-time Martha Stewart. I enjoy my position but as you can see from my schedule, I don't have much time for a social life.

What kind of people do you think would do especially well in your job role?

Marketing communication managers should be hardworking, creative, flexible, and able to juggle 20 or more projects at a time. Someone who is able to manage within a beyond-fast-paced environment—while maintaining a good sense of humor and a thick skin—will do well. You must be a people person. It is a requirement in this position to work with multiple individuals, which of course sometimes includes challenging personalities. It helps to be optimistic and be energetic in order to get through the long, challenging days.

It helps to have a strong background in design or writing and be familiar with programs including Adobe PhotoShop, Adobe Illustrator, Quark XPress, and all Microsoft programs. It's also important to have a good understanding of the Web front-end (the interface) and back-end (the underlying technology that makes it work).

What do you like most about your job?

The diversity of programs I work on. Working with creative people. The excitement of an ever-changing industry. You never know what type of projects you will work on. There is so much opportunity to learn from new technologies and other people. The high-tech industry is changing so fast that you are forced to change along with it. Working for a small company is very rewarding because you are able to affect the entire company or product's image and success.

What do you like least?

The number of hours I have to spend completing the large workload. Lack of social life due to long hours. Daily stress on the job to complete programs on time and preferably under budget. The million tasks to complete a project. It is more enjoyable when you have a strong agency with account reps to help you execute and manage projects. Without assistance, my job is just a very long list of to-do's.

What are some common misconceptions about your job/profession/industry?

That marketing is a glamorous industry and this is a position with plenty of perks. Actually the position requires long hours and daily challenges. Some believe that marketing managers just make things "look pretty," but actually this position requires the manager to think quite strategically—looking out for your company's (and each product's) best interests. We always focus on the bottom line and what will bring the greatest ROI (return on investment).

What would you say is the best way to go about landing a job like yours?

Join organizations, network through friends, family, organizations, school. Learn as much as possible about the position and industry by searching the Web for marketing information. Read the vertical and industry publications, including *DM News, Brand Week, Business 2.0, Fast Company,* and *Red Herring.* Create your resume and show it to several people in the industry. A good resume is key. And since you will be posting it online, it can be two to three pages in length because I have found the HR managers have "spiders" that search online for key words such as "strategic," "leading cross-functional teams," "return on investment," "manage agency," "enterprise," "small business," and "Web marketing." Also, all the standard marcom media, including "advertising," "collateral," "events," "packaging," and "promotions." The more words the better.

Note that I was offered multiple positions during my search and chose this job due to several factors. The way I found the other positions was through headhunters who contacted me because of my resume posted on several online sites, including: **Monster.com, headhunter.net, careercentral.com,** *The Wall Street Journal Online,* **bayareajobs.com, excite.com, yahoo.com,** and a few more. I tried to get as much exposure on the Web as possible by posting my resume on all logical sites. The more exposure you can have to headhunters, the better.

I was offered six jobs during only five weeks of searching for a new position. I got my foot in the door for an interview in several different ways:

* **Posting my resume online.** This piqued the interest of two headhunters. I actually received one to three calls every other day from headhunters and HR managers because of my posting. One of the best Web sites for marketing positions is the marketing section of Career Central. They have a dedicated marketing section in which you can complete an online profile of your experience. They forward positions to your e-mail based on your profile. I receive 2 to 5 job announcements per week from the profile I submitted with careercentral.com.

* **Professional networking.** I found one headhunter through a co-worker at my previous company and another through an account executive at the creative agency I worked with in my previous company.

* **Personal networking.** Several friends were able to get me in the door with their company or other's companies. Some friends have started their own companies and offered me positions.

Resources

Top advertising agencies (main offices)

BBDO Worldwide, Inc.
1285 Avenue of the Americas
New York, NY
(212)459-5000
www.bbdo.com

J. Walter Thompson
One Atlanta Plaza, Suite 3000
950 E. Paces Ferry Road
Atlanta, GA 30326
(404)365-7300
Fax: (404)365-7499
www.jwtworld.com

Leo Burnett Co.
35 West Wacker Drive
Chicago, IL 60601
(312)220-5959
Fax: (312)220-3299
www.leoburnett.com

McCann-Erickson
750 Third Avenue
New York, NY 10017
(212)697-6000
Fax: (212)984-3575
www.mccann.com

Ogilvy & Mather
11766 Wilshire Blvd., Suite 900
Los Angeles, CA 90025
(310)996-0600
Fax: (310)996-0414
www.ogilvy.com

Advertising industry associations

Advertising Research Foundation
641 Lexington Avenue
New York, NY 10022
(212)751-5656
www.arfsite.org

The Advertising Educational Foundation
220 East 42nd St., Suite 3300
New York, NY 10017-5806
(212)986.8060
Fax: (212)986.8061

American Advertising Federation
1101 Vermont Avenue, NW, Suite 500
Washington, DC 20005-6306
(202)898-0089
Fax: (202)898-0159
E-mail: aaf@aaf.org
www.aaf.org

Association of National Advertisers
708 Third Avenue
New York, NY 10017-4270
(212)697-5950
Fax: (212)661-8057

Advertising industry publications

Advertising Age, Adweek, Brandweek,
and *Mediaweek*
1515 Broadway, 12th Floor
New York, NY 10036
(212)536-6527
(212)536-5353
www.adweek.com

American Demographics
P.O. Box 10580
Riverton, NJ 08076-0580
(800)529-7502

Internet marketing firms

Engage AudienceNet
1000 Brickstone Square
Andover, MA 01810
(978)684-3884
Fax: (978)684-3636
www.audiencenet.com

Fusion DM
501 Folsom Street, Suite 400
San Francisco, CA 94105
(415)229-2800
Fax: (415)229-2884
www.fusiondm.com

**Global Technology Marketing
International**
157 Portsmouth Ave., Unit 3
Staham, NH 03885
(888)467-7709
Fax: (603)775-7319
E-mail: info@gtminet.net
www.targitmail.com

Marketing associations

American Marketing Association
311 S. Wacker Dr., Suite 5800
Chicago, IL 60606
(800)AMA-1150 or (312)542-9000
Fax: (312)542-9001
www.ama.org

Direct Marketing Association
1120 Avenue of the Americas
New York, NY 10036-6700
(212)768-7277
Fax: (212)302-6714
www.the-dma.org

**International Association of
Business Communicators**
One Hallidie Plaza, Suite 600
San Francisco, CA 94102
(415)544-4700
Fax: (415)544-4747

Marketing Research Association
1344 Silas Deane Hwy., Suite 306
Rocky Hill, CT 06067-0230
(860)257-4008
Fax: (860)257-3990
Email: email@mra-net.org
www.mra-net.org

**Promotion Marketing Association
of America, Inc.**
100 Marcus Drive
Melville, NY 11747
(516)454-1800
Fax: (516)454-1833
www.pmalink.org

**Sales and Marketing Executives
International**
5500 Interstate North Parkway #545
Atlanta, GA 30328
(770)661-8500
Fax: (770)661-8512
E-mail: smeihq@smei.org
www.sell.org

**Society for Marketing
Professional Services**
99 Canal Center Plaza, Suite 250
Alexandria, VA 22314
(800)292-7677
Fax: (703)549-2498
www.smps.org

Marketing industry magazines

The Marketing News
American Marketing Association
311 S. Wacker Dr., Suite 5800
Chicago, IL 60606
(800)AMA-1150 or (312)542-9000
Fax: (312)542-9001
www.ama.org

Direct Marketing News
and *IMarketing News*
100 Avenue of the Americas
New York, NY 10013
(212)925-7300
Fax: (212)925-8752
www.dmnews.com

Fast Company
77 North Washington Street
Boston, MA 02114-1927
(617)973-0300
www.fastcompany.com

Marketplace 1 to 1
Peppers and Rogers Group
470 West Ave.
Stamford, CT 06902
(203)316-5121
Fax: (203)316-5126

Sales and Marketing Management
355 Park Avenue South
New York, NY 10010
(212)592-6263

Web Marketing Today (electronic)
Wilson Internet Services
P.O. Box 308
Rocklin, CA 95677
(916)652-4659
wilsonweb.com

Top public relations agencies (main offices)

Burson-Marsteller
230 Park Ave. South
New York, NY 10003
(212)614-4000
E-mail: bmwebmaster@bm.com
www.bm.com

Edelman Public Relations Worldwide
211 E. Ontario St.
Chicago, IL 60611
(312)280-7000
www.edelman.com

The Kamber Group
1920 L Street, NW
Washington, DC 20036
(202)223-8700
Fax: (202)659-5559
E-mail: dc@kamber.com
www.kamber.com

PRx, Inc.
97 S. Second Street
San Jose, CA 95113-1205
(408)287-1700
Fax: (408)993-2251

Public relations industry associations

International Public Relations Association
11350 McCormick Rd.
Hunt Valley, MD 21301
(301)771-7305
E-mail: IPRAsec@compuserve.com
www.ipranet.org

Public Relations Society of America
33 Irving Place
New York, NY 10003-2376
(212)995-2230
Job Hunt Line: 212-995-0476
E-mail: hq@prsa.org
www.prsa.com

Public relations publications

IPRA Review
International Public Relations
Association
11350 McCormick Rd.
Hunt Valley, MD 21301
www.ipranet.org

The Blue Book: A who's who of the public relations world, *The Green Book: A guide to Public relations service companies*, *The Red Book: A directory of the PRSA Counselors Academy*, *Public Relations Tactics*, and *The Strategist*
Public Relations Society of America
33 Irving Place
New York, NY 10003-2376
www.prsa.com

Chapter 12

Sales

From e-commerce
to world-class customer care

Destination marketer
Financial sales specialist
Online customer care representative
Outplacement services marketer
Service sales representative
Web sales representative
Best Bets for Entrepreneurs:
Manufacturers' representative, Value-added reseller (VAR)

Forecast

Services continue to dominate the economy, making this a strong area for service sales reps, especially those who sell online, and financial services. Manufacturers are expected to continue outsourcing their sales activities to manufacturers' representatives and value-added resellers rather than maintaining large in-house and direct sales staffs. Although jobs for retail workers will continue to be plentiful in number, several significant trends point to disappointing prospects due to industry consolidation and the automation of a number of functions. Retail sales through the Internet will continue to have a significant impact on store sales in the 21st century. Customer service—in person, by phone, and, increasingly, online—is the next big boom for companies that expect to stay healthy in the years ahead.

Growth

According to the U.S. Bureau of Labor Statistics, employment of service sales representatives is expected to grow much faster than the average for all occupations through the year 2006. Manufacturers' representatives can expect employment opportunities to grow about as fast as the average

---

for all occupations through the year 2006, due to continued growth in the amount of goods they sell.

Overview

A service-oriented economy has opened up a wealth of new opportunities for sales professionals, but an intensely competitive global economy and the rise of Internet "storefronts" promise to quickly separate the winners from the wimps in the new millennium. To make your quota, you'll have to be more knowledgeable and, in most cases, more technically astute—to answer the questions of sharper, more value-conscious consumers.

To weather inevitable recessions and economic downturns over the long term, you'll have to be more creative—and more aggressive. Even the "category killers," such as Toys "R" Us, are reaching out to increasingly narrow and more specialized market segments. Web-based successes like **Amazon.com** are going far beyond store services to actively anticipate what customers will be interested in buying, based on past buying preferences. Land's End has opened a 24-hours-a-day, no waiting, virtual dressing room. Field sales reps are cross-selling or adding value, such as consulting services, to product sales as a way to deepen customer relationships. The only common denominator? Dedicated, responsive, as-close-as-possible-to-around-the-clock customer service.

The new sales "specialist"

The old saying that a good salesperson can sell anything is becoming obsolete. Today's sales professionals have a specialized knowledge of their product lines and their customers. Your choice of services or manufactured goods will determine where you meet prospective customers and how you go about making a sale.

Service sales representatives work in industries as diverse as financial services and telecommunications. Prospective customers in a rep's assigned territory can be found in business directories as well as via leads gathered at trade shows, from business associates, and from other customers. Service sales reps contact and visit prospective customers to introduce them to one or more services. The more "intangible" the service or the more difficult it is to demonstrate results (Web advertising sold by online sales representatives is one good example), the more creative the rep must be to sell its benefits. *Web sales representatives* bring a growing number of advertisers online, selling banner ads or full-scale direct marketing programs. Many banks and brokerage firms are hiring *financial sales specialists* to sell a comprehensive package of financial services and investment products, from electronic banking to IRAs. (See Banking & Financial Services, page 59.)

From industrial pumps to high-tech computer systems, independent *manufacturers' representatives* represent the product lines of one or more manufacturers, usually in a single industry. Leads gathered through cold calling or at trade shows and sometimes from responses to a manufacturer's direct mail or telemarketing efforts introduce reps to prospective retail customers. A manufacturers' rep may spend weeks at a time traveling a territory to visit existing customers and new prospects. *Value-added resellers (VARs)* also act as middlemen, purchasing hardware, software, and telecommunications services from high-tech companies at discount prices and reselling them to companies or individuals along with consulting services or other product add-ons.

A growing cadre of *online customer care representatives* combine technical support and customer service as they interface with customers— primarily via e-mail—to address questions and resolve issues.

Industry snapshot

The 1990s were tough on retailers. First, some of the century's most venerable department stores were swallowed up by greedy developers, in the market for prime real estate. Then, heavy cost-cutting aimed at reducing debt left stores especially vulnerable to a drop in consumer spending.

With excess inventories and falling profits, retailers floundered through several seasons of price wars and promotions only to be faced with the recession of 1990. In that year, a record number of retailers—50 of them with nearly $24 billion in annual sales—went bankrupt. Although the retail industry rebounded to grow an average 4 percent per year between 1992 and 1996, experts call for the growth to slow.

In the years ahead, fewer companies will own the majority of the retail business. The top 10 specialty retailers will control 40 percent of the market. Even the strongest retail contenders are branching into narrower categories with spin-off businesses, such as Toys "R" Us did with Kids "R" Us and Babies "R" Us.

In a market-driven economy, retailers and manufacturers will have to satisfy a more cost-conscious and value-driven customer. Manufacturers' reps and VARs serving niche markets and selling on a global scale will be central to this effort. The Internet will be an asset to Web-savvy customers—and a formidable contender for those who lag behind. With more sales channels and more buying information at their fingertips, consumers will increasingly judge sellers by the quality of the customer service they provide.

Trends to track

E-commerce, or bust. Forget about the mall. A Web address is prime real estate these days.

According to a study by the Boston Consulting Group, total 1998 online revenues across all categories reached $14.9 billion. While that represented 0.5 percent of all retail sales for the year, the firm projects astounding growth of online retailing (or e-tailing) going forward—beginning with a leap to $36 billion in revenues (growing 145 percent) in 1999. The study also makes some interesting distinctions about how "pure-play" (online-only) retailers and multichannel retailers (those who sell through stores, catalogs, or call centers) differ. Multichannel retailers—brokerages, consumer electronics manufacturers, and apparel makers—currently retain an edge over pure-play retailers because they come to e-commerce with established brands and profitable infrastructure.

But watch out. Pure-play retailers are aggressively plowing funds into their own brands, and already dominate the online auctions, books, music/video, and automotive categories. When you consider that the Internet is also becoming the main source of product and pricing information for value-conscious consumers, you get a real sense of its potential.

Customer care in the digital age. Although consumers may be attracted to the self-service convenience of shopping on the Internet, poor customer service isn't cutting it. In a recent survey of e-commerce customers by New York-based Internet market research firm Jupiter Communications, 40 percent reported being dissatisfied with service they received online. Another study conducted by customer care firm Servicesoft Technologies, found that only half of major retail Web sites responded to simple e-mail queries. Retailers like McDonald's, Toys "R" Us, and Wal-Mart have discovered the hard way that the Internet also makes it very convenient for disgruntled customers to publicly air their complaints.

More companies are outsourcing tech support operations or hiring companies to create customer support solutions and software. **Liveperson.com** has designed software that lets consumers exchange instant e-mail messages with living, breathing sales reps at about 50 commercial sites. Users ask questions about products and billing. At any rate, as e-commerce retailers try to smooth out technical glitches, they should create some very interesting opportunities for technical folk. (For more detail on these jobs, turn to Telecommunications & the Internet, page 259.)

The mega-store. The latest marketing maneuver: high-tech mega-stores and malls that use entertainment as merchandising. Levi Strauss & Co. entered the competitive ranks with its flagship store in San Francisco. Among the attractions: a custom tailoring service using lasers to take customers' measurements; a hot-tub-sized pool for shoppers who want to shrink their shrink-to-fit jeans on the spot; a workshop that helps customers ornament their jeans for $8 to $125, and multiple screens on which film clips are shown.

Old standards...and still winners

Manufacturers' representatives. As the economy expands, so will opportunities for outside sales professionals who sell a wide range of consumer and industrial goods. A growing number of firms will rely on manufacturers' reps to market their products in order to control costs and expand customer lists. Imports provide excellent potential. It's often more cost-efficient for importers to delegate sales responsibilities than to hire a sales force.

Opportunities for self-employment vary by industry, however. Some industries, such as pharmaceuticals, prefer to employ a dedicated sales force.

Some reps are more service-oriented than others. Industrial products, such as valves, may sell themselves to a highly technical customer base of building engineers, construction supervisors, or facilities managers. But high technology sales often involve assessing a company's computing needs and recommending a specific combination of software and hardware. Some reps may also assist with the installation of new equipment or software, as well as fine-tuning and training.

Service sales representatives. Selling services such as training, financial planning, advertising, outplacement, and telecommunications plans requires a sales representative who is skilled at solving problems. Service sales representatives begin each sales cycle by gaining a thorough understanding of a prospect's business needs and then developing a strategy for meeting them.

Service sales reps often work as part of a team to compile detailed, technical Request for Proposal (RFP) documents that show how one or more specific services will meet a unique set of needs based on specifications provided by a customer or prospect. Many sales representatives deal with several prospective clients at once.

From there on, every industry has its unique nuances. Web sales representatives work with advertisers and agencies to sell space online. (See Telecommunications & the Internet, page 259, for more details.)

Many banks and brokerage firms are hiring *financial sales specialists* to sell a comprehensive package of financial services and investment products, from electronic banking to IRAs. (Also see Banking & Financial Services, page 59, for more details.)

Outplacement services marketers have the tough task of justifying the expense of providing career resources and job-hunting services to employees who have been laid off. (See Human Resources & Employee Services, page 165, for more details.)

Destination marketers from out-of-the-mainstream cities provide incentives to woo corporate travel managers and convention groups to bring their meetings—and attendants' spending—to smaller cities. (See Travel & Hospitality, page 275, for more details.)

A new generation of opportunities

Value-added resellers. Resellers typically make volume purchases of computer equipment, software, and/or telecommunications services from manufacturers or carriers. Then they pass the discounts along to their commercial and residential customers—in conjunction with value-added services ranging from customized billing to customer support and consulting services. Some resellers are small, one- to 10-person operations. Others are large companies with annual revenues in excess of $1 billion. As a group, resellers represent one of the fastest-growing segments in the telecommunications industry.

Online customer service representatives. Not too long ago, only hardware, software, and Internet service providers offered technical support. Now, online technical support—wrapped up with customer service— is becoming a serious, bottom-line-driven business for e-commerce and online trading companies in jeopardy of losing sales. One study of online consumers revealed that up to 40 percent abandon their shopping when they hit a technical snag. The International Data Corporation (IDC) predicts online support services will grow at a compound rate of 48 percent annually. This means that this area is due to explode as other companies see the light and jump on board with online support centers of their own.

The work is challenging and fast-paced. Online customer service representatives answer e-mails or interact with chat groups, answer questions, and help troubleshoot technical problems. Some of the best can juggle multiple requests simultaneously. They also track statistics, analyze trends, and compile feedback that the product development people can use to fine-tune the Web site or products.

Do you have what it takes?

Meeting personal quotas as well as regional and company sales goals can be stressful in this competitive arena. Often sales reps compete against other companies as well as members of their own sales force.

Successful sales professionals are efficient self-starters, ambitious and unflappable mavericks. They are neat, personable, and aggressively focused on solving customers' problems. In some cases, this requires plenty of patience and tact. Good verbal and written communications skills are essential, as well as organization and attention to detail. That means a good memory for names and faces. A working knowledge of data analysis and technical skills is also critical. Perseverance helps in areas where completing a sale can take months.

Sales can be a physical job much of the time. Some reps lug around heavy sample cases; retail sales associates often stand for hours at a time and may need supervisory approval to leave the sales floor. Evening and weekend work is common and longer-than-usual hours may be scheduled during holidays and other peak periods. Sometimes weekly schedules make planning a challenge.

Education and training

An inborn talent for selling will take you far. But to get a good first job, you'll probably need a college degree. After that, training and field experience will give you expertise with your product lines and market. To sell industrial products, you'll need a bachelor's degree in science or engineering. Many reps in this area gain expertise in a technical job first before moving into sales. Employers prefer service sales representatives to have a bachelor's degree in business, marketing, or a field related to the service they're selling.

Many companies have formal training programs. Some last up to two years and cover a wide range of products, company services, and sales techniques. In some company training programs, trainees rotate between jobs in manufacturing plants and corporate offices to become familiar with all phases of production, installation, and distribution. In others, trainees take formal instruction at the plant, followed by on-the-job training under management supervision.

In some firms, you may be trained by experienced salespeople who accompany you on real sales calls. As you gain familiarity with the firm's products and clients, you may be given increased responsibility and eventually your own territory.

Pharmaceutical company training programs resemble a college curricula. Classroom-style training concentrates on biology, physiology, and chemistry concepts that sales professionals need to know to successfully interact with physicians.

Keeping current on competing products and services as well as changing technology and market trends is essential. Most companies schedule frequent follow-up training sessions to update sales reps on new products or services and help them maintain and update sales skills.

You'll probably attend a lot of trade shows, conferences, and conventions. In addition, many companies sponsor meetings of their entire sales force where presentations are made on sales performance, product development, and profitability.

You don't have to be a programmer to be an online customer care representative. You probably won't even need a college degree, unless you want to move into management. If you're comfortable with a PC and the Internet and are a quick study, you'll progress to the front lines quickly. Once you're there, you need good written skills so you can fire back answers in concise English. In some jobs you'll need analytical skills as well as a working knowledge of how to troubleshoot various Web browsers and operating systems.

Tips on breaking in

Bone up for the interview. Because the sales process is becoming more complex, some employers aren't taking any chances during the hiring process. Some are going as far as to test applicants' IQs. In many industries, entry-level trainees will need very specific credentials—a degree in chemistry or engineering, for example, to work for a chemical manufacturer.

Be discriminating. True, many opportunities are advertised. But sometimes it will difficult to separate the wheat from the chaff. Avoid ads with flamboyant or provocative headlines, such as "Can you get by on $100,000 per year?" You'll probably find yourself trying to unload swampland in Florida. While advertisements for sales jobs use colorful language such as "unlimited income opportunity," remember that there is no *floor* either.

It's better to identify companies you have a specific interest in, do some research, and apply directly. The best bets are the top-performing companies in industries that are growing. (Use this book as a guide.) Look for corporations that have successfully restructured and managed the tough transitions.

Shop for training. Although virtually every company has a sales department, not all have a good sales training program, which is crucial in the early stage of your career. Companies with a reputation for excellence in this area include IBM, Procter & Gamble, Hilton Hotels, and Johnson & Johnson. (You'll find their addresses in "Resources" at the end of this chapter.)

Speak to the right person. That's not the human resources manager. Ask to speak with the area sales manager. Most sales managers are always willing to meet with new prospects because they never know when one of their reps will be promoted or transferred, or will decide to quit. Sales managers like to have an inventory of applicants so they can cut down on recruiting time.

Get a recruiter working for you. If you have sales experience, you may find the recruiting firms that specialize in sales helpful. There are good local firms in most cities. Get recommendations from people who got their jobs through recruiting firms. If you don't want to leave your current location, focus on smaller companies or firms that have headquarters in your city. Your local chamber of commerce can provide you with a list of the major employers in your city.

Look like a client. The hiring process for sales professionals places a lot of emphasis on the style and image you convey in the interview. You should look like the client you'll be calling on. If you're applying at IBM, dress in a conservative, dark suit. If you want to sell industrial construction equipment, slacks and a blazer might be more appropriate.

Career path

A large number of sales reps decide to make a career of selling. Regardless of your goals, most sales careers require a commitment of a minimum of three to five years of field work.

After that, reps who display management potential may be promoted to district sales manager, area manager, regional manager, divisional manager, and ultimately head of the field sales organization reporting to a corporate vice president of sales. A lot of CEOs at major corporations began their careers in sales. If you are interested in pursuing the management track, be prepared for frequent relocations.

Manufacturers' reps are promoted by taking on increasingly larger accounts or territories where commission potential is greater.

As a rule, large companies prefer to hire recent college graduates. Smaller companies tend to look for people with proven sales experience.

Some manufacturers' or service sales reps move into sales training. Some inside reps go into business as independent manufacturer's reps.

Unless you're a technical whiz, you'll probably start out taking non-technical calls as an online customer care representative. Once your on-the-job training has taken hold and you're comfortable with the process, you'll begin handling more complex questions. If you show real potential, you may become the customer care center manager or move into a technical support position for a customer.

How much can you earn?

A sales career is most satisfying for people who want their earnings to reflect how successfully they sell. But beware: Earnings for all reps may fluctuate with changing economic conditions and shifting consumer preferences.

Compensation methods for manufacturers' reps vary by type of firm and product sold. Most employers use a salary-plus-commission or salary-plus-bonus pay structure where the typical payout is 40 percent salary and 60 percent commission. Depending on the type of products you represent, your experience in the field, and the number of customers you reach, you can earn much more or much less than sales reps employed by a manufacturer.

Sales representatives who establish a strong customer base can earn more than managers in their firm. According to Dartnell Corporation's 1996 Sales Compensation Survey, entry-level sales representatives received $36,000 in average total cash compensation, intermediate-level sales representatives earned $46,000, and senior sales representatives received $63,000.

Sales representatives are paid in a variety of ways. Some receive a straight salary; others are paid solely on a commission basis—a percentage of the dollar value of their sales. Most firms use a combination of salary and commissions. Some services sales representatives receive a base salary, plus incentive pay that can add 25 to 75 percent to the sales representative's base salary. In addition to the same benefits package received by other employees of the firm, outside sales representatives have expense accounts to cover meals and travel, and some are provided a company car. Many employers offer bonuses, including vacation trips and prizes, for sales that exceed company quotas.

Sales managers make more on average than other middle managers, but they earn it with long hours and high pressure.

Sales reps who work directly for an employer are usually reimbursed for expenses like transportation, meals, hotels, and entertaining customers. Manufacturers' reps must cover their expenses and pay for health insurance and other benefits typically provided by an employer.

Salaries for online customer care representatives range from $25,000 to $45,000. Moving on to become a manager can raise your compensation to $55,000 or higher.

Many resellers have annual revenue of more than $100 million.

Where will you work?

The diversity of products and services sold point to employment opportunities in every part of the country.

Job Profile

Julie Kenney, customer care manager in a corporate sales department

What are your general job responsibilitie?

To develop, manage, and execute Intraware's Customer Care Programs, including our Beta testing program, customer references and testimonials, case studies, and customer council. I also manage a team of customer care specialists who make satisfaction/awareness calls out to our customers.

My primary functions include:

* Managing our key customer database (setting up the necessary internal infrastructure for the appropriate people to have access).
* Working with the sales reps to solicit prospects for our Customer Care Programs.
* Working with our business partners to leverage their key customer references for our Web site.

* Guiding our PR agency in developing testimonials and references.
* Ensuring the consistency of corporate message in our customer success stories.
* Developing and designing the Customer Council participants and meetings. Customer Council meetings provide our top customers with a forum for discussing our services and Intraware's business strategy for annual business planning sessions and future direction. In addition to receiving valuable feedback from our top customers, we also have an opportunity to show our appreciation for our top customers.
* Providing ongoing analysis of the effectiveness of our Customer Care Program.

How many years have you been in this business?
Seven years.

How many years of education do you have?
I have a B.A. in liberal studies, with a minor in psychology.

How many hours do you typically work per week?
At least 60, if not more.

What hours do you work on a typical day?
From 8 am to 6:30 p.m. Then I log in from home from about 8:30 to 11 p.m.

How big is the company you work for?
Almost 300 people.

Do you have (or need) professional certification?
No.

How did you get your current job?
Through the **680careers.com** Web site.

Can you describe a "typical" day?
No two days are ever alike. I spend a lot of time with my team, working on projects, running reports, speaking with customers, and so on. It changes each day.

What are your career aspirations?
To be honest, I'm happy as a manager. I want to stay where I am for a while.

What people do you think would do especially well in your job role?
Highly motivated team players with:

* A strong customer focus.
* Three to five years of experience working in a sales and/or marketing role, with a proven track record.
* Strong interpersonal, listening, speaking, and writing skills.
* Excellent organizational skills. They should be detail-oriented— with no hesitation about managing multiple projects simultaneously and at a furious pace.
* An understanding of technology and this industry.
* Proficiency with Microsoft Office and an understanding of database software.
* A great attitude and willingness to remain flexible in a crazy start-up environment.
* Creative ability is also plus.

What do you like most about your job?
It's definitely exciting and no two days are ever the same. I like that my group makes such a difference and is so important to the success of the company.

What do you like least?
The long hours—but, at the same time I love it. It is a very rewarding position.

What are some common misconceptions about your job/profession/ industry?
When I say I am the Customer Care Manager, a lot of people think that I manage the inbound call center. This is not the case. In addition to being the marketing and sales liaison for references, testimonials, and case studies, I manage the team of reps who make outbound calls to promote awareness of our products and overall customer satisfaction.

What would you say is the best way to go about landing a job like yours?
Several years of experience working in a customer service environment with marketing exposure, determination, and networking!

Resources

Top sales firms

Baxter International
1 Baxter Parkway
Deerfield, IL 60015-4633
(847)948-2000
www.baxter.com

Corning, Inc.
One Riverfront Plaza
Corning, NY 14831
(607)974-9000
www.corning.com

Hilton Hotels Corp.
P.O. Box 9003.
Addison, TX 75001-9003
(800)552-0852
www.hilton.com

IBM
5600 N. 63rd Street
Boulder, CO 80314
(914)765-1900
www.ibm.com

Johnson & Johnson
One Johnson & Johnson Plaza
New Brunswick, NJ 08933
(732)524-0400
www.jnj.com

The Procter & Gamble Company
P.O. Box 599
Cincinnati, OH 45201
www.pg.com

Sales associations

**Manufacturers' Agents
National Association**
23016 Mill Creek Road
P.O. Box 3476
Laguna Hills, CA 92654-3467
(949)859-4040 or (877)MANA-PRO
Fax: (949)855-2973
www.manaonline.org

**Sales & Marketing Executives
International**
5500 Interstate North Pky, Suite 545
Atlanta, GA 30328
(770)661-8500
Fax: (770)661-8512
www.sell.org

Sales publications

Agency Sales Magazine, *The Directory of Manufacturer's Sales Agencies*, *The Knowledge Base*, and *MANA Matters*
Manufacturers' Agents
National Association
23016 Mill Creek Road
P.O. Box 3476
Laguna Hills, CA 92654-3467
(949)859-4040 or (877)MANA PRO
Fax: (949)855-2973
www.manaonline.org

Sales Manager's Bulletin
The Bureau of Business Practice
24 Rope Ferry Road
Waterford, CT 06386
(800)243-0876, Ext. 6
www.bbpnews.com

Selling Power
P.O. Box 5467
1140 International Parkway
Fredericksburg, VA 22406
(800)752-7355

Successful Meetings
355 Park Avenue South
New York, NY 10010-1789
(212)592-6403
Fax: (212)592-6409
www.successmtgs.com

Chapter 13

Science

Exploring frontiers in biotechnology and the environment

Agricultural scientist
Biologist
Chemist
Clinical research associate
Hydrogeologist
Regulatory Affairs Associate
Best Bet for Entrepreneurs: *Environmental consultant*

Forecast

An aging population and the rising incidence of terminal illnesses such as cancer and AIDS will throw a spotlight on medical research to find a cure or develop more effective drug therapy. Prospects for biologists and chemists involved in research and development—especially in the areas of biotechnology and pharmaceuticals—should be bright well into the 21st century. Over the long term, the chemical industry will become increasingly important to America's technological progress, especially in aerospace, electronics, agriculture, and medicine.

Growth

Much better than the average in key areas. Fueled by an aging global population and blossoming international markets, the industry has maintained growth rates nearly twice those of the economy at large. Behemoth multinational drug companies such as Glaxo Wellcome, Bristol-Myers Squibb, Eli Lilly, and SmithKline Beecham traditionally clear 30 percent in operating margins—twice what most Standard & Poors' 500 companies can boast. One positive indicator of continued growth: venture capital investment in small biotech companies went up $100 million since 1997, much of it from

European venture funds. Growth in some areas may depend on the economy and government funding.

Overview

Forget the mad scientist muttering over a bank of frothing beakers and test tubes. Today's research scientists are just as likely to be tapping away at the computer or using complex maps to plot genetic mutations in a cell, like modern-day Magellans. Significant discoveries and research advances in recent years make these exciting times for scientists in the lab and in the field.

As the Food and Drug Administration (FDA) steps up its approval process, there are more new drugs hitting the market to keep pace with the needs of a blossoming segment of the population. The over-65 crowd will grow by almost 20 percent during the next decade, all the while contributing more to the pharmaceutical coffers.

All eyes are on about 1,400 biotechnology companies going into the new millennium. Just 20 years young, biotechnology brings together biochemistry, cell biology, genetics, and chemical engineering to create often revolutionary advances in pharmaceutical, diagnostic, agricultural, environmental, and other products and services—everything from bio-engineered tomatoes to Viagra, advanced criminal forensic procedures to (hopefully) the cure for cancer.

The catch is that most research-and-development-driven biotech companies are years away from turning a profit. Funding often comes from big deep-pocketed pharmaceutical companies in return for future royalties and profits. (Funds needed for research have been known to grow by close to 100 percent each year.) This means that most of the plum biotech jobs go to (you guessed it!) scientists—especially in R&D "studios" with fewer than 50 employees.

Prospects are better for business and marketing people at a few larger biotech companies. Chiron and Genentech, for example, each employ between 5,000 and 10,000 people and often turn a profit. A large percentage of Chiron is owned by Novartis, a large pharmaceutical company, and close to two thirds of Genentech is owned by Roche. These alliances allow the smaller companies to distribute their products via the larger companies' global channels.

From the laboratory to the marketplace

Biologists study living organisms, such as the components of a cell, as well as organic substances such as blood and food.

Chemists specialize in developing new polymers, synthetic materials, or foods, as well as drugs based on the research conducted by scientists in biotech companies.

Agricultural scientists focus on improving the yield and quality of a wide variety of crops, increasing the resistance of plants and animals to disease, insects, or other hazards, or improving animal breeding and nutrition. Research in the area of agricultural biotechnology has resulted in the development of BST (a milk production hormone), PST (a lean pork hormone), and insect- and herbicide-resistant cotton.

Success in the laboratory leads to often-lengthy trial testing before the FDA can approve new products for release to consumers. *Clinical research physicians* (CRPs) are specialized M.D.s who develop and implement plans for bringing drugs through clinical trials. Under their guidance, *clinical research associates* (CRAs) conduct experiments and record the results.

Regulatory affairs associates ensure that companies' development and manufacturing processes are in accordance with the detailed and complex regulations imposed by the FDA.

As federal and state regulatory agencies lower the boom on companies for unsafe disposal of hazardous waste and chemicals and other environmental issues, more chemical companies will move into environmental services, increasing the demand for *chemists with an environmental specialty*. A growing emphasis on the environment should also bring new opportunities for *hydrogeologists* in the chemical, petroleum, and manufacturing industries, as well as with environmental services firms and the government. In the years ahead, hydrogeologists will have their work cut out for them, setting standards and testing toxic levels in water tables and local water supplies.

Industry snapshot

The economy and fluctuations in government funding have historically taken a toll on research and development.

Many research labs, biotech firms, and pharmaceutical firms suffered through the recession just as global competition was heating up. Biotech companies in particular were hit hard. After many drugs failed to gain FDA approval, most companies were crippled by a severe shortage of capital and funding for continued research. The tongue-in-cheek definition of a biotechnology company became "any life-sciences company that loses money."

Things began to turn around as the FDA approval dropped from 28 months in 1992 to 19 months currently. A shortage of capital has resulted in the consolidation of established companies and startups. A shortage of qualified research scientists is more difficult to overcome. Each year, fewer science graduates earn Ph.D.s, the necessary educational credential for top research jobs that deal with complex new technologies. In addition, college enrollment in agricultural science programs has dropped off over the past few years.

Leading scientists think the new field of proteomics could be the next big thing in biotechnology. The study of the roughly 100,000 proteins that make up every muscle, nerve, and fiber, proteomics could yield revolutionary discoveries such as memory-enhancing drugs.

Trends to track

Consolidation. Twenty-seven mergers valued at close to $12 billion worldwide have transformed an industry of midsized firms into an arena of giants employing legions. The top 10 pharmaceutical companies posted $127 billion in sales for 1997. The trend in recent years has been for these firms to shed their peripheral businesses and concentrate on drugs. By pairing up with smaller biotech companies, large pharmaceuticals can create vertically integrated powerhouses that control emerging drugs from development to distribution.

Competition from established companies in Europe, Japan, and Canada, as well as rising stars in South Korea, Taiwan, and Mexico, may prompt mergers between the U.S. and foreign companies. It could also lead to mega-science projects, such as the space station, that pool the costs and talents of a number of global participants. U.S. companies may also begin to move some production overseas to take advantage of cheaper labor.

The techno-scientist. In many labs, the test tube is taking a back seat to high-tech research methods. Eventually biology's most important discoveries may come from computers and automated processes rather than from test-tube experiments. Already software based on nonlinear equations is being used to more precisely describe the behavior of the highly unpredictable DNA molecule. Software models allow researchers to closely examine the complex "folding" action within a DNA molecule.

Telling stories. It's the year 2030. Most of us are living well past the age of 100, which is putting a severe strain on public services and products for the elderly. This is just one story line that emerged when a group of major biotech firms convened to imagine how the future would play out. Using a technique called story building, or scenario creation, the group plans to develop a set of if-then strategies by envisioning various possible future realities. The most successful stories are driven by events that aren't well accounted for in long-term business planning, such as political unrest, industrial accidents, or social upheaval.

Going "green." The message is increasingly clear: More pharmaceutical and chemical companies and even university labs will have to find new ways to handle chemicals and toxic waste disposal or face stiff penalties. Stanford University agreed to pay close to $1 million in fines and other costs for violations of state hazardous waste disposal laws in an out-of-court settlement. Regulators from the state branch of the Environmental Protection Agency (EPA) put the university on notice for violations that included improper handling and storage of chemicals, especially incompatible substances that could have ignited a fire or explosion.

Some large chemical companies may form alliances with established environmental services firms. Other companies will bring in consultants or scientists who specialize in environmental concerns to help them carry out cleanup mandated by the Superfund and related legislation and to put future environmental management strategies in place.

The generic game. Fifteen years ago, low-priced generic copies of well-known prescription drugs accounted for 21 percent of the prescription drug market. Today they make up 37 percent of a $60 billion market. The potential for profits has already inspired many large pharmaceutical companies to get in on the action. Before the patent for Xanax (a top-selling tranquilizer) expired, Upjohn introduced its own generic version of the drug. Typically, a generic drug manufacturer can expect to garner a third to a half of the market. Upjohn's preemptive strike gobbled up 90 percent of the market. With patents for today's seventy-five bestselling brand-name drugs set to expire by 2010, competing generic manufacturers could face dire days.

Without regulation by the Federal Trade Commission (FTC), generic manufacturers may be absorbed by large pharmaceutical firms or forced into smaller niche markets. If they can't make a profit, they may abandon the market altogether, leaving large firms little incentive to make cheaper forms of the best selling drugs.

New markets for specialty chemicals. Advanced polymers and plastics designed for very specific uses. Fuel oxygenates that meet Clean Air Act standards. Biotech applications for agricultural chemicals. While regulatory decisions may keep a rein on how fast new products will enter the marketplace over the next few years, it is clear that more research scientists will be at work developing new chemical solutions to a multitude of problems.

Old standards...and still winners

Biologists. New methods of research will open a wealth of opportunities for biologists in the years ahead. Universities and private biotech companies will hire many to conduct research in areas as diverse as genetic engineering and cancer screening and treatment. Biologists will also become more involved in conducting environmental impact studies and solving problems, such as how to treat toxic waste. Many will be drawn back to campuses to fill positions left vacant by retiring faculty.

Chemists. Much of the emphasis in the push for research and development of new chemicals will be on "green" issues faced by American industry. Many chemists will find opportunities in companies that develop environmentally-friendly chemicals such as fuel additives that don't harm the ozone layer.

Agricultural scientists. These scientists will use their backgrounds in molecular biology, microbiology, genetics, biotechnology, and food or soil technology to treat a range of issues from crop protection to animal nutrition. Again, the specialty to watch is agricultural biotechnology. The results of current research already bring us leaner meat, tastier tomatoes, and mosquito-proof T-shirts.

Clinical research associates. With hundreds of new drugs ready for testing, CRAs who represent leading-edge pharmaceutical and biotech companies will be busy working with medical centers to conduct clinical trials necessary before the FDA begins its approval process. Using high-tech laboratory instruments, CRAs monitor experiments, calculate and record results, and develop conclusions.

A new generation of opportunities

Environmental consultants. Environmental consciousness-raising will continue. More chemical companies will step up to provide environmental services. Industrial manufacturers and even university laboratories not already guilty of environmental transgressions are likely to begin planning ahead to ensure the proper use and disposal of waste and chemicals. Environmental renewal (the development of new methods for returning the environment to its natural condition) will provide the next wave of opportunities for these highly specialized scientists.

Hydrogeologists. These New Age geologists specialize in tracing the effects of toxic waste dumped in the nation's lakes, rivers, and streams or buried in landfills. Hydrogeologists are already in short supply in the government and in private companies that produce chemical and petroleum products, as well as in manufacturing firms and environmental services firms. The Geological Society of America lists current jobs in its job bank. (See "Resources" at the end of this chapter for details.)

Regulatory affairs associates. If you're inspired by the potential in science, but don't want to work in a lab, becoming a regulatory affairs associate may be for you. Regulatory affairs associates marry a knowledge of science to a firm grasp of the detailed and complex FDA-imposed regulations to ensure that companies' development and manufacturing processes follow policy to the letter.

Do you have what it takes?

Scientists use science and mathematics principles and theories to solve problems in research and development and to investigate, invent, and improve products. Rapid advances in technical equipment and scientific applications call for well-educated scientist-technologists to work in this highly segmented field. Still, research, not to mention the FDA review cycle, take years to complete. So this is a field for the meticulous—and patient.

Research scientists and CRAs should enjoy working alone or as part of a team. Good written and verbal communication skills are essential to effective research and analysis. An understanding of business principles can come in handy to researchers in consulting and private industry. Scientists who conduct field research in remote areas will need physical stamina.

Education and training

Most companies hiring research scientists place a great deal of emphasis on grades and experience.

Chemists and biologists need a Ph.D. to conduct independent laboratory research, advance into administrative research positions, or teach at the university level. A master's degree is necessary for jobs in applied research and testing.

A bachelor's degree in biology or chemistry is adequate for clinical research assistants, as well as for nonresearch positions in sales, service, or high school education. A master's or bachelor's degree in biology, chemistry, physics, or a related engineering specialty is acceptable for some agricultural science jobs. A bachelor's degree in agricultural science can lead to management positions in businesses that deal with ranchers and farmers—businesses such as feed, fertilizer, seed, and farm equipment manufacturers; retailers or wholesalers; or farm credit institutions. Agricultural scientists with a bachelor's degree may also work in applied research and product development.

A master's degree is sufficient for environmental scientists, hydrogeologists, and regulatory affairs associates. Some regulatory affairs associates earn law degrees.

Clinical research associates should have a bachelor's degree in chemistry, biology, or pharmacology, as well as experience working in a laboratory, hospital, or related setting.

Tips for breaking in

Temp. Major temp firms, such as On Assignment, with offices nationwide, place science grads in temp jobs as lab technicians and scientists.

Be flexible. If you can't find your dream job out of the gate, consider looking for a job in your dream company and work your way into your ideal job over the course of a year or two. There is a lot of movement in entry- and mid-level jobs within this industry.

Map out a career path. If you don't, you may end up facing the "postdoc" syndrome that comes from specializing in an area that offers a low-pay, low-prestige career track. Before you complete your doctoral degree, do some career research. Learn which areas of research offer the best intellectual and financial rewards.

Get experience. According to *Biotechnology* magazine, the right academic background will take you only so far. The key to getting the best job is having laboratory skills. Taking research assistantships while you're still in school and laboratory jobs during the summer will pay big dividends later on.

Use career-building resources. The Environmental Careers Organization offers career conferences, special career publications, and other services. It also places students and recent graduates in short-term professional positions, serves as an on-the-job training organization, and gives associates an inside track for employment.

BioTron, a job bank run by the American Institute of Biological Sciences (AIBS), is a good source for general biology positions. The AIBS and the American Society for Experimental Biology also run another job bank called the Federation of American Societies for Experimental Biology (FASEB) placement service.

The American Chemical Society operates the Employment Clearing House. Also check the classified ads in *Chemical and Engineering News*. (You'll find addresses and telephone numbers in "Resources" at the end of this chapter.)

Pharmaceutical companies recruit graduate students on university and college campuses and advertise jobs in trade publications and *The Wall Street Journal*. There are also a number of executive recruiters who specialize in the pharmaceutical industry. Check your local yellow pages.

Career path

Many scientists spend their entire careers conducting research. Progressive pharmaceutical companies have designed career paths to reward those who choose to advance into management.

Scientists who do decide to move into management often begin their careers as lab technicians and become laboratory supervisors in five to eight years. In eight to 10 years, they may be promoted to department head. It typically takes more than 10 years to take on the duties of director of research and development for a division within a large company, and up to 20 to head all research and development activities as vice president.

Some scientists choose to leave the corporate world to become college professors or entrepreneurs.

Scientists with Ph.D. degrees earn prestige by publishing articles about their research in leading industry journals.

How much can you make?

The unfortunate truth is that the average research scientist often make less money than an experienced plumber! The salary range is $65,000 to $85,000, but it can run to the low six figures at large companies.

A new graduate with a master's degree may begin at $25,000 to $28,000. Ph.D. graduates typically start at $35,000 to $55,000. Many laboratory jobs top out after 20 years at $55,000 to $65,000. Managers and senior-level directors can make $75,000 to $100,000.

Clinical research associates earn salaries in the mid-$30,000 range at the entry level and up to the high $70,000s for upper-level positions.

The salary range for regulatory affairs associates is $35,000 to $50,000. If you have a law degree, expect this range to double.

At large pharmaceutical companies, people in management positions earn significant bonuses in cash and stock options. At many biotech companies, all employees receive stock options, which, if the company does well, can be lucrative.

Where will you work?

The majority of research scientists work for the federal, state, or local government or for universities. Most of the rest work for chemical and pharmaceutical manufacturers, biotech companies, hospitals, physicians' offices, and research and testing laboratories. A small number are self-employed. Chemical consulting already represents as much as 5 percent of the total U.S. consulting market. Nonfaculty agricultural scientists can find some of the best opportunities in agricultural service companies, commercial research and development companies, pharmaceutical companies, wholesale distributors, and food products companies.

Job Profile

Carl Friddle, postdoctoral fellow

What are your general job responsibilities?
Basic research identifying and characterizing genes that affect disease processes. This is primarily independent work, drawing upon departmental resources for capital and labor with advice from my supervisor.

How many years have you been in this business?
I've been in my current position for two years.

How many years of education do you have?
Too many! Four years for my B.A. and five years for my Ph.D.

How many hours a week do you typically work?
50 hours per week.

What are your hours on a typical workday?
8 a.m. to 6 p.m.

How big is the company you work for?
There are 5,000 employees working at this national lab.

Do you have (or need) professional certification?
No.

In what general range does your annual salary fall?
Postdoctoral fellows make $20,000 to $45,000, depending upon their location and the source of funding. Faculty positions (the next step) average $55,000 at entry. Industry positions average $70,000 plus.

How did you get your current job?
Networking. I was recommended by one of my Ph.D. advisors.

What's your typical day like?
On a typical day, I spend half of my time performing experiments and half of my time either analyzing the results or troubleshooting technical problems. On a larger scale, there are periods of intense activity followed by periods of data analysis, and then designing the next experiment.

What are your career aspirations?
I'd like to move into a faculty position at a university or a senior management position at a pharmaceutical company.

What people do you think would do especially well in your job?
You need to be persistent to the point of foolishness. Any rational person would take a career path with more frequent and concrete evidence of accomplishment. A successful person must be able to see how even the most mundane task or experiment ties in to the motivating drive to understand the underlying science.

What do you like most about your job?
The independence and intellectual stimulation.

What do you like least?
The pay scale, insecure funding, and delayed gratification (long periods between designing an experiment and publishing the results, *if* the results are interesting).

What are some common misconceptions about your job/profession/ industry?
There is a common belief that people who follow this career path are entitled to a faculty position upon completion of a long, rigorous training

process. The job market is currently quite good, but you must be willing to relocate and you must be flexible about the type of setting.

It is also frequently believed that the academic freedom you enjoyed as an undergraduate will carry on throughout an academic career. This is simply not true. Compromises must be made to address the concerns of both funding agencies and the university/department in which you perform your work. I believe that the freedom is, in fact, substantial, but it is not unlimited, and this disappoints many people.

What would you say is the best way to go about landing a job like yours?

Choose a field that interests you, whether it is biology or physics, and attend the best graduate school you can. Stress the fundamentals in your training to maintain flexibility in subsequent career steps. Your school and advisor will play a large role in helping you move up, so choose them carefully.

Resources

Leading chemical manufacturers

W.R. Grace
1750 Clint Moore Road
Boca Raton, FL 33487-2707
(561)362-2000
Fax: (561)362-2193
www.grace.com

Dow Chemical USA
47 Building
Midland, MI 48667
(517)636-1000
Fax: (517)638-7238

Monsanto Chemical Co.
P.O. Box 14547
St. Louis, MO 63178
www.enviro-chem.com

DuPont
P.O. Box 540117
Waltham, MA 02453-0177
Fax: (800)978-9774
www.dupont.com

Olin Corp.
501 Merritt Seven
P.O. Box 4500
Norwalk, CT 06851
(203)750-3000
Fax: (203)750-3292
www.olin.com

H.B. Fuller
1200 Willow Lake Boulevard
St. Paul, MN 55110-5132
(651)236-5900
www.hbfuller.com

Union Carbide Corp.
39 Old Ridgebury Road
Danbury, CT 06817-0001
(203)794-5300 or (800)335-8550
www.unioncarbide.com

Leading pharmaceutical and biotech companies

Abbott Laboratories
200 Abbott Park Road
D393, AP51
Abbott Park, IL 60064-3537
www.abbott.com

Amgen Inc. (Headquarters)
One Amgen Center Drive
Thousand Oaks, CA 91320-1799
(805)447-1000
Fax: (805)447-1010
www.amgen.com

Bristol-Myers Squibb Co.
Consumer Sales Organization
225 High Ridge Road
Stamford, CT 06905
www.bms.com

Genentech, Inc.
1 DNA Way
S. San Francisco, CA 94080-4990
(650)225-1000
Fax: (650)225-6000
www.gene.com

Glaxo Wellcome Inc.
P.O. Box 13398
Research Triangle Park, NC 27709
www.glaxowellcome.com

Ciba-Geigy Corp.
444 Saw Mill River Road
Ardsley, NY 10502-2699
www.ciba.com

Warner-Lambert Co.
201 Tabor Road
Morris Plains, NJ 07950
(973)540-2000
www.warner-lambert.com

**Science/pharmaceutical
industry associations**

**Biotechnology Industry Association
American Chemical Society**
1625 K Street, NW, Suite 1100
Washington, DC 20006
(202)857-0244
www.bio.org

The American Institute of Chemists
515 King Street, Suite 420
Alexandria, VA 22314
(703)836-2090
Fax: (703)684-6048
E-mail: AICoffice@theaic.org
www.theaic.org

American Geological Institute
4220 King Street
Alexandria, VA 22302-1502
(703)379-2480
www.agiweb.org

American Geophysical Union
2000 Florida Avenue, NW
Washington, DC 20009-1277
(202)462-6900 or (800)966-2481
Fax: (202)328-0566
www.agu.org

American Pharmaceutical Assoc.
2215 Constitution Avenue, NW
Washington, DC 20037-2985
(202)628-4410
Fax: (202)783-2351
www.aphanet.org

Environmental Careers Organization
2179 South Street
Boston, MA 02111
(617)426-4375
www.eco.org

Geological Society of America
3300 Penrose Place
P.O. Box 9140
Boulder, CO 80301-9140
(303)447-2020
www.geosociety.org

**National Association
of Pharmaceutical Manufacturers**
3279 Veterans Memorial Hwy, Suite D-7
Ronkonkoma, NY 11779
(516)580-4252
Fax: (516)580-4236
Email: info@napmnet.org
www.napmnet.org

Society for Industrial Microbiology
3929 Old Lee Highway, Suite 92A
Fairfax, VA 22030-2421
(703)691-3357
Fax: (703)691-7991
Email: info@simhq.org
www.simhq.org

Science/pharmaceutical directories

BIOSIS
Two Commerce Square
2001 Market Street, Suite 700
Philadelphia, PA 19103-7095
(800)523-4806 (USA and Canada)
(215)587-4800 (worldwide)
Fax: (215)231-7401
E-mail: info@mail.biosis.org
www.biosis.org

Directory of Chemical Producers USA
www.che.ufl.edu/WWW-CHE/topics/
chemicals.html

Science/pharmaceutical magazines

Chemical Engineering
1221 Avenue of the Americas
New York, NY 10020
(212)512-2849

American Scientist
P.O. Box 13975
Research Triangle Park, NC 27709
(919)549-0097

Biomedical Products
Box 650
Morris Plains, NJ 07950
(973)292-5100

Chemical Processing
301 E. Erie Street
Chicago, IL 60611
(312)644-2020

Biotechniques and *Chemical Week*
810 Seventh Avenue
New York, NY 10019
(212)586-3430

High Technology Careers
Westech Publishing Co.
4701 Patrick Henry Drive, Suite 1901
Santa Clara, CA 95054

Pharmaceutical Technology
P.O. Box 10460
Eugene, OR 97401
(503)343-1200

Chapter 14

Social Services
A changing society
opens up new opportunities

Correctional officer
Employee Assistance Program (EAP) counselor
Geriatric care manager
Residential living assistant
School social worker
Social worker
Social/human services assistant

Forecast

More Americans are living longer. Hospitals are discharging patients earlier to control costs. Crime is on the rise. More families are in crisis. Changes in our society will continue to open up employment opportunities for a range of social services practitioners, from social workers to correctional officers. Private social service agencies, job training programs, and residential care facilities, such as board and care homes, nursing old age homes, and group homes for the mentally retarded, will offer the best opportunities for social and human services assistants.

Opportunities for social workers in private practice will expand, especially in rural areas, thanks to the promise of funding from health insurance and public sector contracts. Employment in correctional departments is growing faster than in other areas of state and local government. According to *Corrections Today* magazine, the Bureau of Prisons will experience unprecedented growth during the next five years. In addition to opportunities at the federal level, correctional officers will also be in demand by state corrections and corrections run by private corporations.

Growth

The number of jobs for social and human service assistants—which the BLS ranks among the 10 fastest growing occupations—is projected to increase by nearly 53 percent through 2008. There will be 46 percent more jobs for residential living assistants and social workers can look forward to 36 percent more jobs (mostly in rural areas). The number of jobs for correctional officers will grow by nearly 39 percent.

Overview

The situations are often bleak. The pay is low. The stack of caseloads in never-ending. It takes a special kind of person to establish a career in social services. Someone who tallies rewards in terms of what might seem like minor breakthroughs in other occupations: a client keeps a job; a family averts a crisis. In social services, you live for the rescues and life-changing moments and spend the rest of your time chipping away at a myriad of challenges—from homelessness to caring for the elderly.

Public or private? Big city or rural setting?

The choice is yours. If you're thinking about a career in social services, you can choose from a wide range of work venues including hospitals, schools, mental health clinics, and public agencies, such as the public welfare department.

Most *social workers* specialize. For example, *school social workers* will intensify their efforts to stem the rising rate of teen pregnancy. *EAP consultants* work with corporate clients, providing resources for a range of issues, from financial difficulties to alcohol abuse, that can seriously undermine the job performance of individual employees. *Geriatric care managers* specialize in finding and recommending the most suitable care facility, home health assistance, or community program for aging clients and their families. *Social/human services assistants,* such as *residential living assistants*, work under professional supervision in health agencies, halfway houses, group homes, and other public and private care organizations.

Meanwhile, the American jail system processes more than 22 million people a year, with about half a million inmates in jail at any given time. *Correctional officers* work in the prison system, guarding or counseling inmates and offenders or managing prison staff.

Industry snapshot

A recent emphasis on social work is evidence that we, as a society, are reaping what we have sown over the last decade. Substance abuse and violence are commonplace even in suburban schools. Layoffs leave thousands of workers vulnerable to joining the next wave of homelessness. Mandatory sentencing guidelines, calling for longer sentences and reduced parole, already have our prisons bursting at the seams. In California alone, the number of correctional officers more than doubled in seven years.

Of course, some the current demand for social services is coming from a ballooning population of people who are living past age 85. The number of people living independently past the age of 65 will rise 21 percent to 12 million by the year 2010. This area is wide open and begs for innovative solutions.

Although it appears that the government has cut back on many necessary social services, more and jobs are being contracted out to private agencies that provide and staff drug rehabilitation facilities, group homes, daycare for the elderly, job retraining programs, and even correctional facilities. This has led private agencies to restructure services and hire more lower-paid social/human services workers. However, budgetary constraints at the state and local levels will continue to affect the rate of job growth in schools and correctional facilities.

Despite cost cutting, watch for a handful of innovative programs coming from the private sector. More community-based programs and group home facilities are being built to help homeless families and battered women get back on their feet and to provide support for chronic mental patients, who were de-institutionalized and left to their own devices for too many years.

Trends to track

Privatizing social services. Fewer than half of all social services jobs are in state, county, or municipal government agencies. As government increasingly contracts out social services, more—and better paying—jobs are likely to be in the private sector agencies, community and religious organizations, hospitals, nursing homes, and/or home health agencies.

New solutions for eldercare. Once again, technology—specifically the Internet—provides innovative links to care and community services for people past the age of 65 who want to continue living independently. Crozer-Keystone Health Systems of Springfield, Penn., is using WebTV—the TV connection that provides inexpensive Internet access—and video cameras to connect elderly people at home to health care and social service workers.

Elder clients can request rides and meals during regular videoconferences with care managers. In a Commerce Department-funded test, Kansas doctors will use "telemedicine" to oversee 40 patients at home. Having nurses monitor vital signs by telephone can reduce routine checkup costs by more than half—from $90 to $35. The high- tech links could ultimately encompass scattered family members.

Old standards...and still winners

Social workers. Through direct counseling, social workers help clients identify their concerns, consider solutions, and find resources. Often, they refer clients to specialists in various areas, including eldercare, public assistance, or drug/alcohol rehabilitation programs. In consultation with clients, social workers review eligibility requirements, fill out forms and applications, arrange for services, visit clients on a regular basis, and provide support during crises. School social workers focus on students' problems—ranging from pregnancy to excessive absences. They counsel children in trouble, arrange for necessary services, and help integrate disabled students into the general school population. They also advise teachers on how to deal with problem students.

Employee assistance programs (EAP) staffed by EAP counselors provide a safe and confidential resource for employees coping with problems such as debt, substance abuse, difficult family matters, and stress. Working in human resources departments, at an agency, or in private practice, an EAP counselor provides individual counseling and can recommend appropriate treatment. By reaching out to valuable employees in this way, a company can limit long-term productivity losses. Geriatric care managers specialize in finding and recommending the most suitable care facility, home health assistance, or community programs for aging clients and their families. The goal is always to keep people independent for as long as possible.

Geriatric care managers work with physicians to assess the physical and mental abilities along with the medical and nutritional needs of each client. They then counsel clients and their families, many of whom may be resistant to change. Some work as consultants for nursing homes and home care agencies, but private practice offers the highest income and prestige.

Correctional officers. Correctional officers' duties differ depending on where they work. Generally, they are responsible for overseeing individuals who have been arrested, are awaiting trial or other hearing, or who have been convicted of a crime and sentenced to serve time in a jail, reformatory, or penitentiary. They maintain security and observe inmate conduct and behavior to prevent disturbances and escapes.

To make sure inmates are orderly, correctional officers monitor their activities, including working, exercising, eating, and showering. They directly supervise cell blocks of 50 to 100 inmates via closed-circuit television. Sometimes it is necessary to search an inmate's living quarters for weapons or drugs, to settle disputes between inmates, and to enforce discipline.

In both jails and prison facilities, most correctional officers are unarmed. They enforce regulations primarily through their interpersonal communication skills. Depending on the offender's security classification within the institution, correctional officers may have to escort inmates to and from cells and other areas and accompany them to see authorized visitors. Officers may also escort prisoners between the institution and courtrooms, medical facilities, and other destinations.

A new generation of opportunities

Social/human service assistants. Social/human service assistants play a variety of roles in community settings. They may organize and lead group activities, assist clients in need of counseling or crisis intervention, or administer a food bank or emergency fuel program. In halfway houses, group homes, and government-supported housing programs, residential living assistants help adult residents who need supervision in personal hygiene and daily living skills. They review clients' records, ensure they take correct doses of medication, talk with their families, and confer with medical personnel to gain better insight into clients' backgrounds and needs. They also provide emotional support and help clients become involved in community recreation programs and other activities.

Social/human service assistants may also be employed to establish a client's eligibility for benefits and services such as Medicaid and food stamps, and help clients complete applications for financial assistance or assist with daily living needs. In addition to monitoring and reporting on the progress of clients to their supervisors, social/human service assistants may transport or accompany clients to group meal sites, adult daycare programs, or doctors' offices. They may also help resolve disagreements, such as those between tenants and landlords.

In psychiatric hospitals, rehabilitation programs, and outpatient clinics, social/human service assistants may help clients master everyday living skills and teach them how to communicate more effectively and get along better with others. They support the client's participation in the treatment plan, such as individual or group counseling and occupational therapy.

Do you have what it takes?

Highly valued traits in this field include a strong desire to help others, patience, and understanding.

Social workers and social/human service assistants should be emotionally mature, objective, and sensitive to people and their problems. They must be able to handle responsibility, work independently, and maintain good working relationships with clients and co-workers. Many social workers spend evenings and weekends meeting with clients, attending community meetings, and handling emergencies. The work, while satisfying, can be emotionally draining. Understaffing and large caseloads add to the pressure in some agencies.

Correctional officers must be in good health. The federal system and many states require candidates to meet formal standards of physical fitness, eyesight, and hearing. Strength, good judgment, and the ability to think and act quickly are indispensable. Correctional officers also need good interpersonal and writing skills to complete regular oral and written reports on inmate conduct and on the quality and quantity of work done by inmates.

Geriatric care managers should be assertive yet compassionate in dealing with people and families who may be angry and resistant to change.

Education and training

A bachelor's degree is the minimum requirement for many entry-level jobs in social work; however, a master's degree in social work (M.S.W.) is generally required for advancement.

Besides the bachelor's in social work (B.S.W.), undergraduate majors in psychology, sociology, and related fields satisfy hiring requirements in some agencies, especially small community agencies. Accredited B.S.W. programs require at least 400 hours of supervised field experience. An

M.S.W. is generally necessary for positions in health and mental health settings. Jobs in public agencies may also require an M.S.W. Supervisory, administrative, and staff training positions usually require at least an M.S.W.

An M.S.W. prepares graduates to perform assessments, manage cases, and supervise other workers. Master's programs usually last two years and include 900 hours of supervised field instruction or internship. Entry into an M.S.W. program does not require a bachelor's in social work, but courses in psychology, biology, sociology, economics, political science, history, social anthropology, urban studies, and social work are recommended. In addition, a second language can be very helpful. Some schools offer an accelerated M.S.W. program for those with a B.S.W.

EAP counselors should earn a bachelor's or master's degree in social welfare, as well as have experience as a counselor or licensed therapist. In addition to the ability to assess a range of conditions from alcoholism to Alzheimer's disease, they should be familiar with appropriate resources for treatment. Geriatric care managers should have a B.S. in nursing, social work, or gerontology, and an M.S.W. A background in psychotherapy can be helpful.

Most institutions require that correctional officers be:

* A U.S. citizen.
* At least 18 or 21 years of age.
* A high school graduate.
* Free of felony convictions.

Correctional officers with post-secondary education, particularly in psychology, criminal justice, police science, criminology, and related fields are likely to find better opportunities. In general, advancement requires a bachelor's or master's degree in counseling, rehabilitation, social work, or a related field.

Federal, state, and some local departments of corrections provide training for correctional officers based on guidelines established by the American Correctional Association, the American Jail Association, and other professional organizations. Some states have regional training academies. All states and local departments of corrections provide on-the-job training at the conclusion of formal instruction. Officer trainees receive several weeks or months of training in an actual job setting under the supervision of an experienced officer. Entry requirements and on-the-job training vary widely from agency to agency.

Academy trainees generally receive instruction on institutional policies, regulations, and operations, as well as custody and security procedures, among other subjects. New federal correctional officers must undergo 200 hours of formal training within the first year of employment. They must complete 120 hours of specialized correctional instruction at the Federal Bureau of Prisons residential training center at Glynco, Ga., within the first 60 days after appointment. Experienced officers receive continuing education to help them keep pace with new ideas and procedures.

Social/human service assistants with a bachelor's degree in human services, social work, or one of the social or behavioral sciences have the best employment prospects. Many degree programs require completion of an internship. Some people enter the field on the basis of coursework in human services, psychology, rehabilitation, social work, sociology, or special education. Most employers provide on-the-job training in the form of seminars and workshops.

Professional licensing and certification

Since 1993, all states and the District of Columbia have had licensing, certification, or registration laws regarding social work practice and the use of professional titles. Standards for licensing vary by state. In addition, voluntary certification is offered by the National Association of Social Workers (NASW), which grants the title ACSW (Academy of Certified Social Worker) or ACBSW (Academy of Certified Baccalaureate Social Worker) to those who qualify.

The Employee Assistance Professionals Association administers a certification exam.

Contract workers must be certified by the outplacement firm and then complete one or two weeks of training.

Geriatric care managers are required by 45 states to be licensed clinical social workers.

Hiring requirements in group homes tend to be more stringent than in other settings. In some settings, applicants must meet the Criminal Offense Record Investigation (CORI) requirement. Special licensure or state certifications may also apply. The federal system and some states screen applicants for drug use and require candidates to pass a written or oral examination, as well as a background check.

Tips on breaking in

Roll up your sleeves! Volunteer work, internships, and paid jobs as a social work aide offer a window into in this field. Some universities allow students pursuing a degree in social work to spend a full semester interning. This is also a great way to make contacts with people who do the hiring.

Career path

The best way to advance from social worker to supervisor, program manager, assistant director, or executive director of a social service agency or department is to earn a master's degree (M.S.W.). Although some social workers with a B.S.W. may be promoted to these positions after gaining experience, many employers hire managers directly from M.S.W. programs—especially those that focus specifically on management training. Some social workers choose to move into teaching or research. Others become consultants or help formulate government policies by analyzing and advocating policy positions in government agencies, in research institutions, and on legislators' staffs. They may help raise funds or write grants to support these programs.

Some social workers go into private practice. Most private practitioners are clinical social workers who provide psychotherapy, usually paid through health insurance. Private practitioners must have an M.S.W. and a period of supervised work experience. A network of contacts for referrals is also essential.

With education, experience, and training, qualified correctional officers can advance to correctional sergeant, a supervisor of other correctional officers, or another supervisory or administrative position. Many correctional institutions require experience as a correctional officer to advance to other corrections positions. Some officers transfer to related areas, such as parole. Correctional officers have the opportunity to join prison tactical response teams, which are trained to respond to riots, hostage situations, forced cell moves, and other potentially dangerous confrontations. Team members often receive monthly training and practice with weapons, chemical agents, forced-entry methods, and other tactics.

How much can you earn?

Social workers with an M.S.W. had median earnings of about $35,000 in 1997. Those with a B.S.W. earned about $25,000. The average annual salary for all social workers in the federal government in nonsupervisory, supervisory, and managerial positions was about $46,900 in 1997.

Employee assistance program counselors working inside a company earn an average of $42,000 to $60,000. Counselors in private practice or who direct the function for Fortune 500 companies can earn $100,000 or more.

Geriatric care managers make an average of $50 to $100 an hour, depending on the market in which they work.

According to a 1996 survey in *Corrections Compendium*, a national journal for corrections professionals, federal and state correctional officers' annual salaries ranged from a low of $17,300 in South Carolina to a high of $41,700 in Rhode Island.

Supervisory correctional officers started at about $28,300 a year. Starting salaries were slightly higher in selected areas where prevailing local pay levels were higher. The annual average salary for correctional officers employed by the federal government was $33,540 in early 1997.

Starting salaries for social/human service assistants ranged from about $15,000 to $24,000 a year in 1997. Experienced workers generally earned between $20,000 and $30,000 annually, depending on their education, experience, and employer.

Where will you work?

Competition for social worker jobs is stronger in cities where training programs are prevalent. The best opportunities are in rural areas.

EAP counselors are employed in consulting firms and companies in virtually every industry, mostly in the private sector.

Most correctional officers work in relatively large institutions located in rural areas, although a significant number work in jails and other smaller facilities located in law enforcement agencies throughout the country.

Social/human service assistants are employed by state and local governments, primarily in public welfare agencies and facilities for mentally disabled and developmentally delayed individuals. An increasing number are employed by private agencies, group homes, and halfway houses. Social/human service assistants also hold jobs in clinics, detoxification units, community mental health centers, psychiatric hospitals, day treatment programs, and sheltered workshops.

Job Profile

Neil Hannon, director of court services

What are your general job responsibilities?
My responsibilities are mostly administrative, but I also carry an active caseload of 45 mentally ill, criminally-challenged clients.

How many years have you been in this business?
29 years

How many years of education do you have?
I have a B.A. in public and environmental affairs with a concentration in criminal justice. I am also a candidate for a Master of Public Affairs (M.P.A.) degree. I have also earned more than 1,200 continuing education units (CEUs) since 1971 and have had extensive training in personnel and office administration. (I also like to say I have my M.B.W.A.—Management By Walking Around—degree. It's not worth any formal credit, but I've found it quite valuable.)

How many hours do you typically work per week?
40 hours, plus. I carry a pager and am on-call 24 hours a day for emergencies.

What hours do you work on a typical day?
7 a.m. to 5 p.m.

How big is the company you work for?
Our Adult Probation Department has 24 probation officers and five full-time support staff members.

Have you earned professional certification?
Yes. I have been a Certified Probation Officer (C.P.O.) for 28 years. To earn this certification, I passed a State Probation Officer exam given by the Indiana Judicial Center, a division of the Indiana Supreme Court. I was then interviewed by the circuit court judge. Today, I interview and hire all new staff members who have already passed the exam and attended New Probation Officer Orientation.

What is your annual salary?
My annual salary is $54,500. An entry-level probation officer (P.O.) starts at $24,500. During the next five years, P.O.s receive performance increases of $1,750 to $2,500 per year. Those with a master's degree receive 5 percent more each year. After 10 years, P.O.s can expect to earn $35,000. If they are assigned supervisory duties, they can earn more.

How did you get your job?

I filled out a job application. Then, I set up an interview to discuss my qualifications and learn about the court's philosophies on sentencings and supervision.

Please describe one of your "typical" days?

Morning: I start at the jail to learn whether any of our probationers were arrested overnight. If so, I communicate with the appropriate supervising officer. I answer my voice mail and then visit with offenders who have scheduled appointments. My client base is almost exclusively mentally ill offenders in the criminal justice system.

I also attend meetings, develop policy, and review budgets. I meet with personnel to do case-staffings or address personal issues.

Lunch: I leave to take a mental break.

Afternoon: I check my voice mail and return calls. I average more than 60 phone calls per day, at work and at home. Then I repeat the morning's work schedule.

I also do a lot of work on my computer, and visit with department heads, judges, prosecutors, public defenders, criminal court clerks, and service providers.

What are your career aspirations?

Generally, I like to know that I'm making a contribution by giving offenders the tools to help themselves make a better life. If I wanted career advancement, I could be in charge of special programs or work in the Federal Probation System, where the pay scale is higher.

What kind of people do really well at this job?

People who can balance the needs of criminal justice—meaning: the offender is wrong, but responsible for his or her behavior—with treatment goals. People who are compassionate and empathetic. You must have the patience of a saint and, at times, have big shoulders to accept decisions made by plea bargains allowed in the system.

What do you really like about your job?

Working with individual offenders as well as our staff. Keeping them focused, motivated, and having a positive attitude in an otherwise negative environment. I also like working with the clients and watching their progress. Suddenly, they become responsible—or they complete what we would think of as an insignificant accomplishment and they come back with tears in their eyes to thank you for caring and sharing.

What do you dislike?
Pleading for funds from the county council for necessary programs.

What is the biggest misconception about this job?
That we're dealing with a lost cause. Social programs work great if they're implemented consistently. Those who fail to complete them need to return until they do. The easiest thing to do is to simply go to jail and do nothing. Unfortunately, we can't be successful with everyone. Drugs and alcohol cause more failures on probation than any other single factor. We use a drug called antabuse, which causes them to become violently ill if they ingest alcohol.

However, 95 percent of the time, urine screens show that, in the absence of alcohol, they switch to their drug of choice—basically whatever else is available. Therefore, they need treatment programs combined with education, such as intensive outpatient programs as well as Alcoholics Anonymous (A.A.), Narcotics Anonymous (N.A.), or Al Anon to be successful in abstaining.

How can someone get a job such as yours?
Do an internship while you're still in college. You can earn three to five credit hours. With some universities, you may be able to spend a full semester during your senior year interning and earn 15 credit hours. Spending time in the field will allow you to learn the system and make contacts with people who do the hiring.
Computer skills and command of a second language, such as Spanish, will also make you more valuable.

Resources

Social services associations

American Correctional Association
4380 Forbes Boulevard
Lanham, MD 20706-4322
(800)222-5646
www.corrections.com/aca

American Counseling Association
5999 Stevenson Avenue
Alexandria, VA 22304-3300
(800)347-6647 or (703)823-9800
Fax: (703)823-0252
www.counseling.org

American Society of Criminology
1314 Kinnear Road
Columbus, OH 43212-1156
(614)292-9207
Fax: (614)292-6767
www.asc41.com

American Vocational Association
1410 King Street
Alexandria, VA 22314
(800)826-9972
www.avaonline.org

Child Welfare League of America
440 First Street, NW, Third Floor
Washington, DC 20001-2085
(202)638-2952
Fax: (202)638-4004
www.cwla.org

Council for Standards in Human Service Education
Northern Essex Community College
Haverhill, MA 01830
www.necc.mass.edu

Council on Social Work Education
1600 Duke Street, Suite 300
Alexandria, VA 22314
(703)683-8080
Fax: (703)683-8099
www.cswe.org

National Association of Social Workers
Career Information
750 First Street, NE, Suite 700
Washington, DC 20002-4241
(202)408-8600 or (800)638-8799
www.naswdc.org

National Organization for Human Service Education
Metropolitan State College of Denver
MSCD Box 12
P. O. Box 173362
Denver, CO 80217-3362
(303)556-2967
E-mail: hatchera@mscd.edu
www.nohse.com

Social services publications

Corrections Today
8025 Laurel Lakes Court
Laurel, MD 20797
(301)206-5100

National Employment Listing Service
Sam Houston University
Criminal Justice Center
Huntsville, TX 77341-2296
(409)294-1692
www.shsu.edu/cjcenter

NASW News
National Association of Social Workers
750 First Street, NE, Suite 700
Washington, DC 20002-4241
(202)408-8600 or (800)638-8799
www.naswdc.org

Social Service Jobs
10 Angelica Drive
Framingham, MA 01701
(508)626-8644

Chapter 15

Telecommunications & the Internet
The wireless and dotcom revolutions

Computer security specialist
Interactive media specialist
Intranet developer
Network architect
Telecommunications reseller
Telecommunications technician
Web business development specialist
Web content developer
Web designer
Web programmer/developer
Webmaster

Forecast

Continued deregulation and breakneck advances in technology have created a slew of new Web-related job titles for people (not all of them techies) with a little training and a lot of seat-of-the-pants aptitude. Be careful, though. While many Internet ("dotcom") companies are currently buoyed by plenty of venture capital, most have yet to turn a profit. Some experts speculate that a correction—through consolidation, attendant restructuring, and layoffs—is looming. Over the long term, however, technology will spawn enough products and services to ensure healthy job opportunities in Internet and telecommunications companies.

Growth

Employment will explode during the short term. Long term, expect some bumps due to continued consolidation and restructuring. However, as the evolution of e-commerce and wireless telecommunications continues to unfold well into this millennium, career opportunities will be plentiful.

Overview

In 1995, when this book was last published, fewer than 3 percent of all U.S. households regularly accessed the Internet. By 1997, the government reported that 57 million Americans were regularly logging on to the Internet.

Today, industry researchers believe upwards of 83 million American adults spend time volleying e-mails, hanging out in chat rooms, bidding on auction items, checking stock prices and buying "stuff." Yahoo already showcases two million products from 27,000 stores. By 2002, consumers are expected to be forking over $1.2 billion online annually. Forty percent of all companies are already selling online—portending a boom in business-to-business commerce.

Not bad for a technology still in its infancy. The Web is literally being developed day by day. Those who work in the industry will shape its future. Best of all, you're not tied to one industry. Just take a peek into other chapters and see how the Internet is affecting businesses in just about every field and profession covered in this book.

The Internet is opening the way for advances in telecommunications—from speech recognition to wireless Internet access. With millions of miles of fiber-optic cable and global cellular stations and fewer regulations, the telecommunications company of the future will become a one-stop resource for a range of services—including local and long distance telephone, wireless telephone and Internet access, and cable TV. Expect consolidation first.

Despite any uncertainty about which companies will come out on top in this "survival of the fittest," though you can bet on plenty of opportunity in the freshest crop of new job titles to hit the career mainstream in decades.

Online, or on the line

"All companies will be Web companies in the future, or they won't *be*." In a sentence, a computer executive summed up the biggest revolution in business since manufacturers adopted the assembly line during the Industrial Age. Currently $19 billion is spent annually on business Web site development and companies in almost every profession and industry are clamoring for the skills of a new cadre of professionals whose titles are as new as their job responsibilities. A decade ago, who had heard of a *Webmaster* or an *intranet developer*?

Even titles in existence then have taken on a new patina today. More companies are adding *network architects, Web content developers,* and *designers* to their ranks. Hackers' techniques have become more sophisticated, so corporations depend on *computer security specialists* to defend them against crippling losses. Others are turning to outside vendors such as *interactive media specialists* for help creating and managing Web sites to advertise their products—as well as extranets (secure Web-based connections for customers who want to order online) and intranets (company-specific Web sites designed for the use of employees only.) To remain competitive, companies are also calling on value-added *telecommunications resellers* and *technicians* to effectively integrate the latest telecommunications technology.

Industry snapshot

Believe it or not, the global mega-network known as the Internet began as a part of a defense research project connecting scientists and engineers at major universities in the 60s. Even this brain-trust probably didn't foresee the phenomenon it would become—or what purposes it would be put to, including day-trading and human organs on the electronic auction block.

When the Web first gained popularity in the mid-1990s, the focus was on pure content, with news sites like **CNN.com** getting most of the "hits." A few years later, there was a dramatic shift to e-commerce sites, such as **Amazon.com**. The next wave, according to speculators, will tie consumer queries for information directly to related shopping links. Some call it "contextual commerce."

The next challenge for Internet companies: keeping cyberspace free of taxes and government regulation that that would curb growth. Technology-related lobbying groups such as **www.handsoffthenet.net** are appointed watchdogs.

The telecommunications industry also underwent a major transformation during the 1980s and 90s. It all started in 1984, when a federal court decided to grant seven regional "Baby Bells" independence from "Ma" (AT&T). The wave of court, Federal Communications Commission (FCC), and state Public Utilities Commission rulings that followed opened the way for the twenty-two local Bells, as well as independent long-distance telephone companies and cable television firms, to begin expanding into each other's territory. The Telecommunications Act of 1996 went a step further, lifting regulations restricting cable companies and local and long distance telephone service providers from competing in the same markets.

Deregulation has set the stage for more industry restructuring as telecom companies position themselves for heavy competition. Mega-deals, mergers, and alliances between phone companies, broadcasters, cable television companies, and related communications industries, such as publishing companies and motion picture firms, will position a few super-carriers to woo customers with a full roster of telecom services—from telephone to high-speed data transmission.

As hard wired/mechanical switching systems are replaced by the digital wireless age, a host of new technologies are emerging that will make a worldwide voice-data-video network a reality. Companies will continue to pour money into research and development to stay on the competitive edge.

Trends to track

Wireless Internet access. E-commerce darling **Amazon.com** was one of the first to go wireless, selling its products through new handheld computers that provide wireless Internet access. Watch for other products to go head to head with 3Com Corp.'s new Palm VII—freeing consumers to shop anywhere. Web sites give advice on anything from how to use chopsticks to how to housebreak your puppy.

Testing the waters. Online auctions are the latest in a steady stream of commerce-venues being developed by dotcom companies that are changing the way people buy and sell—and even plan their daily lives. In fact, many auction aficionados have become positively evangelical about this virtual marketplace. The number of registered users of **eBay.com**, the granddaddy of online auctions, almost tripled during the first half months of 1999—ballooning from 2.1 million to 5.8 million in just six months. According to eBay's home page, some three million items are up for bid in more than 2,000 categories at any given second. Best of all, "mom and pop shops" can compete with name retailers, and rural consumers have the same crack at merchandise as their urban counterparts.

Another emerging trend: expert sites. Most sites, such as **eHow.com**, offer free, prewritten advice on a range of topics. Other sites connect "seekers" with live experts qualified to dispense personalized advice (for a fee) on romance, finance, health, and career-related issues.

Privacy and the virtual community. In cyberspace, Memphis and San Francisco are part of the same close community. This poses a problem when it comes to regulating access to pornographic text or images that can be downloaded from online bulletin boards. As more criminal acts, such as pedophiles luring teens away from home or teenagers build bombs, are linked to the Internet, some sort of censorship of content seems imminent.

Customer service. More retailers are spending big bucks on the technology behind the scenes of their e-commerce sites. The key is integrating the Web site to existing business software systems so inventories can be updated in stores, call centers, and on the Web within minutes after a purchase is made. (For more detail about how customer service is changing, please see Sales on page 217.)

An international field. Telecommunications services companies and equipment manufacturers are expanding into foreign markets, such as the Netherlands, Spain, South Korea, Japan, and Eastern Europe. At the same time, increased competition is coming from foreign rivals as formerly state-owned telecom companies like Deutsche Telekom look abroad for new business. Also, expect to see an increase in joint ventures and arrangements between U.S. and foreign telecommunications companies. Finally, an increasing number of multinational companies will need private networks to link headquarters offices with foreign branches. Bottom line: more support services will be needed, opening up more jobs for telecommunications technicians.

Old standards...and still winners

Computer security specialists. The ExploreZip.worm, a computer program masquerading as e-mail, wiped out thousands of PC users' files in at least three countries. In the end, it prompted the temporary shutdown of e-mail servers at corporate giants like Microsoft, Intel, and Lucent Technologies. Computer viruses are only one threat to the security of corporate data. According to the "Computer Crime and Security Survey" conducted by the Computer Security Institute (CSI), a San Francisco trade association, and the San Francisco FBI Computer Intrusion Squad, theft of proprietary data cost the 163 companies surveyed about $1.67 million in 1998. Now 300 of the Fortune 500 companies are hiring computer security specialists qualified to assess the risks they face and design and update safeguards for a range of sensitive data—from financial records to trade secrets to employee information. Working behind the corporate network "firewall," these high-tech security guards are alert to system events like multiple attempts to log on with an incorrect password. They are also skilled at restoring data and systems lost or damaged in the event of a natural disaster, such as the Los Angeles earthquake.

Network architects. These days, almost every company regardless of size, has a dedicated network linking its geographically-distant employees. Network architects construct and maintain what is often a very complex environment of diverse hardware and software components. Any change—from adding a new user to integrating new computer technologies—can send a ripple through the system that will eventually bring some or all of its users to grinding halt. Network architects have the technical savvy to anticipate and plan for these repercussions so they can maintain overall performance every day.

Telecommunications technicians. Telecommunications technicians help design strategies for using technology to increase efficiency and productivity. As sophisticated new fiber-optic lines begin to merge data and voice communications, these two areas of expertise should also merge to create a single telecommunications technician who is able to maintain, repair, and install voice lines and switching equipment and to facilitate the transmission of computer data.

Web content developers. The need is growing for content experts, technical writers, and other communications professionals who can create and communicate compelling content for pages that reside on a Web site. In the online format, content developers often work like traditional print editors, commissioning writers and researchers to develop stories or repackage previously published material. They may also work directly online, responding to user questions and hosting bulletin-board chat sessions.

Web designers. These graphic designers put their traditional graphic arts training—color, proportion, and other generally accepted design principles—into practice for electronic media. Working closely with Web content developers, Web designers create a message that is aesthetically appealing, as to attract the intended audience, yet technologically accessible—that is, easy to download at speeds that are reasonable for the average viewer.

Web programmers/developers. Without these gurus of Web technology, there could be no Web sites. Web programmers/developers configure and manage the Web server and select the tools—such as browsers—that allow end users to access and interact with the Web site. To ensure a Web site is more than just a place to post static text, Web programmers/developers write scripts and dynamic application programs using Web development languages, such as Java and Hyper-Text Mark-up Language (HTML). Some programmers/developers also compile Web usage statistics.

A new generation of opportunities

Intranet developers. The most efficient way for companies to communicate with employees—especially those who travel often or work half a world away from corporate headquarters—is through an internal Web site called an intranet. An effective intranet site can goes beyond the traditional employee newsletter by instantly updating information and providing a dynamic forum encouraging feedback and information sharing that leads to increased productivity. Employees can also complete health insurance forms online and locate an employee (with photo) in another department without dog-earing a paper phone list. Intranet developers organize a wide range of information so that it is easily accessible to employees within the context of design and messaging that is consistent with the company's culture.

Web business development specialists. Internet sites build their business through direct sales to customers as well as through indirect sales resulting from strategic alliances and reseller agreements. Web business development specialists know how to communicate with both groups. When speaking to individual customers, they can reduce the technological complexity of the Web. And they're equally comfortable talking bits and bytes with marketers when negotiating strategic alliances with other Web sites.

Webmasters. Few job titles are as overused and misunderstood in this emerging industry as that of the Webmaster. According to the Webmaster's Guild, a Webmaster designs, implements, and maintains an effective Web site. A true Webmaster is the quintessential project manager, analyzing business requirements, developing a vision and navigation scheme for the Web site, and marshaling the resources necessary to deliver it—from graphic design to writing to network configuration and software development. Because the function of a Webmaster encompasses so many areas, the position is often not held by a single person, but rather by a team of individuals.

Telecommunications resellers. As a group, resellers represent one of the fastest-growing segments in the telecommunications industry. While telecommunications resellers attribute more than 80 percent of their revenues to commercial accounts (mostly small to medium-sized businesses), they been rapidly expanding their share of the $35 billion consumer portion of the long distance market.

Resellers act as full-service telecommunications companies for the customers they serve. Instead of owning and maintaining a network, however, they purchase discounted products and services in volume from manufacturers or network carriers. They then pass along the discounts to their commercial and residential customers—in conjunction with value-added services ranging from customized billing to customer support and consulting services. (For detail on value-added resellers, see Sales, page 217.)

Interactive media specialists. The promise of multimedia will bring video and software engineers, graphic designers, scriptwriters, and other diverse professionals together on a range of project teams. For example, an in-house team designing a demonstration on CD-ROM or Web-based corporate training program might include instructional designers who are experts on human learning patterns as well technical experts who can mold technology to those specific needs.

Do you have what it takes?

To make it in this evolving industry, you should be creative, resourceful, and flexible enough to flow with constant changes. While many professionals, such as Web designers and content developers, can get by without in-depth technical knowledge, the most successful people will be focused on pushing current technology beyond its limits and finding new applications for emerging technologies.

Web designers need a working knowledge of the design constraints of the Web. Content developers should be experts on the services and products presented on the Web sites they develop.

Webmasters and Web programmers/developers need to combine technical expertise with knowledge of business requirements and business processes.

Telecommunications resellers need, along with solid industry experience, a solid marketing plan and sufficient capitalization for their company.

Computer security specialists should understand how data is stored and experience working in a networked environment. The best are innately curious people who enjoy working against the clock to unravel puzzles and solving problems.

Education and training

In this industry, experience is still more valuable than formal education, although that won't always be the case. Some Webmasters and intranet developers have degrees in computer science. Shorter associate and certificate programs are widely available in networking, programming languages, and Web technology. Web programmers/developers should build expertise in general Web technology and have experience working with Web servers and coding in Java and HTML.

Network architects need a working knowledge of UNIX and Windows NT as well as knowledge of TCP/IP (a set of protocols developed to allow cooperating computers to share resources across a network).

Computer security specialists should have a two- or four-year technical degree, with experience in database management systems, C++, Java, and Internet applications. They should also have knowledge of legal and privacy issues. Some computer security specialists are former police officers with technical skills.

Online content developers should have a bachelor's degree with an emphasis on communications as well as work experience or a background in media production or publishing. The field is also friendly to graphic designers, writers, and programmers.

Web business development specialists need a bachelor's degree in liberal arts and should feel comfortable working with and talking about technology.

Telecommunications technicians should have a B.S. in electrical engineering or computer science or a two-year associate degree coupled with significant work experience such as technical training in the military.

Keeping up with technological advances has become the only way to survive in the telecommunications equipment industry.

Professional licensing and certification

Professional certification is available to technical professionals from various vendors, including Novell and Microsoft.

Tips on breaking in

Think small. Employment opportunities continue to be strong at small and medium-sized companies, especially those involved in developing and marketing cutting edge technologies, such as wireless Internet access. NexTel Communications had only a few hundred employees in 1990. Now it employs early 2,000.

Share skills...and business. Network architects may find it easier to break into a company by working with the consultant/systems integrator who installs network systems in banks, insurance and financial service companies, and other companies.

Volunteer. When it comes to Web design, experience can be the best teacher. Once you have a little training under your belt, offer your services—for free—to a nonprofit organization. You'll learn a lot working in a real-world environment and the finished "product" might land you a plum job.

Career path

The good news: Because this is such a new field, opportunity for advancement is pretty much wide open for ambitious people with the right skills. While you may not make it as far as the executive (or want to, for that matter), you will be in the spotlight in most companies. Advancement can come in the form of more challenging projects, supervisory positions, or lateral moves into related areas. Many professionals may decide to take their skills and go it alone as entrepreneurs.

How much can you earn?

Web programmers/developers earn from $40,000 to $85,000. Successful interactive media specialists can earn hundreds of thousands of dollars. Webmasters and intranet developers can earn from $50,000 to $150,000 depending on the size of the company they work for. Network architects earn from $45,000 to $65,000.

Web designers and content developers can earn from $60,000 to $70,000.

Web business development specialists with specialized knowledge of promotion, publicity, or advertising earn from $45,000 to $80,000.

Telecommunications technicians earn an average salary of $40,000 to $60,000.

Computer security specialists earn from $60,000 to $100,000-plus at senior levels.

Many telecommunications reseller companies have annual revenues of over $100 million.

Where will you work?

Computer security specialists, network architects, and Web site development specialists will find plenty of opportunities in private companies and government agencies installing dedicated networks and business-to-business or business-to-consumer Web sites. Web specialists may also find work with ISPs and Web-site development companies.

Job Profile

Christin Gurka, senior training consultant and Web author

What general job responsibilities does your position encompass?
I conduct computer software training sessions, train and mentor new trainers, and create and maintain a segment of our company's intranet.

How many years have you been in this business?
I've been teaching since 1993 and doing intranet design since early 1999.

How many years of education do you have?
I have my M.B.A.

How many hours do you typically work per week?
Usually 45 hours per week.

What hours do you work on a typical day?
7:30 a.m. to 5:30 p.m.

How big is the company you work for?
1,400 employees.

Do you have (or need) professional certification?
No certification is necessary for intranet development. I would need to earn a Microsoft Certified Software Engineer (MSCE) certification if I taught technical courses. Currently I teach Microsoft Office, MS Outlook, and Windows 95/98/NT, as well as similar courses on other software.

How did you get your current job?
Through a headhunter.

Please describe a "typical" day.
My days differ, depending on whether I'm training or doing web development. If I'm training:

7:30-8:30 a.m.: Room setup and prep
8:30 a.m.-4:30 p.m.: Teaching
4:30-5:00 p.m.: Paperwork, room breakdown

If I'm doing Web work...

7:30 a.m.-5:30 p.m.: Various tasks, including the following:
* Gathering content from different people.
* Formatting and arranging content pages.
* User-testing the Web design.
* Revising.

What are your career aspirations?

I'd like to stay within the training and education industry, and move into Web-delivered training.

What kinds of people do really well in your job role?

Some technical comfort is required, but you needn't be a tech wizard. You do need some creativity to design intranet sites. You also need to be able to put yourself in the roles of various users.

What do you really like about your job?

Variety. I do different things and learn different topics every day.

What do you dislike?

Nonresponsive people. As an intranet developer, you often depend on other people to provide content and documentation.

What is the biggest misconception about this job?

That it is boring and difficult. Web design is very easy. Web hosting and setting up domains may be a little more difficult, but putting together sites is actually very easy—and fun!

How can someone get a job like yours?

Most companies have intranets, and if they don't, they should! If your company has one and you see a need for a particular topic to be addressed, learn Web development first, then offer your services. An already-trained employee is much more attractive for the role. Web development is easy, but most people don't know that and avoid it.

Resources

Online companies

America Online, Inc.
22000 AOL Way
Dulles, VA 20166
(703)265-1000
Fax: (703)265-1101
www.aol.com

CompuServe Information Service
P.O. Box 28650
Jacksonville, FL 32226-8650
(614)457-8600 or (800)848-8199
www.compuserve.com

Excite@Home
450 Broadway Street
Redwood City, CA 94063
(650)556-5000
Fax: (650)556-5100
www.excite.com

Genie
190 Main Street
Hackensack, NJ 07601
E-mail: Genie@genie.com
www.genie.com

Prodigy Services Co.
44 South Broadway
White Plains NY 10601
(800)213-0992 or (914)448-8000
www.prodigy.com

Yahoo! Inc.
3420 Central Expressway
Santa Clara, CA 95051
(408)731-3300
Fax: (408)731-3301
www.yahoo.com

Internet industry associations

Association of Internet Professionals
9200 Sunset Blvd., Suite 710
Los Angeles, CA 90069
www.commerce.comstar.net/webpro

Association of Information Technology Professionals
505 Busse Highway
Park Ridge, IL 60068
(800)224-9371
Fax: (847)825-1693
E-mail: 70430.35@compuserve.com

Association of On-Line Professionals
www.aop.org

The HTML Writers Guild
www.hwg.org

International Webmasters Association
www.iwanet.org

Network Professional Association
401 N. Michigan Avenue
Chicago, IL 60680
(888)379-0910 or (312)245-1043
www.npa.org

Webmaster Central
www.wmcentral.com

Webmaster's Guild
www.webmaster.org

Webmaster Resources
www.webmaster-resources.com

World Wide Web Consortium
www.w3.org

World Organization of Webmasters
www.world-webmasters.org

Computer and Web e-zines

BYTE
www.byte.com

CIO Magazine
www.cio.com/CIO

CIO WebBusiness
www.webbusiness.cio.com

Computerworld
www.careers.computerworld.com/
cwnews/subform.html

Information Week
www.techweb.cmp.com/techweb/iw/
current/default.html

InfoWorld
www.infoworld.com

Intranet Design Magazine
www.innergy.com/index.html

Intranet Journal
www.intranetjournal.com

Internet Business Report
www.jup.com/newsletter/business

ISP Business News
www.phillips.com/iw

Internet World Daily
www.internetworld.com

Network Magazine
www.lanmag.com

Web Week
www.webweek.com

Telecommunications and data communications companies

GTE Communications Systems Corp.
1255 Corporate Drive
Irving, TX 75038
(972)507-5000
Fax: (972)507-5002
www.gte.com

Infotron Systems Corp.
Cherry Hill Industrial Center
Cherry Hill, NJ 08003
(609)424-9400
www.infotron.com

Network Systems Corp.
One StorageTek Drive
Louisville, CO 80028
(800)786-7835 or (719)536-4055
Fax: (719)536-4053
www.network.com

Intellicall Inc.
2155 Chenault, Suite 410
Carrollton, TX 75006
(800)800-9091
Fax: (972)418-9455
www.intellicall.com

Motorola Corp.
1303 E. Algonquin Road
Schaumburg, IL 60196
(847)576-5000
Fax: (847)576-3258
www.mot.com

Tellabs, Inc.
4951 Indiana Avenue
Lisle, IL 60532
(630)378-8800
Fax: (630)378-4590
www.tellabs.com

Local, long-distance, and cellular telephone services

AT&T Corp.
32 Avenue of the Americas
New York, NY 10013
(212)387-5400
Fax: (908)221-2528
www.att.com

Ameritech Mobile Communications
30 South Wacker Dr., 34th Floor
Chicago, IL 60606
(800)244-4444
www.ameritech.com

Bell Atlantic Corp.
1095 Avenue of the Americas
New York, NY 10036
(212)395-2121 or (800)621-9900
www.bell-atl.com

Bell Atlantic Mobile Systems
1095 Avenue of the Americas
New York, NY 10036
(212)395-2121
Fax: (215)963-6470
www.bam.com

BellSouth Corporation
1155 Peachtree Street, N.E.
Atlanta, GA 30309
(404)249-2000
Fax: (404)249-2071
www.bellsouth.com

Centel Corporation
O'Hare Plaza
8725 Higgins Road
Chicago, IL 60631
(312)399-2500
www.home.4w.com/pages/centel

Century Telephone Enterprises, Inc.
100 Century Park Drive
Monroe, LA 71203
(318)388-9000
Fax: (318)388-9562
www.centurytel.com

Citizens Utilities Company
3 High Ridge Park
P.O. Box 3801
Stamford, CT 06905
(203)614-5600
Fax: (203)322-7186
www.czn.net

Continental Electronics Corporation
P.O. Box 270879
4212 S. Buckner Boulevard
Dallas, TX 75227
(214)381-7161 or (800)733-5011
www.contelec.com

MCI Communications
500 Clinton Center Drive
Clinton, MS 39056
(601)460-5600
Fax: (601)974-8350
www.mci.com

Southwestern Bell Corporation
175 E. Houston
San Antonio, TX 78205
(210)821-4105
www.swbell.com

U.S. Sprint Communications
2330 Shawnee Mission Parkway
Westwood, KS 66209
(913)624-3000

U.S. West
1801 California Street
Denver, CO 80202
(800)879-4357
Fax: (303)965-0550
www.uswest.com

Telecommunications equipment companies

ADC Telecommunications, Inc.
P.O. Box 1101
Minneapolis, MN 55440-1101
(800)366-3891
Fax: (612)946-3292
www.adc.com

Communications Systems Inc.
213 Main Street
Hector, MN 55342
(320)848-6231
Fax: (320)848-2702
www.commsystems.com

AT&T Corp.
32 Avenue of the Americas
New York, NY 10013
(212)387-5400
Fax: (908)221-2528
www.att.com

Comdial Corporation
Attention: Human Resources
P.O. Box 7266
Charlottesville, VA 22906-7266
(804)978-2239
www.comdial.com

DSC Communications Corp.
54 Rue La Boetie
Paris 75382, France
(800)422-2066
Fax: (201)262-2541
www.dsccc.com

Dynatech Corp.
3 New England Executive Park
Burlington, MA 01803
(781)272-6100
Fax: (781)272-2304
www.dytc.com

Executone Information Systems Inc.
478 Wheelers Farms Road
Milford, CT 06460
(800)955-9866
www.executone.com

Telecommunications industry associations

Competitive Telecommunications Association
1900 M. Street, N.W., Suite 800
Washington, DC 20036
(202)296-6650
Fax: (202)296-7585
www.comptel.org

International Communications Association
3530 Forest Lane, Suite 200
Dallas, TX 75234
(214)902-3632 or (800)ICA-INFO
Fax: (214)902-6521
www.icanet.com

Telecommunications Association
2500 Wilson Boulevard, Suite 300
Arlington, VA 22201
(703)907-7700
Fax: (703)907-7727
www.tiaonline.org

Telecommunications Resellers Association
1401 K Street, Suite 600
Washington, DC 20005
(202)835-9898
Fax: (202)835-9893
www.tra.org

United States Telephone Association
1401 H Street, NW, Suite 600
Washington, DC 20005-2164
(202)326-7300
Fax: (202)326-7333
www.usta.org

Telecommunications industry publications

Telephone Engineer & Management Directory
Edgell Communications Inc.
1 E. First Street
Duluth, MN 55802
(800)346-0085
www.edgellcommunications.com

Data Communications Magazine
3 Park Avenue, 30th Floor
New York, NY 10016
(212)592-8260
Fax: (212)592-8265
www.data.com

Telecommunications
685 Canton Street
Norwood, MA 02062
(617)769-9750
E-mail: editorial@telecommagazine.com
www.telecoms-mag.com

Telephony
55 E. Jackson Boulevard
Chicago, IL 60604
(312)922-2435

Telecommunications/multimedia education

Center for Electronic Arts
250 4th Street
San Francisco, CA 94103
(415)512-9300
Fax: (415)512-9260
www2.cea.edu

Chapter 16

Travel & Hospitality
New vistas for the new millennium

Adventure tour operator
Catering director
Corporate travel manager
Cruise line marketer
Destination marketer
Hotel general manager
Meeting/event planner
Restaurant manager
Travel agent
Best Bets for Entrepreneurs:
Independent travel agent, Independent caterer

Forecast

A new emphasis on international travel, as well as more meetings and conventions stateside, will bring many travel agents back inside companies to manage corporate travel schedules and expenses, meet with destination marketers, and oversee the activities of independent meeting/event planners.

Our changing ideas about how to spend leisure time will produce a wider range of new options from trekking to cruising. Growth in the hotel industry will be concentrated at the management level. However, beccause an increasing number of hotels will be comprised of economy properties, which generally require fewer managers, the number of jobs for hotel managers will not increase as rapidly. Increasingly, new restaurants are affiliated with national chains rather than independently owned and operated. As this trend continues, fewer owners will manage restaurants themselves, and more restaurant managers will find jobs running newly opened establishments.

Growth

While the travel industry is sensitive to economic downturns and international political situations, travel agents can expect 25,000 new jobs to open up by 2008. The number of job openings for restaurant managers and catering directors will grow faster than the average as more new restaurants open to serve busy dual income families. Employment of hotel managers is expected to grow about as fast as the average for all occupations through the year 2008. Although new employment growth is higher in economy hotels, large full-service hotels will continue to offer many entry-level opportunities.

Overview

If U.S. Department of Commerce projections are on target, travel will be the nation's number one grossing industry and line up just behind heath care and business services in the number of jobs it will generate. In a majority of states, the travel industry is among the top three employers.

A strong economy and emerging world marketplace have sparked renewed interest in travel. Thanks to healthy dual incomes, smaller families, and an increasing number of older people who are more likely to travel, spending on travel is expected to increase significantly over the next decade. Many people already take more than one vacation a year, in addition to weekend jaunts. Business travel should also grow as business activity expands.

Meanwhile, competition for travel dollars is revealing a few new twists. Internet ticketing and reservations services such as **Travelocity.com** and **Priceline.com** are catching on with PC-savvy consumers. Air travelers have the option of picking up their tickets from electronic ticketing machines right at the airport.

Travel agents who have survived do so by meeting travelers half way with economical packages, weekend cruises, and a range of "adventure" possibilities—from bicycling the back roads of Vermont to trekking in Nepal. Hoteliers are distinguishing their properties by a offering a range of services targeted at very distinct elements of the marketplace—from multinational business travelers to retiring seniors and families.

Today, business travelers can check into a hotel room as well equipped as any office. There are environmentally "green" hotels, all-suite hotels, and budget hotels. National theme restaurants continue to pop up in local neighborhoods, vying for the discretionary dollars of worn-out working couples and families on the go.

Taking off, checking in, and being served

With the inside line on everything from the weather to local restaurants, *travel agents* continue to act as personal advisors to leisure and business travelers. Some are moving from agencies inside companies to serve the specialized needs of international business travelers as *corporate travel managers.*

Closer to home, meetings, conferences, and conventions keep independent *meeting/event planners* busy handling every detail. And since conventioneers are known to spend double what the typical tourist spends per day, a new generation of *destination marketers* from meeting places as different as Omaha and San Jose are out there in force wooing the nation's corporations.

Adventure tour operators have been successful appealing to active baby boomers and others who need to counteract work stress with physical challenge. Theme cruises and expanded itineraries are part of a wave of success that *cruise line marketers* hope to ride well into the future.

The best jobs in hotels will go to *hotel general managers.* More advanced technology—from the front desk to the back room—means more efficient operations and a wealth of information on guests that can be used to create promotions and new services.

The *catering* business is expanding at 12 percent annually. Increasingly, *restaurant managers* are taking the reins of newly opened chain restaurants and giving local, independently run establishments a run for their money.

Industry snapshot

A combination of skyrocketing real estate values and generous tax incentives granted by the Economic Recovery Tax Act of 1981 lured hotel companies down a risky path. An overly ambitious boom in building—the largest in recent history—was bound to bust when real estate values dipped in 1991. In the midst of the recession, occupancy rates dove to about 61 percent. (The industry break-even point is about 66 percent.)

Mired in high operating costs and too many empty rooms, large hotel chains such as Marriott and Hilton cut costs by downsizing their corporate and headquarters staffs. According to an industry expert quoted in *Fortune* magazine, only about 32 percent of full-service hotels in the country were able to break even. Many small independents weren't able to weather the storm.

By the summer of 1992, airfare wars were stirring up more business and a rebound was in the making. By 1993, nationwide occupancy rates averaged about 68.5 percent, with more than 60 percent of hotels turning a profit.

Now that Americans are back to taking nearly 1.4 billion trips a year, the character of travel has changed. Leisure trips for two-income families tend to be shorter and closer to home, while business travelers are regularly circling the globe. As the world gets smaller, travelers become more savvy—and often less inclined to follow the path beaten by earlier generations. Equally savvy travel agents specialize, offering in-depth knowledge of particular destinations or promoting unbeatable group discounts, travel clubs, and corporate services.

Trends to track

Cutting edge services. The more wired business travelers get, the more digitally equipped hotels are becoming. At the new W San Francisco, rooms with two phone lines are standard. One line boasts 900 MHz cordless dual-line telephone; the other has dataport and speakerphone capabilities. A high-speed direct Ethernet modem connection operates at speeds up to 100 times faster than conventional modems. However, design for the business traveler does not neglect comfort. Goose-down comforters, upholstered banquettes, dark wood desks, and rich natural fabrics make guestrooms homey.

Other hotels are profiting from being environmentally friendly. The Boston Park Plaza features Thermopane windows, reduced-consumption shower heads and toilets, shower dispensers instead of amenity bottles, and recycling containers for paper, plastic, and glass. Although the initial investment may be costly, savings in water use and waste disposal fees have been significant.

The changing face of meetings. While technology can dramatically change the format and role of the traditional meeting, it has become clear that telephones, faxes, e-mail, and even video conferencing cannot replace "face time." Economically savvy companies are leaving one-way presentations and informational updates online—often as a digital introduction.

Face-to-face meetings are for dialogue, interaction, decision making, and hands-on work.

Cooperation: a win-win situation. New marketing strategies will focus on cooperative programs that encourage repeat business. Airline companies have joined with hotel chains and rental car companies, as well as credit card and phone companies, to award frequent flier miles to consumers. In fact, frequent fliers now earn about 40 percent of miles without flying at all, and redeem 10 percent of their accumulated miles for goods and services other than free trips.

In an effort to keep costs down, airlines and cruise lines are bypassing travel agencies to entice customers with economical packages such as three- to seven-day fly/drive package vacations. As these new campaigns cut into travel agent commissions, agencies are getting more creative, too. Many are hooking up with tour operators, city and state destinations, and major attractions to create special promotional packages.

Old standards...and still winners

Travel agents. Depending on the individual needs of their clients, travel agents suggest destinations and make arrangements for transportation, hotel accommodations, car rentals, tours, and recreation. A worldwide computer network puts up-to-the-minute departure and arrival times, rates, and discounts at their fingertips. They may also consult published resources for detailed information on ratings and activities. Travel agents may suggest hotels with corporate facilities, such as in-room fax machines for business travelers, and counsel international travelers on customs regulations, passport and visa requirements, and currency exchange rates. Leisure travelers may need detailed information and prices for tour packages, as well as advice on restaurants and weather conditions. Many travel agents have opportunities to visit hotels, restaurants, and resorts in a variety of locations, so they're able to make recommendations based on personal experience.

Corporate travel managers. Today's corporate travel agent has become an integral part of a company's planning, marketing, and sales structure. Corporate travel managers typically develop and carry out a company's travel policy and manage the overall budget. Most communicate via phone and computer with outside travel agencies that specialize in corporate travel and expense management to plan travel, meetings, and conferences.

Like any good travel agent, corporate travel managers should know the personal characteristics and preferences of every frequent traveler they serve. So today's senior executives are taking a more active interest in establishing travel policy, negotiating contracts with agencies, and even managing expense reporting. These days, a simple two-day trip to Chicago might cost one company $500 and another twice that. Travel agents are being held accountable for seeking out the most economical fares—and many are acting as expense management consultants.

Many companies that depend on frequent travel are also bringing corporate travel managers in-house to ensure efficient purchasing. Some are forging new types of partnerships with their travel agencies. For example, Hewlett-Packard implemented fee-based pricing with its travel agencies. The company receives the standard 10 percent agent's commission plus a 2 percent volume discount from the airlines and pays its travel agencies set fees for service based on tickets issued.

Cruise marketers. Soap opera cruises. Three-day packages. Two-for-one deals. These are the kinds of aggressive marketing tactics that continue to contribute to the prosperity of cruise lines. With new ships and new routes, most plan to increase sales and marketing efforts to create even stronger brand identity.

Hotel general managers. The GM is responsible for all aspects of operations, sales, and marketing in a business that's open 24 hours a day, 365 days a year. Long hours are the norm, but a variety of attractive perks (like luxurious on-site living accommodations) are often the reward. These days, hotels are looking for people with strong business, marketing, and people-management skills. The most successful managers will aggressively seek out new technology and in many cases use it to raise the level of guest services. Marriott's computerized check-in system in the Houston airport allows the majority of its guests to check in before reaching the hotel lobby. A hotel rep meets guests at the airport's underground train and sets up the hotel account using a handheld computer. A room key is issued on the spot.

In smaller hotels and motels, the responsibility for overseeing rooms, food and beverage service, registration, and overall management can fall on the shoulders of a single manager. Large hotels, however, like the Plaza in New York City, employ hundreds of workers. The general manager may be aided by a staff of assistant managers, each with his or her own department to supervise.

Meeting/event planners. Hundreds of thousands of meetings, conferences, and conventions are conducted each year. Add private parties, hospitality suites, and sales meetings and it's easy to see why business is booming for independent meeting/event planners. The catch is that these days, corporations, associations, and nonprofit organizations are pulling together more complex meetings and events in shorter time frames. The challenge for meeting/event planners is to handle every detail, from developing the budget and arranging blocks of hotel rooms to planning individual presentations. Meeting planners regularly communicate with one or more administrative and management people inside companies they serve.

Restaurant manager. Like hotel general managers, restaurant managers are involved in every aspect of running an efficient and profitable operation, from selecting menu items to arranging for maintenance of kitchen equipment. Restaurant managers also investigate and resolve customer complaints about food quality or service and carry out a variety of administrative responsibilities, not the least of which is tallying receipts at the end of each shift.

A new generation of opportunities

Adventure tour operators. These entrepreneurs and small tour operators are enticing baby boomers to part with some of their disposable income in exchange for the adventure of a lifetime. It may be exploring the Galapagos Islands, learning to scuba dive, or bicycling through California's wine country. Ecotourism is a related travel market that should remain strong in the short term. Such package tours or trips are aimed at environmentally-aware travelers interested in enjoying the world's remaining pristine spots and visiting endangered wildlife in their natural habitats.

Destination marketers. New hotel taxes dedicated to funding tourism development have made destination marketing a viable enterprise for communities of all sizes. These days marketers from smaller, rural destinations that want to diversify their economies are rubbing elbows with marketers from larger cities at special trade shows and conventions. Most destination marketers also meet privately with corporate travel managers and make presentations to convention groups. About 800 destination marketing organizations have registered with the National Tour Association.

Catering director. The catering business is growing by the year. Hotels and restaurants are looking for catering directors for on-site events, as well as for off-site catering divisions. Working for a small company, or on your own, you may put in 16-hour days, doing everything from menu planning to setting up chairs. At larger firms, catering directors typically sell jobs and supervise a full staff.

Do you have what it takes?

A love of travel attracts many people to this field. But to succeed in most jobs, you must have a genuine desire to be of service. Travel agents should be pleasant, patient, and have a knack for gaining the confidence of different kinds of clients and motivating them to travel. Much of the work is detail-oriented and repetitive. For example, agents must stay up to date on airline schedules and fares and be familiar with customs regulations, visas, and health permits. Travel agents often work under a great deal of stress during holidays and peak vacation times.

Meeting planners should be creative, resourceful, and have excellent organization and interpersonal skills. Grace under pressure is especially important in this job. Crises, such as a blizzard that closes an airport, or a hotel that mixes up reservations, are to be expected. The ability to think on your feet often spells success.

Hotel general managers need initiative, self-discipline, and the ability to organize and direct people at all levels of the hotel. They should be able to concentrate on details and be good problem-solvers, ready to avert last-minute crises. Above all, they should be friendly and accommodating— even when they have been working for 12 hours on Thanksgiving Day without a break.

Destination and cruise line marketers and adventure tour operators need sales skills as well as the creativity to make a city or trip come alive for prospective customers who may be sitting in an office hundreds of miles away.

Education and training

Education is becoming increasingly important for travel agents because fewer agencies are willing to train agents on the job. Many vocational schools offer three- to 12-week full-time programs, as well as Saturday and evening classes. Make sure to select a school that is "approved," "registered," or "licensed" by your state's Postsecondary Education Bureau or a recognized accreditation association. Before you register, check your choice with your state's department of education and/or the Better Business Bureau in the city where the school is located.

Community colleges offer two-year associate's degree programs and a few four-year colleges and universities offer bachelor's and master's degrees in travel and tourism. Courses in business, computer skills, foreign languages, and geography are especially useful. Courses in accounting and business management are a wise investment if you think you might want to start your own agency.

Several home study programs provide a basic understanding of the travel industry. The American Society of Travel Agents (ASTA) and the Institute of Certified Travel Agents (ICTA) both offer travel correspondence courses.

A bachelor's degree in hotel and restaurant management carries the most clout for hotel general managers and restaurant managers. Cornell University is one of the top schools in the nation, offering both undergraduate and graduate degrees as well as executive education programs.

Many hotels are looking for good businesspeople. Some large hotels sponsor specialized, on-the-job, management training programs that allow trainees to rotate through various departments to gain a thorough knowledge of the hotel's operations. Other hotels may help finance training in hotel management for outstanding employees.

A bachelor's degree in marketing or communications and knowledge of advertising or public relations provide the right background for destination marketers. George Washington University and Purdue University offer degree programs in tourism management and leisure-time marketing.

In addition to formal training in the culinary arts, catering directors need sales and restaurant experience.

Professional licensing and certification

There is no federal licensing requirement for travel agents. Currently, the following nine states require some type of regulation, registration or certification of travel agents: California, Hawaii, Illinois, Ohio, Rhode Island, Washington, Iowa, Florida, and Oregon. For specific requirements contact your state's attorney general's office or department of commerce.

If you have some experience and plan to start your own agency, you must gain formal approval from the suppliers (airlines, ship lines, and rail lines) you'll be working with before you are authorized to receive commissions. You can either contact each supplier directly and work out an agreement on how bookings will be made and how commissions will be awarded, or you can receive appointments from the Airlines Reporting Corporation (ARC) or the International Airlines Travel Agency Network (IATAN). (See the "Resources" section for contact information.)

Experienced travel agents who pass an eighteen-month course administered by ICTA can become Certified Travel Counselors. Another recognized professional credential is the certificate of proficiency from ASTA, awarded to those who pass a three-hour examination.

Hotel general managers can accelerate career advancement by completing certification programs offered by some of the industry's associations. These programs generally require a combination of course work, exams, and experience.

The Society of Corporate Meeting Professionals (SCMP) provides scholarship money to members who wish to earn the Corporate Meeting Professional certification. The Convention Liaison Council administers the Certified Meeting Professional (CMP) designation.

Tips on breaking in

Choose the right school. Before selecting a school, check out the success ratio of placement assistance for graduates. Ask if you can contact recent graduates of the school who are working in the area you're targeting.

Speak another language. If you speak, or have at least studied, Japanese or another foreign language, brush up on your skills for better opportunities in either the travel or hospitality industry.

Women: Jump on the fast track. The hospitality industry has a reputation for encouraging women—even working mothers—and minorities to complete management development programs. Women account for 88 percent of frontline agents. Agency managers are 80 percent women.

Internships and part-time jobs are a huge asset when it comes to getting hired for a managerial-track position.

Career path

Most travel agencies are small, with fewer than 10 employees, each handling all types of business. In larger agencies, agents may specialize in either vacation or commercial (business) travel. In franchise travel agencies or agencies with many offices, agents may advance to office manager. Experienced agents often break away to start their own agencies. Some are becoming destination marketers.

Destination marketers often enter the field from the public relations, advertising, or hospitality industry. They may begin in sales or marketing and advance to the head of a department of tourism, conventions, and communications, or run entire bureaus, such as the San Jose Convention and Visitors Bureau.

Corporate travel managers move from travel agencies to one-person, in-house operations. For large corporations they may supervise a department of two to five agents and administrators.

In the past, most hotel general managers were promoted from the ranks. The hotel's food service and beverage operations were considered the key to the profitability of the entire establishment. These days, however, the right degree combined with solid experience (gained from an internship or part-time job) is the surest route to top management.

Graduates of hotel or restaurant management programs usually start as trainee assistant managers. New hotels without formal on-the-job training programs often prefer experienced personnel for higher level positions. Large hotel and motel chains offer better opportunities for advancement than small, independently owned establishments, as well as transfers to other hotels or motels in the chain. Hotel personnel are encouraged, almost required, to move around to different hotels several times in their careers.

How much can you earn?

According to 1997 Salary and Compensation Survey by the Institute of Certified Travel Counselors, the average frontline travel agent makes $23,700 a year. Thirty-one percent receive only a salary, while 21 percent are paid by commission-only structures. Thirteen percent receive a combination of salary and commission. Twenty-seven percent of frontline agents report receiving a bonus.

Travel agency managers are paid an average of $32,100 per year.

Airlines recently capped the commissions that they used to pay travel agents to a flat rate for fares over $500, whereas previously an agent received 10 percent of the total fare, regardless of the price. This has driven many agents out of the industry, since the commission caps reduced many of their salaries by half.

Salaries of hotel managers vary greatly according to their level of experience, responsibilities, and the segment of the industry in which they are employed. In 1996, annual salaries of assistant hotel managers averaged around $40,000, based on a hospitality industry survey conducted by Roth Young Personnel of Oklahoma City. Salaries of assistant managers also varied because of differences in duties and responsibilities. For example, food and beverage directors averaged $43,000, whereas front office managers averaged $28,000.

In 1996, salaries of general managers averaged nearly $54,000, according to the Roth Young survey. Their salaries ranged from $39,000 to $81,000, depending on the size and type of establishment. Based on limited information, it appears that managers may earn bonuses of up to 25 percent of their base salary in some hotels. In addition, managers and their families may be furnished with lodging, meals, parking, laundry, and other services.

Working in a small bureau with an annual budget less than $200,000, a destination marketer in a sales position starts at $30,000. The CEO of a small bureau makes an average of $45,000. In large bureaus with budgets of more than $5 million, destination marketers with fewer than five years of experience can earn $45,000. Sales directors and marketing directors can earn $100,000 or more. The CEO of a large bureau can make $150,000 or more.

Salaries for catering directors range from $22,800 to $42,600.

Earnings of restaurant and food service managers vary greatly according to their responsibilities and the type and size of establishment. Based on a survey conducted by the National Restaurant Association, the median base salary of restaurant managers was about $30,000 in 1995; managers of the largest restaurants and institutional food service facilities often had annual salaries in excess of $50,000. Besides a salary, most managers received an annual bonus or incentive payment based on their performance. In 1995, most bonuses ranged from $2,000 to $10,000.

In addition to typical benefits, most salaried restaurant and food service managers receive free meals and the opportunity for additional training depending on their length of service.

Where will you work?

Many individual travel agents have specialized skills and work exclusively as commercial agents, catering to business travelers, or leisure agents, assisting individuals or groups in making vacation plans. Travel agencies, hotels, and restaurants are found throughout the country.

Job Profile

Carolyn Johnson, cruise and international travel specialist

What general responsibilities does your job encompass?
I book travel, collect the money, and follow through with customers.

What level of education have you reached?
I have a two-year diploma from a travel school.

How many hours do you typically work per week?
45 or more hours per week.

What hours do you work on a typical workday?
8 a.m. to 6 p.m.

How big is the company you work for?
We have 75 travel agents and 25 accounting and corporate staff.

Do you have (or need) professional certification?
No.

How did you get your current job?
I answered an advertisement in the local newspaper.

Please describe one of your "typical" days.
I really don't have a typical day. What I'm working on from hour to hour depends on the kinds of the trips my customers want me to book.

What are your career aspirations?
I'd like to continue doing what I'm doing: booking and selling travel.

What people do you think would do especially well in your job role?
People skills, people skills, people skills! Also you should detail-oriented and be excellent at following through with customers.

What do you like most about your job?
Talking with all kinds of people about their travel plans.

What do you like least?
The pressure to rush. Everyone wants to be called back first.

What are some common misconceptions about your job/profession/ industry?
That my job is all fun and we travel for free.

What is the best way to going about landing a job like yours?
Attend a good travel school.

Resources

Hospitality associations

Council on Hotel, Restaurant, and Institutional Education
1200 17th Street NW
Washington, DC 20036-3097
Fax: (202)973-3955
www.chrie.org

American Hotel & Motel Association
1201 New York Avenue, NW, Suite 600
Washington, DC 20005-3931
(202)289-3100
Fax: (202)289-3199
E-mail: infoctr@ahma.com
www.ahma.com

Top hospitality employers

Best Western International
P.O. Box 10203
Phoenix, AZ 85064
(602)957-5700
www.bestwestern.com

Hilton Hotels Corp.
9336 Civic Center Drive
Beverly Hills, CA 90209
(310)278-4321
www.hilton.com

Embassy Suites, Inc.
1023 Cherry Road
Memphis, TN 38117
(901)762-8600
www.embassy-suites.com

Holiday Inns
3796 Lamar Avenue
Memphis, TN 38195
(901)369-5895
www.holiday-inn.com

Marriott Corp.
Host Marriott Services Corp.
6600 Rockledge Dr.
Betheseda, MD 20817
(301)380-7000
www.hmscrop.com

Omni Hotels Management Corp.
500 Lafayette Road
Hampton, NH 03842
(603)926-8911
www.omnihotels.com

Hospitality industry magazines

Hotel and Restaurant Administration Quarterly
Cornell University School of Hotel Administration
327 Statler Hall
Ithaca, NY 14853
(607)255-2093

Hotel and Motel Management
7500 Old Oak Boulevard.
Cleveland, OH 44130
(216)243-8100

Hotel and Resort Industry and *Hotels*
1350 E. Touhy Avenue
Des Plaines, IL 60018
(708)635-8800

Top travel employers

Royal Caribbean Corp.
903 S. America Way
Miami, FL 33132
(305)379-2601
www.royalcaribbean.com

American Hawaii Cruises
550 Kearny Street
San Francisco, CA 94108
(415)392-9400

Holland America Line
300 Elliott Avenue W.
Seattle, WA 98119
(206)281-3535
www.hollandamerica.com

Thomas Cook Travel
100 Cambridge Park Drive
Cambridge, MA 02138
(617)868-7500
www.thomascook.com

Vistatours
1923 N. Carson Street, Suite 105
Carson City, NV 89710
(800)647-0800
www.vistatours.com

Carnival Cruise Lines
3915 Biscayne Boulevard
Miami, FL 33137
(305)573-6030
www.carnival.com

Princess Cruises
10100 Santa Monica Boulevard
Los Angeles, CA 90067
(310)553-1770
www.princess.com

Travel industry associations

American Society of Travel Agents
1101 King Street
Alexandria, VA 22314
(202)965-7520
www.astanet.com

Institute of Certified Travel Agents and International Association of Tour Managers
North American Region
1646 Chapel St.
New Haven, CT 06511
(203)777-5994
www.icta.com

Travel Industry Associations of America
1100 New York Avenue, NW, Suite 450
Washington, DC 20005-3934
www.tia.org

Airlines Reporting Corporation (ARC)
1530 Wilson Boulevard, Suite 800
Arlington, VA 22209-2448
(703)816-8000
Fax: (703)816-8104
www.arccorp.com

International Airlines Travel Agent Network (IATAN)
300 Garden City Plaza, Suite 342
Garden City, NY 11530-3302
(516)747-4716
Fax: (516)747-4462
www.iatan.org

Travel Industry magazine

Travel Agent magazine
825 Seventh Avenue
New York, NY 10019
(212)887-1900

Meeting/event planner magazine

Corporate Meetings/Incentives
63 Great Road
Maynard, MA 01754
(508)897-5552

Index

Index

Index